Other Books by June Callwood:

PORTRAIT OF CANADA

A WOMAN DOCTOR LOOKS AT LIFE AND LOVE
(with Dr. Marion Hilliard)

MAYO: THE STORY OF MY FAMILY AND MY CAREER
(with Dr. Charles W. Mayo)

LOVE, HATE, FEAR, ANGER AND THE OTHER LIVELY EMOTIONS

HOW TO TALK WITH PRACTICALLY ANYBODY ABOUT
PRACTICALLY ANYTHING
(with Barbara Walters)

THE LAW IS NOT FOR WOMEN
(with Marvin Zuker)

Emma

JUNE CALLWOOD

Beaufort
New York • Toronto

First published in 1984 by
Stoddart Publishing
A Division of General Publishing Co. Limited
30 Lesmill Road
Toronto, Ontario

First published in the United States by
Beaufort Books

Canadian Cataloguing in Publication Data

Callwood, June
  Emma: Canada's unlikely spy

ISBN   0-7737-0226-X   (Cdn.)
       0-8253-0251-X   (Amer.)

1. Woikin, Emma.   2. Women spies — Canada — Biography.
I. Title.

FC581.W65C3 1984   327.1′2′0924   C84-098920-2
F1034.W65C3 1984

ISBN 0-7737-2026-X (Cdn.)
0-8253-0251-X (Amer.)
Printed and bound in Canada by
T. H. Best Printing Company Ltd.

Acknowledgments

My thanks first and most to Fred and Doreen Konkin of Blaine Lake, who welcomed me into Emma's family with generosity and kindness, and to Emma's husband, Louie Sawula, an honourable and gentle man. I am indebted also to countless patient and resourceful archivists in Ottawa, Regina, Saskatoon and Toronto, but especially to James Whalen of The Public Archives Canada and Catherine Shepard of the Ontario Archives. My gratitude also to Phyllis Clark, who gave permission for access to the papers of her father, J. L. Cohen.

When she was sentenced, the content of the cables was kept secret. Even her lawyer had difficulty getting permission to see them. The impression created was that the cables Emma deciphered for the Russians contained matters of great sensitivity to world security. In fact, there was little in them that hadn't been reported in the newspapers.

It wasn't noted in Emma Woikin's defense that she could have given the Kremlin something of real value, namely the code the British foreign office was using, but did not. It was not revealed, either, that Igor Gouzenko had testified in a closed hearing that the Soviet embassy in Ottawa didn't think it prudent to ask Emma Woikin for the code.

Winston Churchill, wartime prime minister of Britain who had chafed under the necessity of appearing to be a comrade of the Communists, had just given the speech in which he coined the phrase "the Iron Curtain." The Soviets' postwar belligerence, arising from its dark suspicions of the western world's intentions, rapidly had eroded the euphoria of goodwill that prevailed through the years when the Russian army was fighting Hitler. When Emma Woikin came to trial in the spring of 1946 it was hard to remember that only the summer before, when she was memorizing cables, the Russians were regarded by most North Americans as heroes and freedom fighters.

The Ottawa judge who sentenced Emma Woikin on the afternoon of 10 April, 1946, to two years and six months in prison did not comment on the unusual treatment she had received prior to arrest. She had been stripped of all the protections that have accrued in English common law since the Magna Carta. Taken from her bed in a police raid before dawn, she was detained in isolation for three weeks, during which no charges were laid and no contact was allowed with a lawyer, her family or friends. She was interrogated by the Royal Canadian Mounted Police and brought before two justices of the Supreme Court of Canada in a secret hearing. She was not informed that she had a right to the protection of the Canada Evidence Act or that she was entitled to a lawyer. Instead, she was bullied for five hours by the judges and by two lawyers who later became Supreme Court judges. After the questioning a statement was issued to the press declaring that she was a traitor.

That done, she was arrested. Her trial followed briskly and in exactly a month she was on her way to Kingston Penitentiary.

On her last day in court, Emma Woikin took the stand to describe her life, testimony that many in the room found piteous and unforgettable. She said she had been raised on a farm near Blaine Lake, Saskatchewan and was married, at sixteen, at a time when the prairies were experiencing the worst depression and drought in their history. Because of poverty, her baby had died and her young husband committed suicide, leaving her an estate of seventy-five cents. She had the impression, she said — she might be wrong — that in the Soviet Union conditions for working people were better than that.

She was only twenty-seven but her hair was almost white when she was discharged from prison in August, 1946. She returned to Saskatchewan to live in Saskatoon, and found anonymity in another marriage that gave her a new name, Emma Sawula, a profession in the offices of respected legal firms, and an honourable place in the community. For twenty-five years she appeared happy and carefree: the perfect wife, the best legal secretary in town, the most thoughtful hostess, the most loving auntie, the finest cook, gardener, housekeeper, seamstress; a woman who stopped to greet friends five times in every block.

On 22 May, 1974, Emma Konkin Woikin Sawula died of acute alcoholism. This is her story.

Chapter One

The last of the Doukhobor refugee ships left the Black Sea port of Batum in the summer of 1899 carrying twenty-three hundred people, the largest single shipment of immigrants in Canadian history, on a journey that would end on the steep, eroded banks of the North Saskatchewan River on the prairies of Canada.

The people aboard, cramped miserably in a hold designed for cattle, were mostly young. The finest farmers in all Europe, they were fleeing persecution for their anarchist refusal to obey either the czar or the prevailing church. For resisting service in the Russian army, Doukhobors had been flogged to death, raped, put in prison and exiled to starve in mountain caves. Their rescue had come suddenly through a network of Quakers in Britain, the United States and Canada, led with frenzied zeal by Russian intellectuals who sympathized with their pacifism, and by a Canadian, Professor James Mavor of the University of Toronto, whose imagination had been seized by their plight.

Twenty-seven days from Batum the rescue ship, the *Lake Huron,* was below the stark cliffs of Quebec City; the passengers were forbidden to land because there was smallpox aboard. After a month in quarantine on Grosse Island, the Doukhobors were loaded into Canadian Pacific Railway trains, which the women promptly scrubbed spotless, and transported, at six dollars a head to Winnipeg.

For five days and nights they rode across the Canadian Shield's bare rock and brush, around glittering lakes, to emerge suddenly on the flat black earth of Manitoba, so like the steppes of southern Russia that they were deeply thrilled at the sight. Immigration sheds, newly vacated by Doukhobors who had gone before, were waiting for them in Winnipeg. There they would stay until transportation was available to take them to their land allotment further west.

The men found temporary jobs cutting wood, building houses, loading wagons, whatever they could get. Like the Doukhobors who came earlier they sent a shock of outrage through the ranks of local wage-earners, because they worked their heads off and accepted whatever employers chose to pay them.

Eventually they boarded a Canadian National Railway train bound for Yorkton where the track ended. On either side, stretching empty to the skyline, were empty prairies where ripe wild grasses tossed in the wind. Occasionally they saw clumps of motionless Indians wrapped in shabby blankets, staring at the train with dark, fathomless eyes. Bleached buffalo bones, some piled in mounds that could be seen for miles, were a mystery.

At Yorkton they descended from the train and were greeted by teamsters who hovered at the station like crows at a carcass. There were a hundred fifty miles more to travel over a wagon trail, mercifully dry after baking in the summer's sun, before they would reach the area on the North Saskatchewan River that had been designated for the last of the Doukhobor migration. It was the most remote of all the land granted Doukhobors, but these people were the best prepared of all the immigrants who had been described as "the curious people." They were from Kars, and were considered the most able and intelligent of the Doukhobors. They brought more than the meager collection of wooden utensils, tiny hump-backed trunks containing clothing, trinkets and rudimentary tools that were the possessions of earlier Doukhobors. These had glowing Persian rugs in their bundles, a few books, fine clothes, and some had money to purchase horses.

The long trek by wagon ended by a shallow yellow river, a lazy giant that had carved a deep trench in the prairies, the North Saskatchewan. Doukhobors unloaded their possessions and the teamsters departed. These were not the first settlers to be left on open ground to face the winter, and they would not be the last. The money set aside to help Doukhobors migrate had been spent on the first three surges of immigrants. This group would survive, or it wouldn't.

They looked around, finding it an encouraging omen that the thousands of birds they saw were so unaccustomed to humans that they were almost tame. Men rubbed the soil with their fingers and grinned. It was a miracle of richness, almost black with nutrients. But the summer was gone: the sun lay low on the horizon even at midday; it was too late to plough and seed. There would be no crop for almost a year, and no food.

The settlers met to decide what to do. Quakers were raising money to buy food supplies, and the immigrants could only hope that some of it would reach them. The young men were sent to walk five hundred miles to Winnipeg to find jobs and send money back to the community. To save precious shoes, they went barefoot.

It was only fifteen years since Louis Riel and Gabriel Dumont had led an uprising of Métis and Cree a few miles from where the Doukhobors had been dumped. Around them were communities with haunting names — Duck Lake, Batoche, Frog Lake. Big Bear's Cree were back on their reservations, clearly starving, and the Doukhobors feared what little food they had might be stolen by desperate tribespeople.

Nikito Popoff, who had brought a pony cart from Batum, was assigned the task of making contact with the Cree. He drove across the tractless prairie until he found them. Using gestures and drawing in the dirt with a stick, he managed to convey the message that Doukhobors were peaceful people, brothers of all that lived, and hoped to be left alone.

Meanwhile the huge colony had to be housed at once; mornings already were frosty. There was no time to build houses for more than twenty-three hundred people, so the elders turned to their recent past for a solution. They had survived exile in the mountains of Russia by living in caves. The North Saskatchewan River has astonishing high banks, remnants of a torrential youth. These steep flanks are covered with weeds and scrub but the soil is sandy, drains well, and yields to a shovel.

The Doukhobors, even the children, dug huge, roomy caves, each big enough for several families, put in timber floors and wooden doors to keep out the wind. They were then ready, those people from a part of Russia where rice is planted, camels pull ploughs and palm trees grow, to face a Canadian prairie winter.

Two of the people who lived in the caves that winter were to become the parents of Emma Woikin, the first woman spy jailed in Canada's history. One was Alexander E. Konkin, then twenty-two, a short, stocky, handsome youth with bristling black eyebrows. The other was Pearl Wishloff, at twenty-one already desirably stout, proof that she could endure on a farm.

Both had come to Canada with their families; both were unmarried. The Doukhobor youth were not marrying and starting families because copulation was forbidden, even to married couples. Some five years earlier an order banning sex had come from Peter Vasilievitch Verigen, a tall, dashing Doukhobor whose wisdom was believed to be divinely inspired and whose authority, therefore, was as binding on his flock as that of a pope on Roman Catholics. Verigen reasoned, accurately as it turned out, that the Doukhobors were about to be subjected to persecution and would need to flee. Because a flight would be encumbered by babies and small children, Verigen imposed celibacy as a birth-control device, and he was obeyed. If a Doukhobor woman became pregnant, her shame was great. There were stories of babies being born in secret and tearfully smothered.

Doukhobors fascinated the Canadian writer George Woodcock, a great admirer of anarchy. He called them "the most interesting of Canada's small minorities" and, in 1968, wrote a book about them in collaboration with Ivan Avakumovic. The Doukhobor migration across half the world, Woodcock wrote, was one of the largest ventures of a Utopian, self-contained model community in human history.

This sect of Christianity bears some resemblance to Quakerism in its rejection of ritual and priesthood. The Doukhobor philosophy developed among peasants in southern Russia in the seventeenth century as a revolution that was as much political as religious. Existing in a period of wealthy and corrupt clergy and czars, the Doukhobors equated the two with evil and evolved a faith devoid of liturgy, icons, fasting, baptism, funeral services, festivals and clergy, and with little reference to the Bible.

They turned their backs on altars and saints' days but kept what they needed: the concept of eternal life, a standard of community behaviour resembling the Golden Rule, personal decency. The wisdom is child-like but not childish. The angels of God are good thoughts and life after death is "a return to mature fruit, to its source," lacking the dark vision of conventional Christianity.

Doukhobors do not accept churches as houses of God; they believe, as Thomas Paine did, that each living thing is a church that contains God. It follows naturally that Doukhobors can not participate in killing other humans, since this would be tantamount to slaying God, and therefore will not fight in wars. It was this pacifism that most rankled their emperor.

Their rejection of the state and of established churches resulted in isolation and in periods of intense persecution. That persecution strengthened their resolve and deepened the bonds of community and family. To protect themselves from the seduction of heretical beliefs, they avoided literacy. Their prophesies, psalms, prayers and history were passed along orally. Doukhobors developed splendid memories, and their family life was enriched because they sang and prayed together to keep the liturgy fresh.

The Doukhobors turned their backs on "priests, deacons, princes, unrighteous courts," but they still hungered for a centre, and for one person who would provide inspiration and leadership. They distanced themselves from much of the Bible but not from Jesus Christ, whom they believed to be a complete Doukhobor. God was more present in Jesus than in others, they believed, and God would be concentrated in one leader in every generation. However unlikely the personality in which it resided, that spiritual density would exist in a Doukhobor among them who would be treasured and obeyed.

It may seem odd and contradictory that Doukhobors are egalitarian and fiercely opposed to regulation and authority, but at the same time unquestioning of a designated leader. However, the paradox has served Doukhobors well for centuries.

The earliest Doukhobors who turned away from the church were burned at the stake as heretics. Fire has become the Doukhobor symbol for religious commitment.

Despite pogroms and harassment, Doukhobors gained adherents. By the early nineteenth century, they were prospering in the Caucasus, which lies between the Black and the Caspian seas, their farms provided them by a protective and admiring emperor, Alexander I.

They lived in villages made of double rows of lodges in which several families could live together, the lodges surrounded by gardens and granaries. The farms were owned and worked communally and were vastly more economical than the singly owned and operated farms of their neighbours. Their efficiency aroused as much jealousy and hostility then as the productive Hutterite farms of Alberta do today.

Their leader in the mid-nineteenth century was Peter Kalmikoff. At the age of twenty, Kalmikoff fell in love with a beautiful sixteen-year-old, Lukeria Hubanova, and for her divorced his wife. Their relationship was childless, and his death left no logical heir. Though Doukhobors then and now are male chauvinists, they could not bear to be leaderless, and Lukeria Kalmikova, a woman of compelling intelligence and strength, was established as leader. Under her able administration, the Doukhobors continued to flourish. As well, she attempted mild reforms, some of which might be viewed as early feminism. For instance, she challenged the Doukhobor assumption that it wasn't offensive for a man to beat his wife. She sentenced heavy-handed husbands to a night in the chicken coop, from which they emerged soiled and embarrassed.

In 1877 Russia launched a war against Turkey for possession of the rich lands of the Caucasus. Because they lived near the border, Doukhobors were caught in the traffic of war and were under considerable pressure to supply the Cossacks with food. Though it horrified pious Doukhobors to assist men bent on killing, Lukeria Kalmikova agreed to the emperor's demand because she hoped to spare her people a blood-letting.

The Cossacks rode against the Turks and captured the thriving town of Kars, which was surrounded by good farms.

To keep the land, the czar offered it to Doukhobors. Older Doukhobors were unwilling to be uprooted but there were hundreds of young couples anxious to accept. It was from this zesty, enterprising group that many of the North Saskatchewan River Colony Doukhobors were to come.

Meanwhile, the long-widowed and beautiful Lukeria Kalmikova had found a mate, a dashing, six-foot twenty-two-year-old called Peter Vasilievitch Verigen. He was married, and his wife was eight months pregnant, but Verigen left her and became Lukeria's consort. The official explanation was that he was being tutored to succeed her.

Their relationship lasted five years, until 1887, when Lukeria died. Doukhobors quarrelled over the succession. Most of them favoured Verigen because Lukeria had wished it, but some opposed him because he was a hard-liner who promised to stop Doukhobor transactions with the czar's armies. The emperor stepped into the dispute and exiled Verigen to Shenkursk, a village fifteen hundred miles from the Caucasus. Support for Verigen's leadership was solidified.

Verigen soon became so admired in Shenkursk, which was boiling with dissenters, that the czar moved him to what is now Murmansk, some eight hundred miles northeast of Shenkursk, where he had a splendid view of the Arctic.

Again Verigen adapted, holding luxurious court for all who came to pay him homage. In 1892 the exasperated czar returned Verigen to Shenkursk, where Verigen encountered the writings of Russia's most radical aristocrat, Count Leon Tolstoy. Tolstoy's view of egalitarian communal life, simplicity and *agape* had some points of resemblance to Doukhobor philosophy. Verigen grasped the nobility of Tolstoy's ideal of human conduct, and began to practice it himself.

He gathered village children to his home and provided food. Then he sent word to his flock in the Caucasus that they were to rid themselves of all personal property; possessions would be shared freely with the community. Further, all debts were to be erased; money was not to be individually owned. Doukhobors obeyed, because they believed that a chosen leader is infallible.

Verigen's next instruction was to abandon the use of alcohol and tobacco; which they did promptly. He fixed a date, 14 November 1894, on which they were to become vegetarians. On the appointed day the women stopped cooking beef and mutton and prepared barley soup instead. Then he forbade sex; Doukhobors could not face an uncertain future with babies in their arms. This decree, too, was followed rigorously.

The crisis Verigen had been expecting came on 29 June, 1895, a day that has become the most important Doukhobor celebration of the year. On Verigen's command, Doukhobors demonstrated against the military by burning guns and other weapons in large bonfires. Cossacks rode into the crowd, flailing their whips. Public floggings followed and four thousand Doukhobors were banished to the Wet Mountains.

They lived in caves. There was no food. Within a year six hundred were dead, and the plight of the Doukhobors received world attention. Leon Tolstoy, touched by the idealism that so resembled his own, instructed his London publisher, Aylmer Maude, a Quaker, to assign the royalties from the English edition of his novel Resurrection to the cause of Doukhobor relief. It proved to be a princely gift worth more than three thousand pounds.

American and British Quakers also rallied to the cause. It was agreed that the first group that should be helped was the exiles dying in the mountains. The Quakers obtained permission from the Russian government for the Doukhobors to leave. The island of Cyprus, nearby, British and underpopulated, was chosen as a stopping place. The Quakers, afraid that the government might suddenly decide the Doukhobors could not leave, moved quickly.

In August, 1898, the first Doukhobors, numbering 1,126, sailed from the port of Batum, on the Black Sea, to Cyprus. The Doukhobors looked around the island and realized their new home was not much of an improvement on the mountain caves in which they had starved. The soil was rocky and would not sustain such a large population.

By a quirk of history, Canada had been selected as the final destination for the Doukhobor refugees. In the autumn of 1897 a Russian prince, Pytor Aleksevich Kropotkin, a disciple of Tolstoy's and a friend of University of Toronto professor James Mavor, had toured the Canadian west and been delighted with what he saw. The land reminded him of the Russian steppes and he found Russian Mennonites, a pacifist and anarchist people, living in villages much like those they had left, untroubled by Canadian authorities. Kropotkin wrote effusive praise of Canada in a widely publicized article.

By happy coincidence, the Canadian government, desperate to stave off ruin for the railways, wanted to populate the Canadian west. James Mavor spent a feverish summer negotiating with politicians to obtain support for settling thousands of Doukhobors in the west. As Pierre Berton discovered when researching his epic history of the Canadian west, the Doukhobors did not take part in the negotiations. Their enthusiastic benefactors failed to obtain for them two concessions vital to their religion: that they not be required to take an oath of allegiance to the Queen, and that they be permitted to farm their land communally, rather than have individual deeds. The Doukhobors did not realize their sponsors hadn't obtained the concessions. As Berton noted, because of the oversight, the Doukhobors would be forced out of Saskatchewan at a frightful sacrifice.

The first site chosen for the Doukhobor migration was in the Beaver Lake area, near Edmonton. The site had to be abandoned when Conservatives, anxious to keep farmers off ranching land, gave furious speeches in the House of Commons denouncing the "cruel and murderous" Doukhobors, who would be endangering the peaceful people of Edmonton.

The Liberals went back to their surveys and decided instead on three other locations. They assembled the land by making swaps with the CPR.

The prairies had been surveyed in squares six miles by six miles, and each thirty-six-square-mile block was divided into mile-square sections. These sections were cut into homesteads of 160 acres each. Every Doukhobor male older than seventeen would be eligible for a homestead. The price — ten dollars — was to be paid in three years. There also would be a cash grant of six dollars and fifty cents for each homesteader, to be used for seed and other start-up necessities. This was the plan — but such elaborate plans take time to execute. While the Canadians were beginning to implement their idea, Tolstoy, in Russia, began to fear that the authorities would forbid the emigration. While Canada was still far from ready to receive such huge numbers of people, Tolstoy hired two cattle freighters, the *Lake Huron* and the *Lake Superior*, which were converted crudely for passenger use. Most of the crew was dismissed to make more room for passengers, who would be pressed into service as crew.

The refugees were moved by train to the port of Batum, where they huddled in an adorous iron shed which had been used for the making of naphtha, while the loading of the two freighters was completed.

The ships made two voyages each. The *Lake Huron* sailed first, on 17 December, 1898, with a cargo of two thousand Doukhobors. The crossing was terrifying. The ship was shaken by an eight-day gale so violent that the screw was sometimes out of the water. Thirty-two ghastly days after leaving Batum, the *Lake Huron* was in Halifax harbour, where the Canadians stared at the men in sheepskin pants and the women in embroidered vests and flowing skirts.

The immigrants then went to Saint John, where five CPR trains were waiting to take them west. Meanwhile an immigration official in Winnipeg, William McCreary, was trying to find food and shelter for the Doukhobors. When they arrived on the prairies, McCreary housed them in drafty holding sheds in Winnipeg, Brandon, Yorkton, Dauphin, Birtle and Qu'appelle, and there they waited in their flimsy warm-weather clothing until spring.

The *Lake Superior* left Batum a few days after the *Lake Huron* and on 27 January, 1899, after an easier crossing, landed at Saint John, New Brunswick, with Leon Tolstoy's son, Sergei, on board as a delighted observer.

The shuttle was repeated in the spring. The *Lake Superior* went to Cyprus, where sixty Doukhobors had died of malaria and hundreds were in a frightening state. The *Lake Huron*, meanwhile, was back at Batum to receive the final group, from Kars. Their destination was the North Saskatchewan River.

The Kars emigrants looked like Doukhobors in every respect, but were significantly different. Some of them, for example, did not embrace vegetarianism; some were almost prosperous, by Doukhobor standards; and a few were semi-literate and brought Russian books with them. At least four were substantial property owners, despite criticism from fellow Doukhobors, who saw the ownership of private property as against the faith.

The Kars emigrants, who became the North Saskatchewan

River Colony, respected Verigen but did not follow his pro-
scriptions blindly. A skeptical, pragmatic, ambitious and
intelligent people, they came to be known as "the Independent
Doukhobors." In a few years, they would take a token oath of
allegiance, register deeds to own their farms, and embrace
education for their children.

The ordeal of the first winter in Canada in the caves of the
North Saskatchewan River is something the immigrants'
descendants still find painful to contemplate. "They lived like
gophers," said Masha Kalesnikova, her eyes wet with tears.

Masha Kalesnikova was seventy-four when she talked about
the caves on a May afternoon in 1983. She was seated in the
cheerful clutter of her tiny pink-and-white house on the main
street of Blaine Lake, in Saskatchewan, a few miles north of the
river bank where her parents had burrowed. Arthritis has given
her an aching body and knobby knuckles. Something has gone
wrong with her hair, so she covers her scalp with bright wigs,
which are displayed, when not in use, on Styrofoam heads.
She's a kind, sentimental woman, speaking, as older Doukhobors do, in English translated so directly from the speakers'
native Russian that articles are omitted. She's a Woikin from
Langham, ten miles from Saskatoon; her younger brother,
Bill, was Emma Woikin's husband, the one who hanged
himself.

Her husband, Sam Kalesnikoff, seventy-five, is gnarled from
a life of hard labour and bright-eyed with the curiosity and
enthusiasm of youth. He's a social historian of considerable
stature in the Doukhobor community, a gifted artist of the
primitive school who has made exact-scale drawings of the cave
settlement and villages, each labelled with details such as the
location of bushes of Saskatoon berries.

"They couldn't speak, nothin'," he said, meaning that the
people in the caves had no way to appeal for help. "The government not do nothin' at all. Those people come from warm
country. They didn't build no big house for them so they
wouldn't freeze, no nothin'."

He warmed to his outrage, hitching forward in his chair,
stabbing his finger in the air. "You buy a dog, you make someplace for him to stay, but for those people, nothin' at all.
Shameful shame. And people died. The old and the young, the
children. Oh, it was so bad."

Casualties undoubtedly would have been higher but for relief supplies. Philadelphia Quakers sent goods worth thirty thousand dollars — food, wood, yarn, leather, lamps, spinning wheels, cows and grain. California responded with three carloads of dried fruit. The Canadian Council of Women, which had been founded a few years before the immigrants arrived by Lady Aberdeen, wife of the governor-general, provided enough to fill two boxcars: tools, stoves, flannel and spinning wheels.

Few of the goods reached the caves that first winter. The Doukhobors were stranded as surely as if they had been shipwrecked on a rock in the Atlantic. Saskatoon, a village of a hundred people, founded by prohibitionists, was more than fifty miles south. A few Ukrainians lived somewhere in the region and there was a Mennonite community around Rosthern, twenty-six miles away, where the nearest store was located.

But the Doukhobors had no clothes warm enough for the walk to Rosthern, and no money to buy food there. Women stretched out what little flour they had, making bread and blintzes. The community subsisted on pickled grass, tea made from rosebush roots and wild raspberry canes, and dried Saskatoon berries picked before the snowdrifts covered everything.

Rickets struck the children. Old people died of the cold. Malnutrition weakened eyesight; Doukhobors called it "night blindness." In the spring of 1900, sick as they were, the Doukhobors' first priority was to plant. They chopped trees with axes and broke the virgin earth with ploughs unchanged since the days of the Bible. That year they would thresh with flails and winnow their grain in the wind.

The elders searched for suitable sites for their villages. One was selected on a hill above the river and called Petrofka, after a village near Kars in their homeland in the Transcaucasus. They levelled the ground and found remnants of cooking pots and arrows. In their wisdom, they had chosen a place used by a past civilization.

Each of the Doukhobor villages was the same: a double row of twelve to twenty lodges in which two hundred people would live, two families to a lodge. The buildings were made of logs plastered with clay and roofed with sod packed on branches, with floors of clay that took a long time to dry. Families moved in gratefully, finding privacy as best they could. Celibacy no longer was required. Most of the married women were pregnant and courtships were flourishing under stern supervision by parents.

That summer, the men away or building the lodges, women hitched themselves to ploughs to prepare the fields for seed. The heaviest and strongest women took the most brutal position at the rear nearest the blade. A picture of Doukhobor women ploughing appeared in newspapers across Canada and scandalized city dwellers, who had no concept of the desperation of settlers too poor to buy oxen. People thought the Doukhobors were a bovine people who mistreated women.

All summer Doukhobor men sent money from their wages, though some earned as little as fifty cents for a fourteen-hour day as farm labourers. The pool of funds mounted and each village had a modest amount of purchase power. They agreed on priorities: a harness, a cow, chickens, seed, boots. Doukhobors were seen in the store at Rosthern, cackling like chickens to indicate they wanted eggs, pointing at what else they needed on the shelves. Merchants found that sign language, devised for transactions with Cree customers, worked well with the newcomers from Russia. That summer Sam Kalesnikoff's grandfather walked to Rosthern and returned — twenty-six miles one way — with a one-hundred-pound sack of flour on his back.

By the end of the summer there were more than fifty Doukhobor villages scattered across the land of the North Saskatchewan River, each with its own hay fields and herd of cattle. The first crop was ready for harvest, a meagre one but enough to see the settlers through the winter. The men began to trickle home from their labours.

That autumn, the work done, Pearl Wishloff married Alexander Konkin in the Doukhobor way; that is, by mutual consent witnessed by their families and friends, followed with a sumptuous feast. On Sam Kalesnikoff's drawing of Petrofka their lodge is number thirteen, in the centre of the village.

The most heretical of the colony was Gregori Makaroff who was scandalizing his village. He announced he would own his property, "like a Canadian farmer." He would send his son Peter to school. He had habits that were offensive to even his progressive Doukhobor neighbours. When making a trip to Rosthern for supplies, he didn't consult, as others did: he went on his own, swimming his oxen across the river, floating the wagon behind, and not asking for help from anyone. He shocked Doukhobors, too, by his outspoken cynicism about Verigen's divinity; a person might have doubts, but no one else spoke them aloud.

A wealthy Russian, Alexander Bodianski, arrived among them to urge them to resist the perfidious Canadian government's demand that they take an oath and register their deeds. Since they lacked leaders, his influence was profound in the Thunder Hill Colony and the South Colony, where Doukhobors were conservative, but he made less impression among the Doukhobors of the North Saskatchewan River Colony. Gregori Makaroff, in particular, gave him fits. Bodianski spread assurance wherever he visited that God was on the side of resistance. The earth did not belong to bureaucrats, he told the troubled Doukhobors. A long letter from patron Leon Tolstoy caused further consternation. The message was muddled and confusing, but Tolstoy seemed to believe that Verigen was Christ and should be obeyed.

In the next year, 1901, the west had a harvest of miraculous proportions. Even though Doukhobors had been able to clear and plant only a small part of their land, their returns were astounding. The CPR was unprepared for the unprecedented crop and failed to provide enough cars to take the grain to market. The Doukhobor farmers had no storage facilities, and saw their harvest spoiling in the weather.

One of the prairie farmers, William Richard Motherwell, sued the railway and won, a victory that launched his political career. He eventually became the minister of agriculture in Mackenzie King's government.

Prosperity on the North Saskatchewan brought a ferry service to the river below the village of Petrofka, a raft on which wagon and team could be floated. It was known as "the Doukhobor ferry" for many years; later it took the name of the village, and has been replaced by the handsome Petrofka bridge.

The bountiful crop was both a blessing and a pain for Doukhobors. They were torn between the demands of their faith, which would mean refusing to sign the oath and thereby losing the wonderful land, and the demands of their farming instincts, which would require them to sign the oath and lose their self-respect.

A new factor was emerging to disrupt sleep. It was proving to be inconvenient and even impossible to tend to farms that were great distances from the villages. Passionate as they were about the conviviality of the village, commuting to the far-flung herds and fields was becoming difficult. The scale of farming had been smaller in the Caucasus; on the western plains, size defeated the village model the Doukhobors dearly loved.

The lodges emptied gradually, a few families every year. Among the earliest to go were the young Konkins. Alex and Pearl were expecting their first child. It was time to build a home of their own, on their own land. The first building was a wooden shack with a sod roof, which Pearl resodded regularly. Still, when it rained the roof dripped mud, and when it was hot and dry, dust sifted over everything in the house.

A boy was born on 30 November, 1902, and was named William Alexander. The second name of every Doukhobor male is the same as his father's; Doukhobor women, on the other hand, have but one name. Because the pool of Doukhobor names is small, middle initials are an important element in distinguishing a Doukhobor male from his son or cousin.

The second son, Alexander Alexander, came along on 3 April, 1905. His father went to the federal government's land office and signed the deed, paying ten dollars for the homestead. As other Doukhobors were doing, he scratched out the oath clause and replaced it with the word "affirm" to take the sting out of surrender to the authorities.

The third son, John Alexander, arrived on 9 April, 1908. By that time the family was living in a two-story house which still stands on Konkin land. The rooms are small, as the Konkins were: Pearl Konkin measured less than five feet and her husband not much taller. The first floor has a summer kitchen, a later addition, set at right angles to the rest of the house, and two square rooms, one of which sometimes was pressed into service as a bedroom. A fine stairway, still so solid that it doesn't creak, leads to two upstairs bedrooms. One faces east and the other west; between them is a space wide enough to take another bed.

The thick walls are logs caulked with plaster, then covered

with wooden siding nailed to laths. The window frames fit loosely and show marks of having been hand-hewn. Once the house was painted white, but during the Depression paint was an indulgence. For fifty years the Konkin homestead has been silvering beautifully in the sun.

Water came from a well not far from the house, heat from an iron cookstove purchased from the Eaton's catalogue. An outhouse was built over a pit in the ground. In winter the family used a pail with a cover; Alex emptied it, first thing every morning.

The house was graced and protected by lilac bushes and there was a lawn; it was unmowed, but still it was grass. In summer Pearl would close the windows soon after sunrise to keep out the parching heat and the million flies; in winter frost rimed the inside walls every night. When the north wind blew, the linoleum on the floor lifted knee high.

The Doukhobor colonies boiled with argument as the deadline approached on which all homesteaders were required to take an oath of allegiance to the British monarch and register title to their lands. Both actions profoundly affronted their religion, which was imbedded in principles rejecting all state authority. People of the North Saskatchewan River Colony were taking a pragmatic approach that it was better to bend with the wind, but most Doukhobors believed fiercely that the government must be defied. At ten dollars a homestead, the cost of land was seven cents an acre, a great temptation to bend.

Meanwhile the government was becoming more rigid. When the Doukhobors first came to Canada Ottawa was happy to welcome anyone who would open up the west. Few had realized that the 270,480 acres given Doukhobors in Saskatchewan and Manitoba were among the best wheat-growing land in the world. The federal government would not ease its regulations to accommodate the Doukhobor creed.

Leon Tolstoy, aware of the dilemma faced by his protégés, importuned the czar to declare amnesty for the Doukhobors in exile in Russia and to allow Peter Verigen to go to Canada to help his people. In the absence of Verigen's direction, the Canadian Doukhobors were splitting into factions. The five thousand Community Doukhobors wanted to live by their traditions. The three thousand Independent Doukhobors, who lived on the North Saskatchewan, believed in compromise. A small group, the Sons of Freedom, declared all the rest back-sliders. True believers, they felt, should get out of Canada before the poison of assimilation could take hold.

A handful of the orthodox Doukhobors set off in the summer of 1902 in the general direction of the United States border. Royal Canadian Northwest Mounted Police turned them back at Minnedosa, far from their objective.

In the autumn of 1902 Peter Verigen was released from exile in Shenkursk. He arrived in Yorkton, Saskatchewan in December, and went at once to Otradne, the Doukhobor village where his elderly mother was living. When Canadian officials asked him how he planned to advise the Doukhobors, he avoided confrontation by answering that he was sure his people would be cooperative.

In fact, Verigen saw no hope for the situation. His plan was to move the Community Doukhobors to a location where they would not have to sign documents. Meanwhile he asked the Sons of Freedom to stop making trouble for the community. (The Sons of Freedom decided that Verigen was misled.)

Adding to the tension, Gregori Makaroff announced that his son's education would not stop at simple literacy, which was the most education a few Doukhobors had ever possessed. Peter, then eight, would have "a whole education." Makaroff was making himself so unpopular with his radical views that other Doukhobors didn't want their cattle to associate with his cattle. Peter spent the summer keeping his father's herd, known in the community as "the devil's cattle," away from the "holy cattle" of the neighbours.

Peter Makaroff was one of ten Doukhobor sons attending school in 1903. The teacher, Michael Sherbinin, came from St. Petersburg to live among the Doukhobors, in the way modern young idealists volunteer in Third World countries. In 1905 Philadelphia Quakers supplied teachers and built two school-houses in the North Saskatchewan River Colony, one of them at Rosthern. The school was a distance from the colony; sons would have to live apart from their families to attend, a separation abhorrent to Doukhobors. Peter Makaroff was one of two children who attended. Later the kindly-intentioned Quakers offered to move entire families to Philadelphia so the children could be with parents while getting their education. A few accepted, but soon returned to the colony. Peter Makaroff, however, went alone and stayed.

At the urging of the Quakers, one-room schoolhouses soon dotted the prairies, shacks that were moved as requirements changed. One, called Ospennia, was a half-mile from the Konkin farmhouse. William Alexander, Alex Alexander and John Alexander attended and became literate. For many years, the Ospennia teachers boarded with the Konkins.

Peter Vasilievitch Verigen felt the need of family. He sent for the wife he had deserted twenty-four years ago and the son he had never seen. Peter Petrovitch Verigen, twenty-four, was more than the elder Peter expected. Handsome and charismatic like his father, he was possessed of a hot temper, a thirst for vodka and a passion for gambling.

However, young Peter showed unexpected skill at handling the Sons of Freedom. He encountered a small group of them protesting the imposition of the oath by parading in the nude, symbolic for the Sons of Freedom of a return to innocence and purity. He told them they were crazy. They were so stunned that all but one dressed at once and went home.

The elder Peter decided it would be prudent to return Peter Petrovitch Verigen to Russia, and his son was dispatched speedily.

The deadline for signing the deeds and taking the oath was the end of 1906. Frank Oliver had replaced Clifford Sifton as secretary of the interior in the Liberal cabinet and, in the unbridled bigotry typical of the era, he did not disguise his hatred of Doukhobors. He issued warnings that their land would be forfeit if they didn't comply. Few Doukhobors believed that the government would be so monstrously unfair to such a great number of people. In six years they had broken into virgin prairie, built homes and farm buildings, erected fences and purchased cattle and horses, sewn curtains, dug roads, seen their babies born, buried their dead.

Oliver, however, was determined, and the situation in the west had changed dramatically since 1899 when 7,500 Doukhobors had arrived. The first Doukhobors were part of a total immigration to the west of only 31,900 people. As the fame of the rich, dark soil of the Canadian prairies spread through Europe, whipped along by government and CPR publicists, immigration soared. In 1905 it was necessary to create two new provinces, Saskatchewan and Alberta; 200,000 settlers moved west in 1906. Canada no longer needed Doukhobors. Oliver was pleased at the opportunity to evict them legally.

Peter Verigen, the elder, diplomatically removed himself to the United States to avoid being caught in the tragedy he saw ahead. When the deadline came, Ottawa did as it had threatened, seizing 256,000 acres of Doukhobor farms valued at between three and ten thousand dollars, for a total of some eleven million dollars. The government took title to 1,605 homesteads and to everything on them, leaving each dispossessed family a plot of fifteen acres in areas adjoining their villages.

Some five thousand Doukhobors lost everything they had worked six years to build. The two thousand Doukhobors of the North Saskatchewan River Colony, however, complied by signing the deeds and paying ten dollars for each homestead. About a thousand more living around Yorkton also yielded.

Broken-hearted, the hold-outs packed their clothing and possessions, loaded them on wagons and left, raising clouds of dust that blotted out the sun.

Land offices opened in 1907 in Prince Albert and Yorkton to dispose of the Doukhobor farms at bargain prices. No newcomers to the west had an easier start than the men who stood in line to buy. The crowd was so large and unruly that police had to be summoned to keep order.

Peter V. Verigen thought of a scheme to move the Community Doukhobors. He would purchase land in British Columbia and hold title in a limited company. Doukhobors who lived on the land would not own it, and therefore would not be required to sign deeds.

Sons of Freedom Doukhobors, furious at the Doukhobors who were eating meat, drinking liquor, and taking oaths, chose as a target for their outrage the schoolhouses. Many of the schoolhouses were being used as storage sheds, but the Freedomites torched a few to get the attention of blasphemers.

They were arrested and sent to prison, where they were the most frustrating convicts wardens had ever seen. In perfect consistency with their beliefs, they refused to cooperate with prison rules. When compelled by force to obey, they stopped eating. One died of starvation in Stony Mountain Penitentiary.

Peter Makaroff, meanwhile, was in high school. His teacher was a Dutch pacifist, Herman Fast, who had acquired a knowledge of Russian from his wife. Peter was proving to be a brilliant student.

The Doukhobor exodus to British Columbia took place in 1909, a long line of covered wagons stretching to the horizon. Two-thirds of the Doukhobors who had opened up great parts of Manitoba and Saskatchewan, some five thousand people, were in that sad parade to the CPR station at Broadview.

In the Kootenays they built villages and worked together, sharing tools and pooling the profits, which would be reinvested in the community. In a few years they had farms and orchards humming all over the valley and had established a brickyard, a jam factory, a lumber mill and a pumping plant on the site of a future power-generating station.

The Independent Doukhobors who remained in Saskatchewan were proving to be superb farmers. Many of them, especially those with sons who would need farms of their own, were acquiring land as rapidly as they could. Alex Konkin was advised to do so by a friendly land agent but needed little urging. At ten dollars for a 160-acre homestead, expansion was irresistable.

Bumper crops on the North Saskatchewan created a demand for railway service. Doukhobors protested having to haul their harvests to Duck Lake, a three-mile round trip. In 1911 the Canadian National Railway purchased a homestead from William Johnson and put a station on it. The station was not far from the log cabin of Hugh Gillies, a pioneer from Wingham, Ontario; his cabin was one of the stops on the horseback mail-delivery route.

A grain elevator with a capacity of twenty-five thousand bushels was built and the first train puffed into the new station. A village sprang up, first a general store and then the Bank of Commerce in a shack eight feet wide. Gillies moved his post office there. A lumber yard opened for business not far from a harness shop. An early resident was William Diehl, one of three scouts from Prince Albert who captured Louis Riel.

The community was declared a village on 15 March, 1912, by the Honourable A.P. McNab, Saskatchewan minister of municipal affairs. It was called Blaine Lake, though the lake itself, named for a man who drowned in it, was three miles to the east. The Royal North-West Mounted Police established a post on the main street to keep an eye on bootleggers, paying the constable in charge fifteen dollars a month. A public well was dug and a sidewalk of tamarack planks went down.

Two Russian-speaking doctors, J.I. Perverseff and B.P. Batanoff, whose wife also was a doctor, hung up their shingles. A newspaper, the *Blaine Lake Echo*, was launched and Tom Lee opened the Blaine Lake Café. On shopping days as many as two hundred yoke of oxen filled the dusty main street as farmers came to town, their children hopping with excitement in the backs of the wagons.

Pearl and Alex Konkin had their first daughter, Mary, on 30 July, 1915. An easy-going, sweet-dispositioned child, she was adored by her parents and big brothers, Bill, thirteen, Alex, ten, and John, seven. The Konkin way of raising children was low-keyed and relaxed. Both parents were openly affectionate and expected that the children would be pious, obedient and uncomplaining when required to do chores. None of the children was spanked; the response to a misdemeanor was a request for an explanation in a tone that conveyed disappointment, distress and perplexity that such a fine young person could have done something thoughtless.

Pearl taught her children Doukhobor psalms and prayers and both parents told them bedtime stories by the light of the coal-oil lamp. There was a division of labour in the job-training: Alex took his sons into the fields, while Pearl showed Mary how to cook and to care for the chickens.

Young Peter Makaroff returned from Philadelphia and at seventeen was ready for university. His proud father sent him to study law in Regina at the University of Saskatchewan. In the two hundred fifty years of the faith, Peter was the first Doukhobor who went to university.

War broke out in Europe in 1914 and Canadians enlisted to fight. Doukhobors were afraid the government would not respect their pacifism. Peter Verigen suspected they would be conscripted and confided his concerns to his flock. It was an unsettling warning, but Canadians were enlisting in great numbers and there appeared to be no immediate danger of conscription.

The war was bringing enormous prosperity. In 1917, Northern wheat was selling for $2.40 a bushel at Fort William and wages for hard-to-get field hands ranged between $6 and $9 for a fourteen-hour day. The Kootenay Doukhobors, who called themselves the Christian Community of Universal Brotherhood Limited, had assets of a million dollars.

The Blaine Lake community also organized, calling itself the Society of Independent Doukhobors. Its secretary-treasurer was Peter Makaroff, who had just established his law practice in Saskatoon. Doukhobors in the Kootenays sneered that the Independents were "non-Doukhobors." The Blaine Lake people had accepted government regulations, were sending their children to school, and were drinking vodka, smoking cigarettes and eating meat.

Canada suffered thirteen thousand casualties in the battle of Vimy Ridge in 1917, a massive tragedy that created a frantic need for recruits. Enlistments had dried up. There were demands, particularly in Ontario, that the government impose conscription. The first step was registration of all men of military age, a move that resulted in protests in Quebec and elsewhere, notably at Blaine Lake.

The small Royal North-West Mounted Police detachment at Blaine Lake rounded up young Doukhobors who refused to register. It was August and there were crops standing in the fields, but within twenty-four hours a thousand Doukhobors had poured into the village, boiling mad. Nikito Popoff, who owned a car, a McLaughlin Buick, was dispatched to drive the fifty miles over a wagon trail to Saskatoon to fetch Peter Makaroff.

When he arrived in Blaine Lake, Makaroff asked the officer in charge, Sergeant John Wilson, to show his authority for the arrests. Wilson responded rudely, at which Makaroff lost his temper and promptly was arrested and taken to the Blaine Lake jail. He wrote a message to Ottawa, which he smuggled out of his cell to a friend who put it on the telegraph wire.

Sergeant Wilson proceded to try the thirty Doukhobors he had arrested, pressing a justice of the peace into service as a judge. Makaroff protested heatedly that the trial was improper and was one of the first convicted. The justice of the peace fined some of the defendants and sentenced Makaroff and others to prison with an order that they were to be conscripted into the army on discharge.

Harvesting stopped for miles around as furious Doukhobors,

ready to explode, gathered in Blaine Lake. They were threatening to burn their wheat fields when a telegram arrived from Ottawa ordering Sergeant Wilson to release the prisoners. Makaroff went to Ottawa and was assured that Sergeant Wilson had acted without authorization. There were no further attempts to pressure Doukhobors.

Wilson proved not to be a stable man. A few years later he blew his wife's head off with a shotgun, hid her body in a culvert, and the following day was married. On 23 April, 1920, he was hanged for the crime.

Pearl Konkin was forty-two years old in 1920, and her husband forty-three, when they realized they were having another child. Their sons were almost grown. Bill was eighteen that year, Alex fifteen and John twelve. Little Mary, everyone's darling, was five.

"It was a menopause baby," Mary explained as she sat in her spotless living room in Saskatoon on a cold February morning in 1983, a box of family photographs on her lap. "There were no precautions at that time. My mother didn't know what to do."

Mary and her husband, Pete Perverseff, are living in retirement, both in their late sixties, after a lifetime of the hard labour of farming. Like all the Konkins, Mary is gregarious and hospitable, open about her feelings, weeping over the family deaths, chuckling at the fond memories of good times, but her eyes are shrewd and watchful of a stranger even when she is laughing. She had a fond expression as she recalled her sister's birth.

The new Konkin baby was delivered in the homestead, like all the Konkins, by a Doukhobor midwife. Pearl was in no great pain, and the baby was pink and healthy, though small: a little girl the family named Gruna. The closest English translation is "Emma."

The date of the birth was 30 December, 1920. Alex went to Blaine Lake a few days later to register the arrival and placed it on 1 January, 1921. Fathers were casual about birth dates in that era. Many Canadians now in their sixties and seventies have discovered, when searching the records, that they were not born on the day, or even in the year, in which they always believed they were born, and that their registered names are entirely different from the ones they assumed to be theirs.

Mary Konkin Perverseff described Emma's early years as a doting mother might, her face full of pride and affection, no trace of resentment at being replaced as the family's baby. "Our parents treated us like little dolls," she remembered fondly. "Our brothers too."

The Konkin family is tightly loyal and loving. A wedding, a death, a Konkin in trouble brings them running. Of the five children, two were surviving in 1983, Mary and Bill. Bill, seventy-nine and vigorous in defiance of a seriously weakened heart, travelled across the country in 1983 on a sentimental quest for family, visiting every Konkin he could find, giving them fussy advice about keeping well.

When the Konkin children were growing up, the language of the household was Russian. Pearl was never comfortable in English, although the young Konkins spoke it among themselves. Older Doukhobors still lapse into Russian when they want to be clear about what they are saying. When they do, their faces loosen and they laugh more readily.

Each Konkin child developed a set of similar characteristics. All were affectionate and honest; all had an element of Russian darkness in their natures; all kept their troubles to themselves and believed that the way to meet disaster is to cope with it and then forget it; and all had a limitless capacity for hard work and a passion for perfection.

They constructed minor personality differences on that bedrock of attributes. Bill was the family bulldog, full of muscle and opinions, the most assured; Alex was a genius with machinery, an advanced agronomist, a shrewd land-holder; John had the greatest social conscience, the neighbour to call when someone died; he was the man to elect as school trustee, the host who would give hospitality to travelling strangers. Mary was the light-hearted one; Emma was the most intelligent.

"She was so-o-o-o smart," Mary said with satisfaction. "You couldn't believe how smart she was."

Chapter Two

Emma Konkin was not pretty, even as a child. Her face was narrow, dominated by a high forehead, a long nose and a sharp chin; her mouth was thin-lipped and her wispy hair an indeterminate colour between blonde and brown. Her loveliest features were her large, deep-set, extraordinarily blue eyes. Slender, light on her feet, quick-moving, full of music and generosity and laughter, she was popular all her life, even in Kingston Penitentiary.

Rumour hung over her parentage because she bore little resemblance to the other Konkins. Some, and Emma was one of them, believed that her father was Trofem Kurchenko, the hired man on the Konkin farm. He was thirty-five when she was born, and she grew to look very much like him. When he died in 1967 he left her everything he owned, which included a farm and a house in Blaine Lake; she made the funeral arrangements and selected his gravestone.

Asked if Kurchenko was Emma's father, Bill Konkin turned steely and said, "Some thought so and some didn't."

No Konkin is much inclined to explore the subject of Emma's parentage. Whatever the truth, her birth apparently did not upset the calm and warm relationship between her mother and Alex E., nor was there anything in their treatment of her to indicate that she was other than their child.

Lucas Sawula, called Louie by everyone who knows him, was Emma's second husband. In May, 1983, he was interviewed in his apartment in the handsome high-rise in Saskatoon where many well-to-do retired people have taken up residence. At seventy-five, Louie Sawula looked younger than his years, much of his hair still dark, his face merry and responsive. He spoke English with a heavy Ukrainian accent, so he tended to keep his sentences short. When he is amused, which is frequently, because Louie Sawula relishes the human comedy, he has a high-pitched "hoo-hoo" laugh that is infectious.

"Trofem was Emma's father, I think so," he grinned, hugely enjoying the Konkin family scandal. "And Emma thought so too. She look like him, she smart like him."

Emma grew up loved and indulged by all. Her disposition was sunny and she was quick to be helpful. Her smallness and a certain air of frailty brought out protectiveness in her brothers and sister. For one thing, she had an alarming tendency to bleed copiously at the slightest injury.

"If she cut her finger it bled a lot," Mary remembered. "If she got a nosebleed, it was terrible. You'd worry yourself to death."

The two little girls adored their big brothers and followed them everywhere. "When they went to pick tomatoes," Mary said, laughing, "we were right there." All three youths accepted the constant presence of their small sisters with good grace but the youngest brother, John, seemed to have the closest bond.

On Sunday mornings the family dressed in its best for the wagon ride to Blaine Lake for services in the Doukhobor prayer home. Doukhobors divide their congregation, the men to the left of the central aisle and the women to the right. The hall is bare of all ornaments except for two framed messages which hang on the confronting wall. One reads TOIL AND PEACEFUL LIFE and the other THE WELFARE OF ALL THE WORLD IS NOT WORTH THE LIFE OF ONE CHILD.

A table at the front of the room bears the Doukhobor symbols, a loaf of golden-crusted, fresh-baked bread, a cut-glass pitcher of water, a cut-glass bowl of salt water and bread being the staff of life, representing peace and hospitality among Slavic people through the ages.

There is no clergy and no formal ritual in Doukhobor services but the congregation knows exactly what to do. An appointed elder, selected for his dignity of bearing and good sense, opens the service with a welcome. Newcomers are introduced and expected to speak. Parishioners who have been travelling give an account of what they have seen. Then there are prayers, which are sung in Russian, men and women standing at the front of the room facing one another.

The selection of prayers is up to the participants. By nods and eye contact, a person makes known that he or she will lead the congregation in the next prayer; the man or woman with the truest, strongest voice moves in smoothly to establish the key. The sound produced is full of profound melancholy, Russian spirituals resonating with exile, reverence and loss. Even when the congregation is small and elderly, as it is now in Blaine Lake, the music is heart-stirring.

Because all stand for the singing, and services can be lengthy, heavy women whose legs ache from a lifetime spent on their feet in kitchens will position themselves prudently near the walls where they can lean.

Singing is the heart of the Doukhobor faith. The prayers and psalms are often narratives, stories of good deeds, courage, peaceful eternity, pure hearts and the well of piety that produces kind thought. Their power, found in all liturgical music, comes from the deep faith they express and the unity of their hope.

Few people consult song books. It is nothing for Doukhobor children to know sixty prayers and psalms by heart before they are six years old; adults know hundreds.

Some of the hymns have been translated into English and appear in a pamphlet, *Historical Exposition on Doukhobor Beliefs,* prepared by Eli A. Popoff. A sampling gives the flavour. For instance one, "He Is Happiest Who Loves All Creatures," begins:

Fortunate is he, who loves all living creatures.
The pulse of creation beats dear to his heart.
For whom all in nature is kindred and near.
Man and bird, flower and tree — none to him
    Stand apart.

The Doukhobor commitment to pacifism is nowhere better expressed than in these lines:

Friends, let's go forward.
Away with guns.
We sing the song of freedom.
Away with political boundaries and with kings,
And with military power.
We sing the song of freedom.

Emma Konkin, a precocious toddler, had learned dozens of Doukhobors hymns by the age of three; her sister, Mary, was walking a half-mile each day to the one-room schoolhouse called Ospennia, at the end of the Konkin homestead road. The little girl watched every day for her older sister's return and pounced on her, avid to know what she had learned.

Mary, good-natured and patient, would open her books and read. Emma committed to memory everything she heard and soon was "reading" to herself, turning the pages at the appropriate places. Mary pointed out the Russian words and was astounded that her little sister quickly learned to read in Russian. Mary thinks Emma was about four when she could read every Russian book in the house.

"I'm giving myself a little bit of credit here," Mary said modestly — but the fact was, she taught Emma arithmetic and reading and writing in English before the child was five.

"We'd sit down and I'd give her all the numbers and the ABCs and everything," Mary recalled, her face bright with the pleasure of it.

Students were allowed to bring their small sisters and brothers to school if the little ones would be still, so Emma became a frequent student long before she could be enrolled officially. She passed the time listening to the lessons and making crayon drawings in a scribbler. She possessed an early knack for proportion and perspective and, even when she was small, she talked of being an artist.

Emma was not eligible to begin classes in September, 1926, since she was only five years old. She objected so much and so persistently that in May, 1927 the teacher yielded. Emma Konkin was ecstatic.

The teacher asked Emma if she could write numbers.

Emma nodded her head vigorously.

"Write one to ten," the teacher told her.

Emma hesitated. "I can write to one hundred," she offered, and did so.

"All right," said the teacher. "I suppose you can also print the alphabet all the way through."

Emma wriggled in delight. "I can write words," she said proudly.

"Emma just loved books." Mary beamed telling the story. "She loved to learn and she was so quick, so quick."

In the evenings Mary and Emma returned to the schoolhouse for Russian lessons from an emigré, Alexander Nazarov. In most weather they walked but when the temperature sunk lower than thirty or forty below and the very air seemed frozen, a brother would hitch a team and take them to classes in the cutter with a horsehide over them to keep out the cold.

The highlight of the summer for the children was the two weeks they spent at a Doukhobor camp near Watrous, on Little Manitou Lake, where they lived in a tent and bathed in the waters, which Doukhobors believed had power to heal. Pearl Konkin's crippled sister went every year, as much for the singing and traditional dances as in hope of a cure.

Mary remembered that the singing was beautiful. In that sylvan setting beside the lake, the soaring voices that spoke of aching homesickness and loss touched the heart. Tears were understandable but to Mary's consternation Emma would sob unconsolably and so loudly that their mother would ask Mary to take the child out of earshot.

Mary was bitterly disappointed to leave the gathering. "I had to go away with her," Mary explained. "Back to the tents or around the lake. Anything with feeling, Emma would cry. And not only one time. If anybody had tears, she had tears. She was very sentimental."

Emma's ability to memorize effortlessly was the family wonder. She would read a poem or speech over twice, maybe three times, and know it perfectly. She seemed incapable of forgetting anything that interested her.

The bright scholar was expected to do her share of woman's farm chores. She and Mary milked cows, tended the garden, took care of the chickens, and carried water in pails from the well. They tried not to spill half of it before they reached their destination. They also helped their mother scrub the floors and do the laundry in boilers heated on the wood stove.

Most of all, they cooked.

"My mother had high blood pressure," Mary said. "It was the cooking that did it, especially feeding the threshing gangs."

Young Doukhobor women who can remember feeding the threshing gangs say bluntly that the work was sheer hell for the women. Threshing gangs, some of them hired men and some neighbours, used to go from farm to farm in the late summer in groups of sixteen, eighteen or more. Whatever farm they visited, it was the duty of the woman to cook four meals a day for them, and heaven help the woman who didn't have daughters.

Cooking began at four in the morning with preparation of a huge breakfast, which the men ate before the sun rose. When the tables had been cleared and the dishes done, it was time to bake bread, pies, cakes, tarts. Vegetables were taken from the garden, cleaned, chopped and cooked. By noon dinner was ready, a groaning table of borscht (vegetable soup), potatoes, sometimes meat, vareniki (dumplings filled with cheese), blintzi (thin pancakes), pyrohi (baked pastries stuffed with cheese, or mashed beans, or sauerkraut), galhooptsi (cabbage rolls) and nalesniki (thin pancakes wrapped around some filling such as cottage cheese and drenched in melted butter), rice, bread, eggs, fruit, preserves, pickles, pies and cakes.

At four the women carried lunch to the men in the fields: sandwiches, tarts, coffee, cakes and cookies. The men ate hurriedly, on the run, and when they finished the women went back to the sweltering kitchen to start supper, as gargantuan a meal as dinner, which the men ate when darkness stopped the harvesting, around nine or ten. Men dropped into exhausted sleep as the women cleaned up and organized breakfast, falling into bed themselves around midnight.

"I'll never forget feeding threshing gangs," Masha Kalesnikova said fervently. "Never, *never*. No wonder I have arthritis, look at my hands. It takes a long time to make borscht. You have to have carrots, beets, peppers, celery . . . you chop and chop and chop. We had to cut potatoes on the board. And make bread, so *much* bread."

Emma developed into an instinctive cook. She could follow her mother's recipes but she was disposed to add an unexpected ingredient or an unusual flavouring that transformed them. It became part of her legend that she could produce, seemingly without effort, great quantities of delicious food.

All her life Emma expressed her affectionate nature and her need for approval by cooking.

On summer nights families visited one another, travelling in dusty buggies. Men gathered to discuss farming and the perfidious bankers in the east while women knitted and talked about the children. Children could play, but quietly, waiting for the best part when they would be drawn into singing Russian folk songs, after which the hostess served a "lunch" that sent them home glassy-eyed.

The toys of the children were homemade kites and boomerangs. When there were enough children, they started a game of Russian baseball. In winter their pleasure was sliding on the ice since few had skates, or sledding on contraptions they made themselves.

When Mary Konkin was fourteen she graduated from grade eight, which was as far as the Ospennia schoolhouse could take her. A friend was going on to high school in Blaine Lake. Mary wept and begged to be allowed to go too but her mother said it was out of the question. Blaine Lake was ten miles away. How could the family take her there and back every day? Mary argued that some farm children boarded in the village, but Pearl rejected that solution. "What would you do in the evenings?" she asked her daughter. "You would be all alone."

Mary protested in vain. She wasn't surprised. Some seventy percent of her friends went no further than primary school. Still she had a sense of loss that was hard to swallow, though she kept her disappointment to herself. The Konkin household did not accept whining.

"It wasn't so bad," Mary said stoutly during an interview in Saskatoon in February, 1983. "I had lots of work to do at home helping my mother. There was crocheting, knitting, mending clothes; lots to do."

As farm children Mary and Emma had no illusions about animal procreation, but they were mystified as to its application to humans. They would never ask their father, and their mother gave no hints. They came to the conclusion on their own that babies came from being married. When they heard of a pregnant woman who wasn't married, they were baffled.

They asked Pearl how this could happen, a baby but no husband. Pearl pondered a moment and then answered amiably, "Well, that's a problem all right."

Winters were periods of comparative rest, the fields buried under glittering snow that squeaked underfoot, the herd in the cold barns, preserves lining the shelves of the root cellar. Farm families were rarely snow-bound. They travelled by cutter to see their neighbours and to go to Blaine Lake for Sunday services.

The homestead was comfortable enough by day but at night, when the fire in the cookstove was low, the rooms were so cold that water froze in pails. The Konkins went to bed in socks and long underwear, warm hats or scarves on their heads, sleeping on down-feather tickings and wrapped in Pearl's quilts. Despite the cold, Emma rose chipper and singing in the morning, a happy little girl.

Relations among the surrounding Doukhobors, however, were far from idyllic. To the annoyance of the Konkins and other Independent Doukhobors, the Sons of Freedom were still creating trouble in the Blaine Lake region. In 1923 and 1924 there were more mysterious burnings of schoolhouses, for which the Sons of Freedom were blamed. On 28 October, 1924, the dispute among Doukhobors turned ugly. Peter V. Verigen, travelling west in a CPR coach through the mountains of British Columbia, was blown to bits by a bomb that had been placed under his seat.

Mourning Doukhobors sent for his son, Peter Petrovitch Verigen, who was living with his family at Rostov-on-Don, in Russia. The younger Verigen showed little enthusiasm for returning to Canada. He said he would need money first, and funds were sent. Still he didn't come, and British Columbia Doukhobors grew desperate for his council. They were holding out against the insistence of an increasingly hostile provincial government that they send their children to school. Heavy fines were being levied and Doukhobors were filling the jails.

Verigen finally arrived in New York in September, 1927, on the luxury liner *Aquitania*; he left his wife and children behind in Rostov. Asked what he planned to do about the Doukhobor school question, he replied ambiguously, "We will take everything of value that Canada has to offer, but we will never give up our Doukhobor souls."

He promised to unite the three factions of his people: those living communally in British Columbia, who formed the majority; the Independents on the prairies; and the Sons of Freedom, who could be found in both regions. Verigen was a compelling orator who could fire up an audience, but sometimes he seemed drunk and incomprehensible. Sometimes he wept, occasionally he displayed a burst of violence that was shocking. Still he was Peter Verigen, in whom Jesus was presumed to exist, and he could not be rejected.

He called the coalition of Doukhobors who believed in him "Named Doukhobors," and retained the Doukhobor lawyer, Peter Makaroff, as his legal advisor. In a document he called the "Protocol," he set forth a list of concessions he wanted from the federal government and went to Ottawa to present his conditions.

He, Makaroff and others of the delegation stayed in the Chateau Laurier until the prime minister, William Lyon Mackenzie King, reluctantly agreed to see them.

King told them their demands were pointless. In most cases, he said, the government was respecting Doukhobor practices. The critical issue of compulsory schooling was out of his hands because it was a provincial matter. The request that Doukhobors be allowed to divorce in their traditional manner, which was whenever a husband said so, was out of the question; marriages could not be dissolved except by courts.

The Sons of Freedom grew more active the following year. Schoolhouses for miles around Blaine Lake were torched, and in nearby Kamsack there was a nude demonstration which the police dispersed with fire hoses. Verigen, known as "Peter the Second" to distinguish him from his father, talked of riding out of Canada "on a white horse" to find a new land where Doukhobors could live according to their beliefs. He spoke of raising half a million dollars for the migration and proposed South America as a destination.

The times were against him. In October, 1929, the crash of the New York Stock Exchange helped to send the world price of wheat plummeting. The financial disaster reached Blaine Lake and caught the Konkins when they were overextended. William A., twenty-seven, the oldest son, had been married for ten years to Hannah Demoskoff. In the manner of farm families, the couple lived with his parents for about two years until his father was able to give him a quarter section about six miles from the homestead. An ambitious man, Bill was farming there but reaching out for more land.

Alex A., twenty-four, who inherited his father's bushy black eyebrows, married Annie Planidin in 1922 and they lived with his parents almost seven years before his father could provide him with a quarter section of his own. During that period, when the small homestead was packed with people, Annie was a treasure. She got along beautifully with Pearl, her mother-in-law, and was devoted to her nieces, Mary, emerging as a happy-go-lucky teenager, and little Emma. Annie made clothes for them as a mother would and romped with them like a sister, even after her own two daughters, Agatha and Mabel, arrived. The onset of the Depression found Alex, Annie and their daughters, aged five and one, newly settled in their own place about a mile north of the family homestead.

John A., a burly twenty-one-year-old, had married Lena Padowski in 1928 and the young couple moved into the east room of the homestead just vacated by his brother.

Mary was fourteen and had just finished school when the Depression struck; Emma was almost nine.

The harvest of 1929 was even larger than the previous year's bumper crop and much of the 1928 crop was still in the grain elevators. The world market had been glutted by unprecedented bounteous crops everywhere and Canadian wheat, at $1.60 a bushel, was overpriced.

Blaine Lake suffered another calamity in the spring of 1930. A fire broke out in the bowling alley and burned down much of the business district, threatening homes and cracking windows in stores across the wide street. The village was rebuilt with bricks, but it was not until after the Depression that all the ugly gaps left by gutted stores were filled.

There was almost no rain in Saskatchewan in the summer of 1930. The southern part of the province, the desert-like Palliser Triangle, felt the drought the most severely. Average per-capita income fell by seventy-two percent as hot, dry winds wailed over the parched earth and lifted off the topsoil, blowing away the precious seed.

Dust was the despair of all. There was no way to keep it out of the house, out of food, out of eyes and dry throats. Women wrapped newborns in swaddling blankets and watched hopelessly as dust filled the folds of the cloth and the babies' eye sockets.

People put Vaseline in their nostrils to help screen out the dust and wrapped wet towels over their faces to work outdoors.

Graveyards filled with those who committed suicide or succumbed to what was called "dust pneumonia." The mental hospital at Weyburn received women driven mad by the wail of the pitiless wind.

Banks foreclosed on mortgages and people lost the work of a generation. In 1932 wheat sold on the world market at the lowest price in three hundred years. Number One Northern sold for thirty-nine cents a bushel at Moose Jaw, where yearling steers were fetching an average of $2.75 per hundredweight. Hardest hit of all the provinces, Saskatchewan abandoned the Liberals and elected eight Conservatives in the summer of 1932, helping to make Richard B. Bennett prime minister of Canada. An Unemployment Relief Act was passed, but the federal government provided little money, pointing out that welfare was a provincial responsibility. Most of the relief offices were in the cities, out of reach of farmers in desperate need of food, clothing, fodder and fuel.

Churches opened food kitchens to feed the starving. Stories of deprivation on the prairies brought relief supplies from Ontario. Blaine Lake got some fruit, vegetables and clothing to distribute to the needy; everyone was needy.

One of the Konkins, Fred, the younger son of Emma's brother John A., on an icy morning in February, 1983, talked about the destitution. Bitterly he told of an old couple, both blind, living about seven miles from Blaine Lake, who were put out of their home by a bank foreclosure. At fifty-one, Fred Konkin was a man grown too heavy, his belly straining his shirt buttons. He's a room-warmer, the kind of person who can fill an awkward silence with pleasantries, a beatific beam on his face while his eyes watch for the shy ones. When he told about the blind couple, he put himself in their shoes.

"They knew how far to walk to the well, they knew how far to walk to the woodpile, they knew how far to walk to the out-house," he said, gesturing to indicate the locations. "The bank came and took possession and led them out to the road. They sat all night by the road, two old blind people."

Indignant neighbours found them the next morning. Despite their own poverty, nearby farmers raised enough money to cover the mortgage payment and put the blind couple back in their home.

That incident, one of the most poignant of hundreds of evictions in the early thirties, led to the decision of R. B. Bennett's government to pass an amendment to the Homestead Act called the Farmers' Creditors' Arrangement Act, which gave Saskatchewan farmers protection from seizure. The Konkins were to avail themselves of every bit of help they could get from it to hang on to farms they had bought with a down payment. Wheat often could not be sold at any price.

Meanwhile, Doukhobor stubbornness was becoming more than British Columbia could bear. The attorney general talked of putting five thousand people in jail if necessary, as judges increased sentences and wardens placed mattresses on prison floors to accommodate the dissident Doukhobors. Even Peter Verigen was in jail in Prince Albert for perjury, in a tangled case involving a debt. His unconscionable sentence of three years was an indication of the mood of the courts. Work began on a new prison on Piers Island off Sidney, Vancouver Island, which would house Doukhobor women. The first group took up residence behind bars in 1932.

Peter Makaroff succeeded in having Verigen's sentence reduced to eighteen months. Verigen had served half of this in 1933 when the government made a clumsy attempt to deport him. He was taken from the prison in secret and placed on a train to Halifax, where he would be put on a ship to Russia. A Doukhobor rescue team travelled by airplane to Halifax; they arrived in time to protest before a Halifax judge, who declared the deportation illegal.

Makaroff, newly appointed a KC in recognition of his skill, was drawn into a group who talked of a new political party that would be founded on pacifism and a more fair social order. Makaroff was among the first to join the Cooperative Commonwealth Party after the Regina manifesto of 1933 created the party. In the summer of 1934 he was the provincial CCF candidate for Shellbrook.

Doukhobors who had avoided polling booths all their voting lives turned out to elect one of their own, but Makaroff was defeated by his Liberal opponent whose party formed the government that year.

Saskatchewan farmers thought the millionaires of Montreal and Toronto were the source of their misery. The Saskatchewan branch of the United Farmers of Canada argued for "social ownership and cooperative production," which sounded like a Doukhobor prayer meeting, and linked with a leftist labour group, the Independent Labour Party, forming in Regina. The Canadian Communist Party, led by the imprisoned Tim Buck, was also attracting supporters across the west. The movement to overthrow capitalism grew quickly on the blighted prairies and young men frightened their elders by arguing for the Marxist ideal that was found in the people's government of Russia. In 1934 young Doukhobors established the Progressive Society of Doukhobors, which Peter Verigen dismissed disgustedly as "no-Doukhobors and Bolshevists." None of the Blaine Lake Konkins joined. They liked the socialist ideals of collectivism and pacificism but they were attached to private ownership as well.

Doukhobors seemed to be as disparate a group as could be found in any Canadian community. James F.C. Wright, a journalist who lived in the Blaine Lake district in the thirties, wrote a book about them, *Slava Bohu,* and said, "Borscht soup, the steam bath and pickled cucumbers now remained the only three things with which the Doukhobors were in unanimous agreement."

Nonetheless, whether Communist or Conservative, Sons of Freedom or Independent, all Doukhobors still considered themselves to be profoundly Doukhobor. Wright saw better than any outsider before him the contradictions and the bonds within the faith. Despite the universal commitment to pacifism, for instance, there were Doukhobors who fought in the Spanish Civil War on the side of the Loyalists. Others continued to think of themselves as Doukhobor while joining the United or Baptist churches in search of more structure in their religious ceremonies. The Independents followed the ownership pattern of Canadian farmers but farmed like Doukhobors, helping one another harvest, move buildings, build barns.

Federal legislation to protect farmers against eviction from their land did not help farmers who owned property communally, and in 1937 thousands of Doukhobors in the Kootenays faced being thrown out of their homes by the Sun Life Assurance Company and the National Trust Company. The Canadian Communist paper *Clarion Weekly* earned the gratitude of the community by protesting fiercely against this second eviction. Eventually the crisis was averted when the British Columbia government paid off the mortgages, a total of $350,000.

The trouble had sapped the well-being of Peter the Second Verigen, who was gambling heavily. He was a big loser at poker games in Yorkton and Kamsack in the winter of 1937. In the autumn of 1938 he complained of pains in his chest and was taken to Saint Paul's Hospital in Saskatoon, where three infected ribs were removed. He failed to recover and on 11 February, 1939, he died. His heir was his son, Peter Petrovitch Verigen, known as Peter the Third, who was still in Russia. Peter the Third disappeared, probably to a Soviet prison, and is believed dead. There is some uncertainty now as to who is the Doukhobor spiritual leader.

No one who lived through the Depression of the thirties in Saskatchewan ever forgets the dust, desolation, poverty and injustice. On a cold rainy afternoon in May, 1983, Emma's oldest brother, Bill Konkin, seventy-nine, sat in the home of his nephew, John J. Konkin, in the Toronto suburb of Mississauga and talked of that long ordeal. Bill Konkin is a small oak of a man with an assertive, alert manner and a shock of pure white hair.

In the thirties he didn't lose his land, thanks to the legislation; he acquired more. Sometimes in partnership with his younger brother Alex A., sometimes on his own, he bought and rented property. In 1934 he and Alex took over an abandoned farm, three quarter-sections, in Marcelin, a hamlet ten miles from Blaine Lake. A farmer ruined two years earlier had left it to the weeds, so the brothers got it for a bargain, thirteen hundred dollars down and the promise of sixteen thousand bushels of Number One wheat, or its equivalent, to be paid in installments.

He described how he and Hannah moved into the farmhouse and in the spring of 1935 Bill broke the land to the plough again. The harvest that year was a disaster. "It was wet and cold, the wheat no good, hard to get rid of it," he summarized bleakly. "Had to sell it very cheap. Could hardly pay nothing for the land. To make up one-third crop of Number One for the payment, I had to give up half that crop."

Bill kept his quarter section east of Blaine Lake, his dowry gift, bought another and rented a third. He worked them all himself, then rented himself out as a well-digger, harvested other men's crops, and kept a herd as well. It was a stack of cards that depended on the price of wheat and beef, and both were falling. The government ordered a bottom price for beef, three-quarters of a cent a pound. It was better than nothing.

On a day so cold that breath frosted eyebrows, Bill prepared to take his herd to Blaine Lake to sell for the government's price.

"I'll tell you that story," he said fifty years later, watching his nephew John light a cigarette. "That story is more interesting than Emma. I had to bring the cattle to Blaine Lake, that's twelve miles, in winter. I brought them on foot and that's cold work. *Hah!* The government only buy at a certain time and you have to bring them in."

A fat young heifer jumped the fence and joined the moving herd. He left her in, looking forward to getting three cents a pound for her, a better price than the rest of the herd would bring. A government inspector weighed the cattle by the railway siding and told Konkin the price.

"How about the heifer?" asked Bill.

"It's all the same price, three-quarters of a cent," the inspector said.

Konkin, furious, announced that he would take the heifer back. That wouldn't be easy, loading the animal on his sleigh, but he wasn't going to sell her cheap. He started for the gate in the cattle pen but the inspector barred his way.

"You're not taking that heifer out of the herd," he shouted. "It's sold!"

"The hell it's sold," shouted the Doukhobor. His plan was to remove the heifer, weigh her, and subtract her weight from the total.

"You know which one and I know too," he told the inspector. "She's the one with one tit torn off, the littlest one of all."

Bill climbed the fence, the inspector yelling behind him to stop, and pushed through the milling cattle. "You can't go in there!" the inspector was screaming.

"Yes I can," Konkin yelled. "I'm going to chase my heifer out the gate."

The inspector asserted his authority. He started to lock the gate and Bill Konkin attacked him. The inspector hollered for the police and a crowd gathered. Konkin was urged to stop before the police arrived. "Who will take care of your farm, your family, if you go to jail? You've got four kids there," his friends said.

Bill Konkin was feeling the loss of that heifer, as acutely as if it had happened a day before. As he sat in his nephew's living room, he was still incredulous that a man would be in danger of being arrested for taking home his own cow.

"That's how they treated us in the thirties," he concluded bitterly. "He took my cow."

The next venture was even worse. The Konkin brothers decided to take advantage of the CNR's offer to ship their cows to market on credit. No one was sure of the market value in Winnipeg, but they reasoned it had to be better than what the government was paying. Approaching Prince Albert, they had a better idea. They would unload and sell the cattle there, saving themselves some of the freight bill. Bill Konkin was still disgusted, a half century later, at their naiveté. The best price they could get in Prince Albert was $2.50 a cow.

"Good big steers!" Bill exclaimed, slapping his hands on his knees. "Three, four years old!"

The Konkins returned to the CNR station and said they wanted to put the herd back on the train for Winnipeg. They were told that the credit deal was off. If they wanted to continue to Winnipeg they would have to pay cash in advance.

"I had no money!" Bill groaned, "I had to sell in Prince Albert for $2.50 a steer!"

There is no telling how many times John Konkin has heard his uncles and father relate the story of $2.50 steers but he listened to it without a sign of impatience, chuckling ruefully and shaking his head. He added, "The way my dad told the story is that when they finished paying the freight bill, they had $11.40 left over for themselves."

Bill Konkin switched to Russian to check something with

John and then nodded. "That's right, that's why we had to sell in Prince Albert, to make sure we could pay the freight. Some farmers who shipped cattle sold so cheap they couldn't pay the railway."

Bill Konkin paused and gave John a long, level look as the younger man struck a match and lit another cigarette. He sat up straighter and he thumped himself at the belt-line. Watching for John's reaction, he bragged, "Look, I'm almost eighty years old and I got no belly." John Konkin, fifty-four, a big, dark, quiet man with a thoughtful, sad face, has a sedentary look; he has a seriously damaged back and hasn't worked in recent years.

Bill Konkin said to him, "I give you ten years and you be dead if you don't quit smoking."

John was amused; this was a familiar exchange. "Never make the old-age pension, eh?"

The older Konkin wouldn't be put off. "No," he said bluntly. "You won't."

John Konkin's life has been a long series of descents from what he hoped it would be when he left his father's home near Blaine Lake in 1955 to strike out on his own. A married man of twenty-six, an experienced, hard-working farmer, he bought a quarter section and rented four others in the pattern of his father, uncles and grandfather.

The first year wasn't bad and he was able to make the payments on the land and the machinery he needed, but the next year he had a crop failure, which he narrowly survived.

"The year after that it was looking like I had made it," he explained in a detached, calm voice. "I had all my own machinery but I was in debt to a couple thousand dollars. Still it looked all right." He stopped studying his big hands, his voice dragging. "But when the crop came in, there was nothing, *nothing*. I had this bill. I owed for the combine, I owed..."

He lost everything. He and his wife went to Saskatoon where she found work readily. It was more difficult for him. "I had no trade, really. I only got grade nine so all I could do was hired labour. I drove a mail truck for a while, and then the guy who had the contract lost it to another guy, and I went to drive a furniture truck."

His marriage fell apart. His wife, Eileen, moved to Toronto and joined the collective bargaining unit of the Ontario

Secondary School Teachers' Federation. John lived with his younger brother Fred and sister-in-law Doreen for a while. They made him welcome, took him everywhere with them, could not have been kinder, he says, but he felt an intruder. He moved east in 1962, met a woman newly divorced and raising two children, and they were married.

"I worked for a construction company for a while, then I went to de Haviland, and from de Haviland I went to a plastics place, but they were on strike for so damned long. I was with the plastics place for about six years, I was a foreman there but I was always looking for more money. I made a mistake. I should have stayed, but I went to work for Douglas and I was making damned good money. They had so many layoffs and so many strikes that went to hell too."

He took his time telling the story in a detached tone. "And then I was a courier for about seven years at the airport. You had to have your own truck; they dealt out the loads. I gave them so much, I guess it was ten dollars a week, to pay for the radio and dispatch services. And then I hurt my back about four years ago. I had a disk removed. I went back to work, I hurt my back again. The doctor says, 'You want to wind up in a wheelchair, you go back.'"

Somewhere in the house a woman was moving around, talking softly, John's step-daughter. Her marriage had broken up and she was living with John and her mother for a time with her baby. There were toddler's toys in the living room and a stroller parked by the front door. John resumed, on a long, indrawn breath, his face tired. "So I'm unemployed at the moment." A long pause. "I didn't want to wander so much. I'm not the wandering type, really. I miss farming."

Bill Konkin had listened quietly, his face full of concern. His sympathy formed itself as indignation. "For a sick man to smoke, you're crazy," he burst out. "You should go to a psychiatrist!"

John gave his uncle an understanding grin.

"I tell him a thousand times he has to stop smoking," the old man continued bright-eyed. "It doesn't penetrate him. He can't decide himself, he's not smart enough. If he was smart enough he would quit already."

"Thanks," said John drily, keeping his expression pleasant.

"I was here last year for one hour and I told him, 'You quit.' And he doesn't quit. He's getting pale, he's sick."

John chuckled gamely, waiting for his uncle to stop.

"I have more blood in my face than you have," Bill continued relentlessly.

It was true. Bill Konkin had a ruddy, outdoors look, while John Konkin's face was marked by pallour. "That means you're not healthy. You're a young man and you're not healthy."

He had gone too far and he knew it. He fell silent and somewhere in the house the baby babbled sweetly.

The conversation returned to the thirties at Blaine Lake. Bill said proudly that all the Konkins held on to their land, didn't lose an inch, through the worst of the Depression. He and his father and his brother Alex all got more land; he wasn't sure about his brother John. "I think he got some land on the Indian reserve."

Asked why John didn't buy land as vigorously as the rest of the Konkins, his son John didn't answer at once. Studying the rug at his feet, he replied in a level tone, "I have no idea."

Bill Konkin, however, was worth about a million dollars at one point. With the onset of heart disease and the deaths of his wife and son Bill, he had started giving his land to his other son, Ken, a pharmacist in Blaine Lake, and a grandson, also called Bill. One piece of land later was sold for a hundred thousand dollars. "Now I give him a quarter more," he said proudly.

John Konkin said softly, appreciatively, "Ouch."

It was a far cry from the poverty he had known in the thirties, the old man went on. "We were selling wheat at nineteen cents a bushel," he recalled. When there were no buyers the government would pay four cents a bushel for crushed wheat that was returned to the farmers to be used for fodder.

"A bushel weighs sixty pounds," Bill explained. "We would have to weigh it, deliver it to the government man at Blaine Lake, crush it there so it couldn't be used for anything but feed, and then take it back to the cattle. I must have crushed one hundred bushels one summer and I got four dollars. Working day and night, sleep in the barn, my wife at home looking after horses and cattle, forty below zero lots of days in the winter."

To make ends meet he hired himself and his threshing machine to other farmers. "I worked all over, on the reserve, all over. I was threshing for Senator Horner, you know him. I had to pull the granary to a place where he wanted, shovel the grain into the granary and thresh it. And board myself, my whole crew, and feed the horses."

His eyes flashed. "So how much I get? I tell you. If I make a thousand bushels, that's forty dollars. And I have to pay the crew, feed the horses, everything." He was breathing hard. "We just slave all day, we just slaves."

John broke in, his voice warm and lazy to calm his uncle. "I remember threshing when I was a kid," he said. "By that time things were a lot better, the machinery was better, but it's still the hardest work in the world. I ploughed fields with horses. Not that there weren't tractors around, but nobody could afford them in the forties."

Bill Konkin resumed, relaxed again. "I had a well-digger machine. I dug a lot of wells, we were always short of water on the farm. Dig down, thirty or forty feet, then I got water. Not always, missed it sometimes. That was a hard job. And dangerous."

John nodded. "When you get down thirty, forty feet, and you hit rock," he said, "you have to go down there and put some dynamite in, blast it."

Bill laughed suddenly. He had a picture of John down the well, fixing the dynamite. "You didn't wait for the horse to pull you out," he said merrily, "you just climbed the cable." Both men laughed uproariously. John shook his head. "I sure climbed that cable fast."

Bill Konkin remembered the grasshopper plagues that came after the drought. The first time he saw the grasshoppers he thought they were a rain cloud. They came over the horizon, giving off a strange, dry noise, black against the sky. "They set on the whole farm and in a couple of hours that field was completely finished. Just a whirr, whirr, whirr, and they ate the whole crop."

John shifted his bulk, lit another cigarette. "Too bad we didn't think about it then," he offered laconically. "Chocolate-coat them."

The Depression was ending in the summer of 1939 when

King George VI and Elizabeth came to Canada. It was the first royal visit to Canada by a ruling monarch. They crossed the country by railway and in May stopped briefly at Saskatoon. The road from Blaine Lake wasn't paved — it was little more than a rutted trail — but it seemed the entire population made the trek. People jammed into available cars, eight to a vehicle. When they got to the steep banks of the North Saskatchewan River, everyone got out and pushed the cars up the hill.

The Konkin family's favourite story about royalty concerns a later royal visit, when Elizabeth II and Prince Philip made a transcontinental trek. The Konkins drove to Saskatoon, this time on pavement, and bunked with Mary Konkin Perverseff. On the day of the visit Alex A., the second brother, splendidly dressed in his best suit, was standing near the dignitaries who would be presented to the queen. Alex mistakenly was included in the line-up. He may have lacked sophistication but his poise was impeccable. When it came his turn he put out his hand and grinned. "Hello Mrs. Queen. I'm Alex Konkin from Blaine Lake."

The Konkins think royalty is fine but most of them, in the style of prairie farmers, are ardent establishment-knockers. "The first time I voted, I voted CCF," said Bill Konkin. "I never change; I won't change. Now I vote NDP. The Conservatives got us nineteen cents a bushel for wheat and five cents a dozen for eggs and twenty-five cents a pound for beef. That's the Conservatives."

His temper rose again. "When we got the CCF government in Saskatchewan, then the roads were built."

John added, "That's when the power went through to the farms. You couldn't buy the bloody power even if you *had* the money. It was the late forties, something like that, before anyone in the area got power to the farmers. After the CCF came, that's when everything got modernized."

"Saskatchewan leads all of Canada," Bill Konkin said, excited and pleased. "We had the first CCF government, the first car insurance, the first hospitalization, the first medicare, all those things. Saskatchewan leads it. Nobody else produce that but the CCF."

Bill Konkin is a skeptic to the bone. When he visited the Soviet Union in 1982, he gave his hosts a lecture on the benefits of the free-enterprise system. Laid up with pneumonia in a hospital, he told the doctors that in Canada a hard-working person could have a good house, a fine car, lots of land, and a pension.

"Here you got seventy-year-old women who have to scrub floors in this hospital," he told them severely. "That's no good."

All the older Doukhobors around Blaine Lake have stories of the Depression similar to Bill's. Masha and Sam Kalesnikoff spoke of the time they had no feed for their stock and had to sell a cow for seven dollars and a sucking calf for three dollars. Their hungry horses ate poisonous weeds and died. "We lost them all, poor horses," Sam grieved. Masha churned butter, which Sam tried to sell door-to-door. He had a hundred pounds, but no one was buying. He dropped the price, then dropped it again. Finally he made one sale: two pounds of butter for a quarter.

Masha had her mind on the good side of the Depression. Her expression was soft. "People were so good," she crooned. "So-o-o-o good. Everybody wants to help one another."

Alfred Svoboda, an aged Blaine Lake lawyer, remembered that part of it, the Doukhobors helping one another. He was interviewed in May, 1983, in a sunny room in St. Paul's Hospital in Saskatoon, giving his age as 172 and looking it.

"I knew the Konkins, sure," he said, his shaking hands pulling at the lapels of his dressing gown, his gaunt frame slumped in a wheelchair. "In the thirties the banks were trying to take the farms. The Konkins had expanded too much, like many others. They made small down payments and then fought to hang on to the farms."

The old lawyer had a direct style of answering questions. About Alex E. Konkin, Emma's father, he said with a derisive snort, "You couldn't call him a fool. He was smart, and not smart. He knew what was going on. That was all you could say about any of the Konkins. They were always a little hurt because they didn't think their creditors treated them fairly."

His face registered contempt. "Was John the smartest of the brothers? He may have thought so, but many had other opinions."

His mind wandered. For a few minutes what he said made little sense. Then he pulled himself upright and stared at his visitor. "You know about Emma? She was ganged up on. A lot of what they said about her wasn't true." He waved a long hand in dismissal; he hadn't finished his custard.

The doctor treating Alex Svoboda was Donald Boyd, a prominent Saskatoon surgeon raised in Blaine Lake, who also knew the Konkins well. His father, John Albert Boyd, one of three lawyers in Blaine Lake in the Depression, helped the Konkins hold on to their land.

"Father was handling their legal problems in the thirties," Donald Boyd explained. He is a medium-sized man of medium girth and colouring, with the distracted manner of someone perpetually running behind schedule. He agreed to an interview, but he was cautious. It was not until he had written authority from Emma's second husband, Louie Sawula, and had confirmed it by a witnessed telephone call, that he was willing to talk about her medical problems at all. On this first meeting, he stuck to the safe topic of the Konkins' legal struggles in the Depression.

"A lot of farms were broke then but the legislation saved their land. A Debt Adjustment Board was set up with authority to reduce debts so people like the Konkins could hang on."

Quarter sections, 160 acres each, were selling then for about eight hundred dollars, the doctor said. Now a quarter section is selling for about a hundred thousand dollars.

Chapter Three

Emma Konkin was twelve when she finished grade eight in the spring of 1933. She had skipped grades effortlessly and was looking forward to high school in Blaine Lake. Despite their poverty, her proud parents were inclined to agree that she should have more education. The high school, however, rejected her; they thought she was too young.

Her brother Bill said indignantly, "She was so *smart,* but they said she was too damned young. They wouldn't take her."

"I think Emma was even more sorry to leave school than I was," Emma's sister Mary observed. "Everybody told her she could have done well if she had stayed. I was fourteen, fifteen, when I finished school but Emma was only twelve. It was too bad."

Mary sympathized with her tearful sister, remembering her own pain when her schooling stopped, but she had had more important matters on her mind that summer. She was sixteen and in love for the first and only time of her life, with Peter Perversoff, son of Doukhobors farming near Pelly, east of Blaine Lake.

"Emma and I were the same," Mary reflected. "Mother used to call us by a Russian word, which meant someone who falls in love and doesn't care about anything, not even if they would be shot by their fathers. I fell in love when I was sixteen and didn't get married until I was nineteen but I didn't have any other boyfriends. I just had the one man in my whole life. Emma was like that, too."

By the time Mary and Pete Perversoff were married in 1934, Emma was fourteen and blindly in love herself. The man was Bill Woikin, a six-foot, blond, raw-boned Doukhobor of nineteen from Langham, about twenty miles northwest of Saskatoon. His family's farm was a small one and the soil was poor, weakened by the drought, which was even more severe in Langham than at Blaine Lake. The Woikin family sent Bill to live with his sister Masha and her husband, Sam Kalesnikoff; Bill rented himself out as a day labourer.

Emma adored him on sight. He was a laughing, attractive youth as devoted to music as she was to art. He had a knack for playing almost any instrument he tried, but his favourite was a battered guitar. He loved to play the guitar and sing Russian folk songs and tunes of his own composition. Bill Woikin was as taken by Emma as she was by him. Her devotion to him was impossible to resist. He was enchanted with the vitality and whole-heartedness of her, her quick and sunny ways.

The Konkins are reticent about discussing the Woikins of Langham. The impression they leave, though none would say so, is that the Woikins were a rougher, less affectionate people than the Konkins: hard-working, but not imaginative. Emma's mother made no bones about her disapproval of the match.

Mary quoted her mother: "She said to Emma, 'Nothing doing, you're not getting married into that family. You're not going to live with those Woikins.' " Mary shrugged, somewhat embarrassed. "They were so poor," she explained. "All the kids had to go out and work. Mother didn't like the Woikins, the old folks especially. She thought they weren't that bright."

Parental disapproval is rarely effective against the torrent of adolescent love, and it proved useless this time. Mary said, "Emma was in love with that guy like you wouldn't believe. She was in love so much."

The household was torn by arguments between the unmoveable Pearl and her furious daughter. Pearl said that Emma could do better, that she was so intelligent she could "get ahead" with someone else. If she married a Woikin she would spend all her life in toil and poverty on their poor land.

"It got so bad that mother told Bill Woikin he was not to come to the house at all to see Emma," Mary remembered.

The couple could meet only when Doukhobors gathered for work or a party. However ardent their passion, there was no possibility, however, they could have consummated their love. "There was no way," Mary said firmly. "Everybody knew everything that was going on between everybody. We had a group of about ten couples who went to parties and all of them got married but nothing ever happened between any of them before the marriage. Parents never had to worry what was happening if a girl wasn't home by ten o'clock. We always knew where everyone was every minute."

Mary and Pete Perversoff were married in 1934 or 1935, depending on how you look at it. She explained, "We have a different way to be married, the Doukhobor way. There are two parts."

The first is a gathering of families and friends, who witness that the two people want to be married. The second is a celebration, a feast of glorious and gargantuan proportion, attended by as many people as the family can afford to feed. After the feast the marriage is registered with the authorities and can be consummated.

"Pete's parents were not too fussy for him to get married," Mary said with amusement. "He was the oldest so he was needed in the fields, and the Perversoffs had three daughters, so they didn't need a daughter-in-law, another mouth to feed in those hard times."

Pete's parents resigned themselves to the inevitable and went ahead with wedding plans just before Christmas, 1934. The ceremonial part of the wedding is always at the home of the bride. "Someone who knows how to talk, how to preside, takes charge," Mary explained. "My brother Bill did the marriage for us; he's a very talented man that way. He asked, 'Do you want to get married?' Yes. 'Are you in love?' Yes. 'And do you promise to be good to each other?' Yes. Of course we would promise anything."

Pete and Mary kissed and the people packed in the living room of the homestead cheered. Supper was served with a bit of wine.

The celebration banquet was to take place soon after, on 20 December, but Pete's mother surprised everyone by having a baby. In the midst of the first blizzard of the winter, Pete arrived at the Konkin homestead with the news that he had a new sister. There was nothing to do but postpone the celebration until Pete's mother was on her feet and could contribute her share of the work.

The wedding feast date was moved to 20 January, 1935. The ceremony was held at the Ospennia schoolhouse to accommodate the crowd. Pearl Konkin, who was in charge of the invitations, asked Masha and Sam Kalesnikoff but deliberately omitted Masha's brother, Bill Woikin.

Emma was wild with disappointment. She turned on Mary, blaming her, and Mary protested that it hadn't occurred to her to interfere.

"Why didn't you tell me to invite Bill?" she admonished her weeping sister. "I would have done it."

"You should have known," Emma replied, sobbing.

After the wedding Mary and Pete moved in with his parents. A year and a half later, in June, 1936, their first baby was born. The little girl was three months old when the bad news came that Pearl Konkin was dying. One of the Konkin brothers came for Mary and took her to the homestead, where Emma explained what had happened.

Alex E. had been threshing the day before at a neighbour's farm and went to bed around midnight. As he settled beside Pearl, she awakened and asked if he had finished with the field. He answered her and fell asleep, then was wakened by a convulsive movement. Pearl had thrown up her arm violently and was lying stiffly, her breathing odd. Alex, thinking it was a nightmare, asked what was wrong.

"I'm dying," Pearl said.

Alex E. shouted for Emma, the only other person in the house, to bring the coal-oil lamp. "Light the light," he yelled. "You're mother is sick."

Emma was so frightened by the terror in her father's voice that she lost her bearings. In the pitch-black country darkness she couldn't find the door. She felt the walls, searching for the door, as her father continued to yell for her to hurry. When finally her groping hands located it, she couldn't find the handle right away.

Finally she opened the door and lit the lamp. She went to her parents' room, looked at her mother contorted in the bed and fainted. She told Mary she didn't know what happened for a while after. As sensibility returned, she heard her father saying someone should get a doctor and call the boys and Mary.

"The brothers, of course, were all threshing," Mary related. "They came for me and we all went to the homestead. I took one look at mother and I knew. She was talking and you could understand her, and then all of a sudden you couldn't understand her. She kept throwing up one arm, like she couldn't control it." She was having a stroke.

Grieving husband and sons took turns sitting beside Pearl's bed as her condition worsened and she slipped into a coma. Mary could not bear to look at her. She kept away, helping Emma in the kitchen. Emma seemed about to collapse, crying without end, twisting her hands and unable to be still.

Pearl died at four in the afternoon of 27 August, 1936, during a second stroke. She was fifty-eight. Neighbours came to wash the body, shampoo her hair, and arrange it in the braid she always wore, as men found pine boards and nailed together a coffin. Women conferred about the material to line the coffin, selecting something Pearl would have liked, and they dressed the body in the finest Doukhobor clothing available.

The homestead rang with the singing of mourning prayers and psalms. The singing continued day and night to ensure that Pearl's soul would be launched on its six-week journey to a place of eternal peace. Her body was never left alone; the family took turns sitting beside her. Since Pearl had died in the blazing heat of summer, it was necessary to abbreviate the customary three days of mourning before burial. Doukhobors left their fields and gathered at the Konkin homestead for the funeral dinner; they ate at long tables arranged in the yard while Pearl lay, exquisitely dressed, in the open coffin nearby. The funeral outfit is important to Doukhobors. Women, as they age, begin thinking about the clothes they will wear when they are dead.

When Pearl Konkin died, Emma and Mary and their sisters-in-law cooked the funeral banquet and fed the mourners who came and went to share in the singing. In recent years Doukhobors use the services of a funeral home but the ritual of the food is unchanged. A bereaved family may expect to pay as much as eight thousand dollars to feed guests at the funeral service and at the banquet six weeks later, which follows a service of celebration that the soul has reached its rest.

Doukhobor family albums are full of pictures of farmyard funerals, the open coffin in the foreground and the mourners gathered around. Photographs taken at Pearl's funeral show the truck on which her coffin was loaded for its journey to Ospennia cemetery, where most of the Konkins are buried. After the funeral the guests resumed harvesting; Emma and her father were left alone with their grief.

That winter, however, John and Lena Konkin returned to live in the homestead again. A fire had destroyed John's barn, leaving his herd without shelter, so it seemed sensible to put his herd in with his father's and reunite the families in the nearly empty homestead.

They brought with them two sons, John J., who was seven, and Fred J., four. The boys were given a bed in the upstairs space where Emma and Mary had slept for most of their childhoods; Emma kept the small east bedroom into which she had moved when John and Lena left a few years earlier. Alex E. obligingly moved downstairs into the parlour, and John and Lena took his bedroom.

Fred Konkin's memories of that time are ecstatic. He lived in a small-boy's paradise, indulged and petted by all the adults. He listened to bedtime stories in Russian, English and a combination of the two. Goldilocks and the three bears, he recalled, dined on *kasha*, the Doukhobor version of porridge.

His young Aunt Emma doted on him and would scoop him up by his suspenders to give him a hug. One joke between them involved cookies. Whenever she baked, he would steal a cookie or two and she would pretend to scold him. They played that game, or a form of it, all their lives. At her funeral, Fred Konkin found himself describing how good those cookies were. What he really was saying was that she had loved him and he had loved her.

Fred remembers Emma as a cheerful companion that year, but the fifteen-year-old was shaken by her mother's death and drained by the effort to appear her normal, happy self. "It was very hard for Emma when mother died," her sister Mary observed. "The rest of us had our lives and were gone, but she was at home. I think it bothered her that she and mother had been having so many difficulties, all those arguments about Bill Woikin. She was really sorry about that."

Bill Woikin, free to visit now that Pearl could no longer object, came to comfort Emma. He taught her to play the guitar and they sang together, their eyes on one another.

Fred Konkin has fragments of memories about their courtship. His most vivid impression is that the two were madly in love and full of fun. He can still see Bill Woikin pulling into the farmyard at the wheel of a borrowed touring car that today reminds him of *Bonnie and Clyde*, two guitars sticking out of the back seat. Emma would come out running, wiping her hands on her apron, and Fred would wait blissfully for the music to start.

Four months after Pearl's death, Emma celebrated her sixteenth birthday. She felt she was old enough to marry and announced that she would wait no longer than April, 1937. None of the Konkins was pleased. Small, skinny and coltish, she looked about fourteen.

Alex bought his daughter a wedding dress, a child's dream of city sophistication made of blue crêpe with lots of pleats and copious amounts of trim. The couple went to Saskatoon to pose for a wedding photograph, Emma seated in a chair, erect and dignified, a bouquet of artificial flowers in her hands and a tiara on her head. Bill Woikin balanced uncomfortably on the arm of the chair, dressed in a good dark suit and a wide tie.

Both attempted the fixed, vacant expression they deemed appropriate for such an important photograph but there is something uncertain in Emma's face and Bill looks like a man swallowing an embarrassed laugh.

There was no money for a big wedding. The ceremony took place in the homestead, where Emma's brother Bill, the family's best and most assured master of ceremonies, did the talking. Mary and Pete Perversoff had the wedding supper at their place a few miles away; then Emma packed up and went with Bill Woikin to Langham to live with his parents.

The Woikins are as well known around Langham as the Konkins are at Blaine Lake. Like all Doukhobors, they are indifferent about the spelling of their name in English. Bill and his sister Masha spelled their name "Woikin," but there is also "Woykin," "Voyken" and "Voykin" — all related.

As illustration of this easy accommodation to the exigencies of incompatible alphabets, one branch of the Konkin family recently switched to Conkin to simplify mail delivery, while Mary and Pete Perversoff now spell it Perverseff.

The Woikin homestead was smaller than the home Emma had left and bore marks of a poverty deeper than her own. The Woikins did mixed farming and kept cattle but relied for survival on the produce from their garden, mainly potatoes. Tending potatoes is stoop labour; it's a brutal way to make a living.

To the young bride, the older Konkins seemed censoring and cold after the warmth of her upbringing. They must have wondered if someone so young and frail would not become an invalid, a liability the family could not afford. The adjustment Emma found most difficult was the food. The Woikins ate a lot of meat, while Emma was accustomed to an almost completely vegetarian diet. In later years, whenever she discussed her first marriage she spoke of her difficulty with the heavy, unfamiliar food.

The summer of 1937 was the worst year of the Depression for Saskatchewan. The drought continued, especially in the southern part of the province, and the sky was full of dust and grasshoppers. People called it "the black blizzard" and kept their children indoors to protect their lungs. It was the last of nine unbroken years of crop failures; most farms took in less than they spent. Russian thistle, a weed that thrived on disaster, took over abandoned fields.

The average crop yield in Saskatchewan in 1936 had been seven and a half bushels an acre; wheat yields were even lower, less than three bushels an acre. People thought it couldn't be worse, but 1937 was the worst year for crops in the province's history. Some farmers didn't harvest enough grain for the next year's seed.

The time was ripe for political change. A new party, the Cooperative Commonwealth Federation, was rising under M.J. Coldwell, who promised a fairer distribution of wealth. The Saskatchewan Conservatives had a new leader, John Diefenbaker, a lawyer from Prince Albert. He was a great orator, spell-binding in a courtroom, but the Liberal government felt secure. After R.B. Bennett, the west would never vote Tory.

That bitter summer the Woikins toiled for an income that averaged five dollars a month. Emma, living on bread and potatoes, developed an extravagant craving for oranges. Bill Woikin somehow would find the necessary coins, hitch up the team, and drive into Saskatoon to buy her one.

Emma's father found life intolerable without a wife. He astonished his children by marrying again. His bride, Natasha Woikin, is best remembered in Blaine Lake as the woman whose daughter married Dr. J.W.T. Spinks, who became president of the University of Saskatchewan at Saskatoon. Alex and Natasha were married for about ten years. For those years John and Lena had the homestead to themselves; Alex lived in a tiny house he towed into Blaine Lake. Emma and Bill Woikin came to visit the Konkin family, all smiles and hugs, as though life were a lark. Fred Konkin remembers the lift it gave him to see them because their arrival signalled that a party was about to start. Bill wrote songs on the back of old calendars and would pass them around like sheet music. The sound of voices and guitars drifted over flat prairie fields, drawing passers-by. Emma and Bill became central figures in the young married set of the Langham region, a sociable group of hard-working newlyweds who loved to get together to talk and sing and eat, and forget the toil that dominated their days.

The couple glowed with love. People in Langham still talk about the aura of happiness around Emma and Bill and how devoted they were. A picture of them was taken on a bridge near the Woikin farm on a summer day a few months after their marriage. Bill is sitting on the wall above Emma, who is standing, her uplifted face cupped in his big hands. The two people are oblivious to the camera; their eyes are locked in a moment of poignant intimacy and sweetness.

"He would grab Emma and put her on the table and sing to her and then hug and kiss her," Mary Perverseff recalled. "He was that kind of happy-go-lucky guy. He'd put her on a post somewhere, high up — she couldn't get off — and he'd walk around below, looking up at her."

After a year in the Woikin homestead, Emma was desperate to have a place of her own. Her father-in-law assigned a bit of land to his son, and Emma and Bill cleaned out a storage shed, fixed it up, and moved in. It became the hub of the social life of people their age, a place full of music and the fragrant smells of Emma's cooking.

A year passed and Emma was not yet pregnant. Early methods of contraception on the prairies are a lost piece of social history, but they did exist. Fewer babies were born in the Depression. Stress and poor nutrition certainly reduced fertility, but there was also a woman's underground that passed along such folk recipes as cocoa-butter suppositories to block the cervix. For whatever reason, Emma Woikin did not become pregnant until the second year of their marriage.

The pregnancy was a difficult one from the beginning. Emma was so sick and uncomfortable that she consulted a Saskatoon doctor, J.J. Perverseff, formerly of Blaine Lake. As the time of delivery neared, he thought there was something wrong about the baby's position. He advised her to go to St. Paul's Hospital for x-rays.

St. Paul's, the second largest hospital in Saskatoon, sits on top of Pleasant Hill, which was the site of the Victorian home of one of Saskatoon's most prosperous doctors at the turn of the century. During the 1906 typhoid epidemic, the house was used as a hospital and two Grey Nuns, fortuitously visiting from Montreal, functioned as the nursing staff. In 1907, the Sisters of Charity, a nursing order, bought the house and opened Saskatoon's first hospital in it.

The building to which Emma Woikin came in the spring of 1939 was a brick box, built in 1912, high-ceilinged and rigidly administered in the hospital style of the day. On 4 May, 1939, she checked into Room 312 and then went to radiology. The x-rays of her abdomen revealed that she was in her eighth month of pregnancy and that the position of the fetus was breech. In all likelihood the baby would be delivered feet first.

Birth at home with a Doukhobor midwife was out of the question, and Dr. Perverseff was unwilling to take the chance that she might deliver before Bill Woikin could bring her back to Saskatoon. She was ordered to remain in the hospital to await the onset of labour.

For almost three weeks she wandered the hospital corridors restlessly, frantic at the money her stay was costing. Bill came infrequently; he was getting the fields ready for seed. When he could visit, he brought her an orange.

Emma's labour began in the afternoon of 20 May and lasted eight hours. At one-forty the following morning, the baby was delivered, a perfectly formed little boy. The umbilical cord had wrapped around his throat and strangled him in the birth canal; he was dead.

Breech deliveries are not uncommon and they usually present little risk, but even with the best of modern obstetrics, breech babies sometimes die during birth. Sometimes the umbilical cord collapses because it must pass through the bony pelvis alongside the baby's head. Sometimes veins in the infant's head rupture. Sometimes, as with Emma's son, the cord twists around the baby's throat and hangs him.

Caution suggests that sometimes a Caesarian section is the safest procedure when the fetus is in the breech position. In 1939, however, that operation was extremely rare. The rate of Caesarian deliveries at St. Paul's was approximately one percent of all births; by contrast, the rate in the early eighties was about sixteen percent.

Hospital records show that every effort was made to resuscitate the baby, but they failed.

When Emma emerged from the anaesthetic and was told that her baby was dead, she screamed. Bill Woikin and her sister were there to comfort her, but she was out of control. She cried that she wanted to see the baby. Mary told her that he was "real cute." She thought he looked like Emma. She and Bill went to arrange to have the baby brought to his mother.

Permission was refused. "The doctors wouldn't allow it," Mary related in an outraged tone. "They said we can't bring Emma downstairs and we can't bring the dead baby upstairs, so there is no way. Emma could never forget that; it was terrible. She was begging us to let her see the baby. We talked to the doctors, we talked to the nuns. No, there was no way. They said she wouldn't be able to stand it, it would upset her too much. We tried to talk Dr. Perverseff into it, but we couldn't. And Emma kept crying, crying, 'Why can't I see my baby?'"

The period in which the Woikin tragedy occurred is one marked by a widespread belief among hospital administrators that situations which cause patients to become emotional should be avoided. To this end, parents were discouraged from visiting their children in hospital on the grounds that the child cried when the parent left. It was not until doctors understood that quiet docile children on their wards were severely depressed that changes gradually were made in the policy.

Similarly, it was the practice on obstetrical wards to "protect" grieving parents from the sight of their dead infants. There has been a dramatic change in recent years. To help parents express their grief, hospitals provide an opportunity for them to hold the dead baby and spend as much time as they need with the infant. When a baby simply vanishes, as the Woikin boy did in 1939, as most still-born infants did at the time, the problem of coping with the loss can be devastating.

Whatever the age, the death of a child is not bearable. There is a special horror, however, in the death of a newborn. Instead of what has been expected, a beginning of life, there is what could not have been foreseen, the end of life. The bereavement is deeply damaging to the mother's sense of worth: did she perhaps not want the baby enough? did she not deserve a baby? was she negligent during the pregnancy?

It is assumed that the father's grief is different than a mother's, which may be true, and that therefore it is less, which may not be true at all. Nevertheless, what comfort a family and friends can provide at such a time goes mainly to the mother; the father is expected to put aside his feelings and give support as well.

In 1939 it was considered weak and self-indulgent to display grief beyond the first few days after a death. People were expected to behave as if nothing had happened, and did so. The bereaved did not refer to the tragedy. Those around them, intending kindness, never mentioned the loss. An entire industry has sprung up within the health profession to undo the damage of that kind of repression. It is now acknowledged that denial of grief only drives it deeper into the bones. Parents need to talk about their lost baby in order to accept the reality of the death.

The death of a newborn is not the death of a stranger. A baby carried in the body for nine months, stirring ever more strongly, is a real person, unique and irreplacable. Assurances that there will be more babies have a heartless ring. To prepare for the baby, the parents have done more than fix up a cradle. They have been looking at children from a different perspective, seeing their individuality and how vulnerable they are. They have formed a definition of themselves based on what kind of parents they want to be. They plan the twenty years that lie ahead as their child sweetly unfolds.

When the doctor says the baby is dead, grief is immeasurable.

The next day, 22 May, Bill Woikin signed a form and took the infant to Langham to be buried. Emma picked a name for him, George, the name of her maternal grandfather. Mary believes that a photograph was taken of the baby in his coffin and that Emma kept that picture all her life. She described Emma, dying in St. Paul's Hospital thirty-five years and one day later, holding that picture in her hand and crying over it. Others, Louie Sawula among them, think there was no such picture; Louie, at least, never saw it, and it did not turn up in her effects. Emma had nothing to show that a baby boy named George Woikin had ever existed.

Everyone who knew Emma Woikin agrees that the death of the baby was the most shattering of all the tragedies in her life. She remained childless, and was so drenched in maternal longing that she mothered almost every child she met. She was drawn like a magnet to other people's children, bought gifts for them, baked cookies for them, knitted a thousand miles of pink and blue yarn into booties and bonnets, sang nonsense songs to them, read them stories, invented games, paid attention to their scrapes and boasts, distracted the weepy ones, and drew out those who were shy.

Though there was a great deal about herself that she told no one, she found an opportunity early in a friendship, however casual, to mention that she once had a baby who died. At the deepest level of her being, she seemed not to have separated from that boy. She carried her dead son within her all her life.

People born in that same year, 1939, had a special attraction for her. There were two in her own family, Doreen, who married her nephew Fred Konkin and Pearl, the third daughter of Emma's brother Alex. Pearl Konkin is married to George Sherstobetoff, who has a substantial farm in the Blaine Lake area. Pearl is an outgoing, jolly, sensible and appreciative woman. On a morning in May, 1983, she visited Doreen Konkin in the latter's home across from the Blaine Lake rink while waiting for her son to finish hockey practice and they talked about Emma.

"I was Aunt Emma's pet, right from the beginning," Pearl acknowledged, "She was so kind, to me she was always nice. She liked to hold me on her lap and hug me."

Doreen nodded, picturing that. Doreen Konkin has the look of someone who would be the first on the doorstep of someone in need, and she is. She has porcelain-fine skin, a wide brow and large blue eyes. She and Fred live in a white frame house which Doreen keeps in spotless order.

While she and Pearl talked comfortably, Doreen set the table with a noon meal for four consisting of marinated lamb chops fried with onions, cauliflower with cream sauce, buttered carrots, two kinds of tarts, one filled with mashed kidney beans and the other with cottage cheese, which are eaten with melted butter and sour cream, a bean salad, another salad of lettuce, tomatoes, avocado, cucumber and black olives, a bowl of feta cheese, a basket of homemade braided brown rolls, tea and a dessert of fruit tarts, either raspberry, apple or Saskatoonberry, to be topped with homemade ice cream or sour cream. Fred Konkin had hunted through the cupboard to find something to drink with this. He hospitably produced a bottle of crême de Cacao, which he poured into tiny glasses. Pearl sipped a little, nibbling on the tarts.

In the way of Doukhobor women, Doreen was on her feet throughout the serving of the meal. She prepared more lamb chops, refilled Fred's glass of tea, hunted in the refrigerator for more butter, popped down to the cellar to fetch a jar of preserves. Older Doukhobor women don't even set a place for themselves at the table. They expect to serve the family and eat afterwards. "You get used to eating cold food." Doreen grinned.

While the bustle of serving went on, Doreen and Pearl talked about Emma. "You were the same age as Aunt Emma's son would have been," Doreen reminded Pearl.

Pearl nodded. "Maybe that's why she liked me so much. She would always say I was so nice-looking, eh? And such a nice person."

Doreen took rolls out of the oven. "She also thought I was so beautiful," she said with an embarrassed laugh. "I'm not, but she always saw beauty in me. She would say, 'You're so smart and so nice and so beautiful and you dress so well and you're so petite.' She considered herself too big and yet she was smaller than we were most of the time."

Doreen recalled that once, during an idle conversation with Emma, she asked where her baby was buried. To Doreen's consternation, Emma's eyes filled with tears and she could not speak to answer.

"She never got over that baby's death," her sister Mary said with finality. "Never. It went on hurting her, especially when it turned out she couldn't have any more."

When he discharged her from St. Paul's Hospital on 6 June, 1939, Dr. Perverseff instructed Emma to avoid becoming pregnant again for a year. There is no suggestion in the medical records, now on file in microfilm, that she was sterile. She was only eighteen and her husband was twenty-four; everyone assumed they would have a large family eventually, since both were so fond of children.

The Konkins aren't sure how the medical and hospital bills were paid. They know the Woikins couldn't have paid them and believe that Emma's father must have provided at least some of the money. In Emma's mind her baby's death always was linked to her poverty. Though she never said so, many people had the impression that her baby died of starvation, so strongly did she emphasize her lack of money at the time. She may have believed that if she had not been a dirt-poor woman from a destitute farm, a Caesarian section would have been performed and her baby would have lived.

"Doctors were not free at that time, that's for sure," Emma's brother Bill commented when asked about Emma's month in hospital. He told of a time when his children were sick with diphtheria and a doctor came a few times from Blaine Lake. Bill paid him with five tickets, each one good for a load of wheat.

"He looked at them and gave me one back." Bill related. "'I take pity on you,' he said. 'Four is enough.' When the harvest was in I brought the wheat to pay that doctor, sixty bushels on every load."

When Bill's son Billy broke his arm, they took him to St. Paul's Hospital to have it set. That debt was paid with a load of vegetables, which Bill piled high in his 1929 Chevrolet convertible. He drove at twenty miles an hour over the rutted road to deliver them to Saskatoon.

Blaine Lake people understandably are passionate supporters of state medicine. Sam Kalesnikoff is a compulsive record-keeper, to whom future archivists will be deeply grateful. He proudly produced evidence that before the CCF government brought in free medical services, only three Doukhobors lived beyond the age of eighty-one; since 1956, when Tommy Douglas's government introduced the scheme, fifty-six Doukhobors have lived past their eighty-first year.

Older Doukhobors have memories of the days when most Saskatchewan doctors went on strike against medicare. One of the reasons so many of them admire Dr. Donald Boyd is that he remained on the job.

Emma and Bill Woikin seemed unchanged after their baby's death. She was thinner and a bit subdued, but still hard-working and anxious to please, while he seemed as full of laughter and music as ever. Only a few people knew that he was prone to severe headaches. Fred Konkin has a memory of Bill Woikin pacing the floor, his face pale, gripping his hands to his head in pain.

Mary said, "He couldn't sleep when he had the headaches. He was an emotional, nervous man but he seemed happy all the time. *Too* happy."

Bill's sister Masha said that the baby's death was more than he could bear. His problems seemed to begin with that, she thought.

Emma confided to Mary that there was more to it than the headaches. Bill was having terrifying depressions in which he talked of being dead, of being with his son George. The periods of despondency sometimes lasted for weeks, then would lift suddenly.

She begged him to see a doctor. He said there was no money for doctors and, anyway, they could do nothing for him. He may have wondered if he was becoming insane and lived in dread of the diagnosis. His family was beginning to believe that he had something wrong with his head, a brain tumour maybe.

"He didn't have any tests," Mary said, doubting the brain-tumour theory. "He wouldn't go near the doctors. He was afraid maybe that they'd tell him something was the matter with his brain. He would say, 'There's nothing those doctors can do for me. I'll get over it.' He didn't like to talk about his depressions."

The Woikins managed a cheerful front, as was expected of

them, and were grateful that summer that they had a few dollars
to make the shed more habitable. The addition of another room
gave it a profile not unlike the Konkin homestead at Blaine
Lake.

On 10 September, 1939, Canada declared war on Nazi
Germany. Across the country, patriots and the unemployed
flocked to enlist. In August, Hitler had signed an astonishing
pact with one of Germany's enemies, the Union of Soviet
Socialist Republics. The Royal Canadian Mounted Police,
who had been rounding up suspected Fascists for internment in
prison camps, started to collect all those suspected of Communist sympathies as well. On the prairies, most of those
arrested had Russian or Ukrainian names.

It was a jittery period for Doukhobors who had been critical
of the government's response to the cruel conditions the
prairies were experiencing. Once again, the Saskatchewan
community was swept by rumours that Ottawa would impose
conscription. The pacifism of the Doukhobors, which in
peace-time shone with virtue, no longer seemed so admirable.
As the country girded enthusiastically for war, the Doukhobors
seemed an alien people.

The first step towards the conscription the Doukhobors were
dreading came in August, 1940. All adult Canadians —
including women — were required to register so the government could assess the skills of the country's available labour
force. Emma Woikin's registration form is now in the National
Archives of Canada and was entered as Exhibit 83 before the
Royal Commission on Espionage, which sat in the spring of
1946 and helped to send her to prison.

The registration form reveals a nineteen-year-old who saw
herself as unskilled, uneducated, and unable to imagine that
either could be changed. She gave her level of school as
"Primary only," described her health as "Fair," and gave her
occupation as "Housewife." Asked how much experience she
had in her present occupation, she replied, "Three years."
Asked what other work she did well, she answered bleakly,
"None." Asked what other qualifications or practical experience she possessed, she answered, "None."

Only one answer stands out in the singularly spiritless
record. The form contained a series of questions about

nationality or country of allegiance. Emma correctly identified herself as a British subject. She might have skipped over the other questions in the sequence, which applied only to people not born in Canada. Instead, she chose to respond to Question 7 (f): IF NOT BRITISH SUBJECT, TO WHAT COUNTRY DO YOU OWE ALLEGIANCE? She wrote, "Owe allegiance to no country."

The Royal Commission on Espionage asked her why she had made such a statement. She told them that she did it "because my husband wished me to do it."

Whether she was influenced by Bill Woikin or whether her own grief and poverty was speaking can only be surmised. Judging from the element of spunkiness and independence that distinguished her all her life, it is more likely the latter.

That winter of 1940, as Emma turned twenty, the young Woikins had reason to hope that the desperate years were ending. There was enough rain the autumn to settle the dust, and the snowfall was promisingly heavy. Hungry young men were filling the recruitment halls, where some of them were issued blood-stained World War One khaki. The army was paying cash for eggs and beef.

Bill Woikin's headaches grew more intense and his periods of depression lengthened. Emma was frantic, convinced that something was appallingly wrong, but the young man refused to seek help. He said roughly, angrily, that he couldn't afford doctor bills.

Few of the young couples who came for the singing and the chatter in the spotless little shed noticed that anything was wrong. Both Woikins were consummate actors in the cause of privacy and pride. The friends did wonder, and sometimes teased, that the Woikins were enjoying an obviously passionate marriage but did not have a second pregnancy. Her apparent sterility remains a mystery.

Later in her life Emma had difficulty during her menopause and had a hysterectomy. The surgeon's report shows that both Fallopian tubes were blocked with tissue from an old infection. He was unable to guess how long this situation had existed but thought it wasn't likely that it dated back all the way to the birth of the still-born child. Emma, however, appears to have been convinced that her infertility was the direct result of that tragedy, which she associated with her poverty.

The winter of 1941 was a frightening one for the outwardly

Chapter Four

Bill Woikin left a note addressed to Emma. His sister Masha remembered it: "Don't blame anybody. I am tired of this world. There is no truth in this world."

The Konkins arrived in Langham before nightfall. Emma never forgot the gentleness of her father, who put his overcoat around her as she sat shivering with shock, and begged her to rest.

Bill was dressed in a fine suit and his shirt collar and tie were arranged to cover the marks on his throat the binder-twine had made. His pale hair was more neatly combed than it had ever been in life, and his big hands were composed in rest on his chest. Artificial flowers were arranged around his head in the freshly made coffin. The photograph taken on the day of burial shows Woikins and Konkins gathered in the farmyard around the open coffin. Emma, wearing a shabby coat, stands at her husband's head, with her father and brothers protectively beside her. Her expression is dazed and bleak.

Bill's body was taken to Kirioloka Cemetery, on a rise of ground near the present highway from Saskatoon to North Battleford. He was placed near the grave of his son. There was no money to pay for gravestones for either of them. The mounds were left to the weeds and wind for years. Later Emma talked of buying something to mark the graves, but she worried that it might be seen as disloyal to her second husband. Eventually Bill's younger sister, Soozie, paid for a gravestone for her brother. It lies near similar gravestones, arched beds of cement sprinkled with small bits of coloured glass, which mark the graves of Bill's mother, Hanna, and his father, Nikoli, who died in their seventies.

"All the brothers went to Bill's funeral," Mary related, "but I was too sick. They wouldn't even tell me what had happened. They just said that Bill was sick." Mary had just given birth to a daughter, Gail, and was in pain because the placenta was still in her womb. Despite her agony, she knew something awful had happened. Her husband, Pete, would not answer her questions. Visitors came and seemed to be suppressing some terrible news. Finally she guessed. "Did Bill Woikin die?" she asked a neighbour. The woman looked dismayed and turned away. "Well," she said reluctantly. "he's in a bad way." Then Mary knew.

Suicide among Doukhobors is slightly more frequent than among the general population. Some think it is the lonely exile in them, something in the dark Russian side of their nature that speaks when Doukhobors hang themselves or take lethal doses of gopher poison. The demands of stoicism in the face of adversity must exact a heavy price on the spirit; Doukhobors are a passionate, poetic people whose code of conduct imposes a rectitude that is difficult to maintain.

"I don't know why so many Doukhobors suicide," Mary said, sadly looking at Bill Woikin's funeral picture. "No one knows why, really."

Bill's sister, Masha Kalesnikoff, could not talk about Bill's death even forty years later; it was too painful. "It was a terrible thing, terrible, terrible. I can't forget him, never. No, I can't forget."

Violet Woikin, widow of Bill's brother Fred, lives with their son in Saskatoon and used to make dresses for Emma. She knew Bill Woikin well but refused to talk about him at all. In February, 1983, she had agreed to an interview but telephoned to cancel the appointment. The message wasn't received so the visitor went to the modest bungalow and, hearing music within, knocked repeatedly at the front and side doors.

Eventually a heavy young man, her son, answered. His mother was in bed with flu, he said. She came into the kitchen in a dressing gown and slippers and sat, stiff with embarrassment and resentment, her face averted. She would answer no questions, she told the visitor.

"There are Woikins in Langham," she said. "Try them."

There were two in the telephone book, both spelling the name "Woykin." One was William J. and the other John. Both had friendly voices and said they had known Emma and Bill Woikin all the time of their marriage, but could recall little about them. William J., the more forthcoming of the two, remembered that Bill dropped out of school well before grade eight. He was one of two sons and there were four daughters. The whole family was musical. He played the guitar and liked to sing. He was a bit more than six feet tall. His hair was brown, light brown, maybe blonde in the summer.

"He and Emma were like two peas in a pod, really happy together," William J. went on, in response to the disappointed silence on the receiver. "Every time you saw them, they were happy. It was hard for them to scrape by; they had to work hard, milk the cows, take care of the garden. Emma took that death very hard." He paused and added carefully, "People talked too much after Bill died. No one could figure out what happened."

Some say that Bill's parents blamed Emma for the suicide, feeling that she pushed him to better himself. Given the Konkin attitude towards them, they were bound to take as personal criticism any comment she made on their poverty. There was no plan to have Emma remain in the home where she and Bill had lived together for four years. She took all the money that Bill had when he died, seventy-five cents, and went home to Blaine Lake. The brother who took her in was John, who was living in the homestead. Emma moved into the bedroom she had left to marry, the one with the window facing the sunrise.

Fred Konkin was a nine-year-old at the time, thrilled to have his beloved, fun-loving aunt back for keeps. He found her greatly changed. She was weak, run-down, excessively thin, and disinterested in food. She wept for hours at a time, a wailing kind of crying, as Fred's mother, Lena, tenderly watched over her in concern.

The summer passed. Emma, quiet and listless, helped Lena

in the kitchen and did her share of the gardening and milking. Unmarried Doukhobor men came around, ostensibly to visit John and Lena. Emma wasn't rude; but, even more discouraging, she simply didn't notice they were there.

By the end of the summer John Konkin decided something had to be done to put Emma back together again.

"You're twenty-one," he told her one day. "You're young still and you've got a long life ahead of you. If you're not going to get married you should be taking a job. You're smart enough to work in an office so I'm sending you to secretarial school in Marcelin."

His choice of vocation had a lot to do with the Konkin concern that Emma wasn't strong enough for farm work. Living on the Woikin farm, they thought, had almost killed her. She didn't have the girth older Doukhobors thought essential in a woman. When Fred Konkin first brought Doreen home to meet his mother, Lena said approvingly in Russian, not knowing Doreen spoke it, "You picked a big one. She can work."

Marcelin is the first village northeast of Blaine Lake on the road to Prince Albert. Emma's brother Bill was living there with his family. Her niece, Agatha Konkin, daughter of Alex A., was commuting from her father's farm to high school there. Marcelin was predominantly French and boasted a high school run by nuns, who lived in a convent where farmers' daughters could be boarded safely.

Emma lived briefly with Bill and Hannah, but there was little room in their home. She stayed for a short time in the convent, then finally settled in a boarding-house room she shared with Agatha.

Agatha was about four years younger than her aunt and still regards Emma more as a sister than a member of her parents' generation. But Emma, at twenty-one, had buried a husband and son. She felt immeasurably older than the teenagers in the high school. Drawn as she always was to kin, she and Agatha nevertheless became very close.

Agatha Konkin later married a tall handsome Ukrainian Baptist, William Kardash. She is a devout woman who joined the Baptist church herself, and her daughter is married to a Baptist minister. The Kardashes were visited in May of 1983 just as seeding was about to begin. Bill Kardash was on crutches, recovering from a fourth operation on his hip and frustrated that he couldn't be in the fields.

A cold, hard wind was blowing, stinging the eyes; that night it brought six inches of unseasonal snow. Agatha Kardash was taken aback to be asked questions about Emma. Despite her misgivings, she stopped what she was doing to invite the guest courteously into her living room while she covered her alarm with hospitable small talk. One end of the room is dominated by an upright piano covered with family photographs and the other looks over the Kardash fields. Agatha inherited a good deal of land from her father, including the Konkin homestead where Emma was born and raised. Good management has improved the inheritance. The farmhouse in which they live is imposing; about a dozen barns and storehouses of various kinds are scattered near it, all in good repair, and an assortment of cars and trucks is parked in the yard.

Agatha said carefully, "I'm thinking how Emma would feel about all this being dragged up in a book. I don't think there should be a book about Emma." Suddenly there are tears in her eyes. "Emma was wonderful, to me like a sister. I just don't know what I should say to you."

Her husband came into the room to give support, followed by their son, Ernie, a school teacher in Rosthern who had come to help with the chores. Ernie Kardash is a slim young man with a luxurious dark moustache of the barbershop-quartet variety. His wife, Diane, a shy, unaffected woman in jeans, stood in the doorway, her hands stained from helping her father-in-law repair some machinery.

In the awkwardness of Agatha's tears, Diane tactfully gave her mother-in-law breathing room by talking about an aunt, the late Hilda Neatby, a formidable prairie teacher whose views influenced her generation. The distraction allowed Agatha to regain her composure. She said, "I don't know what I can say about Emma anyway, except that she was a wonderful woman and I loved her very much."

Was Emma obviously unhappy while she was going to school in Marcelin?

"Well yes. She cried a lot. She was very sad and lonely." Agatha was again close to tears herself.

"Did she confide in you about the circumstances of Bill Woikin's suicide?"

Agatha won't lie and, even forty years later, she won't betray a confidence. She replied, looking away, "Emma was very close to my mother, Annie. She used to write my mother a lot when she went to Ottawa."

Agatha was asked if she would share some of those letters. She didn't think so, she replied uncomfortably. They were in a box someplace, she wasn't sure. . . .

However, eight months later she changed her mind. She found the letters, sorted through them, and allowed sixteen of them to be quoted in this book about Emma.

On the initial visit to the Kardash farm, Agatha showed obvious relief when her guests rose to leave. Walking through the gleaming kitchen to escort her visitors to the door, she talked about farming as a poet would. It was her habit to take a lunch for them both when her husband was in the fields, she said, so they could enjoy the huge sky and the smell of the earth together.

"You are alone with nature, you know," she said. "It's really lovely."

During the year she spent in Marcelin, Emma was drawn to the biggest church in the community, which was Roman Catholic. She was baffled by the use of Latin in the services, but there was no mistaking the devotion of the sisters who taught her, or the sense of hope the congregation conveyed. She knelt a long time before the statues that brooded over pools of candlelight at their feet, grieving for her son, grieving for her husband.

For a year, Emma poured her energy and considerable intelligence into learning secretarial skills, everything the nuns could teach her about typing, bookkeeping, filing, and shorthand. By the end of her first year in Marcelin she had completed the two-year commercial course, and was graduated.

There were no jobs in Marcelin or Blaine Lake; she would have to move to Saskatoon, a place where buildings were so tall they required elevators, and where almost everyone had electricity and flush toilets. In the summer of 1943 she answered an advertisement in the Saskatoon *Star Phoenix* for a job in a lab in St. Paul's Hospital. The pay was wretched and she discovered why on her first day: "lab assistant" meant clean-

ing woman. She did the work without complaint but read the
help-wanted advertisements in the paper every night.

Her brother John had a suggestion. Because of the war, the
federal civil service was expanding rapidly. He was told,
possibly by Blaine Lake's Member of Parliament, John
Diefenbaker, that Emma had a good chance of finding a secretarial job in Ottawa. Diefenbaker later denied in the House of
Commons that he had ever heard of Emma Woikin or had
anything to do with her employment, but the Konkins believe
otherwise. The suggestion either came from Diefenbaker, they
say, or from Diefenbaker's partner, John Cuelenaere, who was
holding the practice together in Prince Albert while Diefenbaker was in Ottawa.

The Konkins had no fondness for Diefenbaker, whose
reputation around Blaine Lake was soured because the fee he
demanded for defending a man charged with murder was the
deed to the man's farm. However, it would be natural for John
Konkin, concerned for his tragic young sister, to approach
Diefenbaker for advice.

Emma went to the federal-government offices in Saskatoon
and wrote a civil-service examination. She knew she did well,
especially in the typing test, and hoped she might be offered a
job in Saskatchewan. She told Mary that she dreaded having to
go to Ottawa, so far from home, where she knew no one.

When she confided the same fears to a friend, Mary couldn't
remember who, she was given some brusque advice: "You need
a job and there aren't any secretarial jobs in Saskatoon. If you
don't take the job in Ottawa, you'll go on cleaning floors in the
lab."

Emma received a telegram in August 1943 notifying her that
a job as a typist was waiting for her in the Department of
External Affairs. She was to report for work immediately, and
she would be paid fifty-two dollars a month. She packed in a
daze as her brother John tried to find someone who knew if
there were Doukhobors in Ottawa who would take her in.
There were maybe three families, people said, but no one knew
their names.

John, his wife, Lena, and the oldest brother, Bill, drove
Emma to Saskatoon and put her on the train for the east. She
was twenty-two years old, a woman who had lived all her life,

except for a few weeks in Saskatoon, on the prairies among people who knew and loved her. She had never been on a train, almost never bathed in a tub with running water, hardly ever used a telephone, was just discovering radio.

Her train arrived at Ottawa's Union Station at nine in the morning of 10 September, 1943. On the sidewalk outside the station she faced the imposing castle of the Chateau Laurier Hotel. Across Confederation Square, past the war memorial, she could see the Parliament Buildings rising from a swell of green lawn. The streets were crowded with men and women in uniform, the traffic studded with military vehicles; everyone in a hurry.

She asked directions to the Department of External Affairs and found the office. Some formalities had to be observed. Ottawa didn't have her application for a civil-service job. She was given a form and filled it out. The form was entered as Exhibit 80 before the Royal Commission on Espionage.

NAME IN FULL: Emma Woikin
PLACE OF BIRTH: Blaine Lake, Saskatchewan
DATE OF BIRTH: December 30, 1920
RACIAL ORIGIN: Russian
BRITISH SUBJECT: Yes, by birth
CONJUGAL STATUS: Widow
PERIOD OF RESIDENCE IN CANADA: 22 years
PRESENT PLACE OF RESIDENCE: Blaine Lake, Saskatchewan
EDUCATIONAL BACKGROUND (HIGH SCHOOL AND UNIVERSITY): Public school, Grade VIII
CIVIL SERVICE EXAMINATION PASSED (GRADE AND YEAR): Grade 1, 1943, Stenography (Qualified as a Typist)
PREVIOUS SERVICE IN GOVERNMENT DEPARTMENT WITH PERIOD COVERED:
PREVIOUS POSITIONS HELD: Laboratory in St. Paul's Hospital (helper)
COMMENCED DUTIES IN EXTERNAL AFFAIRS: September 10, 1943
PRESENT ADDRESS OF RESIDENT:
PRESENT TELEPHONE NUMBER — RESIDENCE:
UNEMPLOYMENT INSURANCE BOOK: #E656774

DATE: September 10, 1943
(Sgd) Emma Woikin

She started her new job at two in the afternoon of the day she arrived in Ottawa, and her immediate housing problem was solved minutes later. A concerned co-worker, Betty Mac-Donald, discovered that Emma had no place to stay and knew no one in Ottawa. She offered her a temporary room in her own home. Her brother was away in the army; Emma could stay in his room until she found a place.

This impulsive act of wonderful kindness blossomed into a warm friendship. The MacDonalds took the young Doukhobor woman into their home and into their family. They remained loyal after Emma was arrested as a spy, which few of her other Ottawa friends did, and visited her and sent gifts while she was in prison. Years later, when Emma returned to Ottawa for the first and only time, it was the MacDonalds she wanted to see.

After work that first evening, Betty MacDonald took Emma home to the house at 558 O'Connor Street, where she lived with her parents. Her father, Ernest P. MacDonald, worked for the city in the engineering department.

The MacDonalds' house was a pleasant walk from the Parliament Buildings along busy O'Connor Street, which leads past the Victorian Gothic pile that now houses the Museum of Man and the Museum of National Science, down the way from another fine grotesque, the old Ottawa Curling Club, which was built in 1916.

Number 558 is in the middle of a row of six identical units. A short flight of steps leads from the sidewalk to the front door; there is a curved balcony above the doorway; the facades are grimy with city dirt.

When 558 O'Connor was visited on a spring day in 1983, the door was opened by a young woman who had to swoop to keep a kitten from escaping. A baby complained mildly in the background as she answered questions. She said there were three bedrooms upstairs but no closets. The landlord was the original owner of the property, Ellery E. Beamish.

Ellery Beamish himself was available by telephone. Fresh from a winter in Florida, seventy-six years of age, he spoke of the building with affection. The row of six attached houses was built by his grandfather at the turn of the century, he explained. The grandfather had two daughters, each of whom inherited three units. Conveniently, they each had three children, so the units were distributed equally on their deaths.

Ellery Beamish inherited 558, where he and his mother had lived for many years before he moved out and rented it to the MacDonalds. They were good tenants, he said, but he didn't know them at all and certainly had never heard of Emma Woikin. The MacDonalds paid their rent by mail and had few complaints.

The problem with the house, he went on, was that it didn't have a garage and the backyard was only ten feet deep. "Hard to sell, you know," he added genially.

Four days after Emma Woikin began to work at External Affairs she was taken down the hall, to be administered an official Oath of Secrecy in accordance with departmental routine. Ottawa, more than most Canadian cities, was conscious of protecting government secrets from the enemy. But that "enemy" was changing. With Hitler's surprise invasion of Russia in June 1941, the Soviet Union was transformed from a hostile nation to a wartime buddy. To the intense discomfort of many, Communists were released from prison camps. Many of them enlisted in the armed forces, and the Communist Party came out of hiding and into a respectability it was to enjoy for almost five years. In 1943, the Communist Party of Canada renamed itself the Labour Progressive Party and, through dozens of tough, smart, charming candidates, was elected in all three levels of government.

As the Soviet Army fought the Germans with astonishing courage and tenacity, a wave of admiration for all things Russian swept Canada. Film newsreels in movie houses showed the exploits of the heroes of Stalingrad and the tenacity of those who suffered in the siege of Leningrad. Moscow opened a Soviet embassy in Ottawa and staffed it with handsome officers full of social graces. They made dashing figures around town and were much sought after for their glamor.

As Ottawa sunk into its winter blanket of sooty snowdrifts, Emma found a rooming house at 63 Frank Street and left the MacDonalds. Despite their continued kindness to her, she was ravaged by homesickness and was particularly obsessed with the thought that Pearl Konkin, only three years old, a child born to Alex A. and Annie at about the same time as Emma's still-born son, would forget her Aunt Emma.

She wrote long, emotional letters to her family, begging them to write her often. One of those that has been preserved is dated 29 October, 1943, and is addressed to Annie Konkin.

I'm happy here, sure, but I would like to go home for a weekend, certainly drink coffee, and eat some of your good bread and, oh, I guess just everything else. Most of all I want to see Pearl. There couldn't be another darling as sweet as she is.

Don't you think the Lord has been good to me? For all He has taken away from me, in a measure He has repaid me by giving me these opportunities, like work and a wonderful place to stay where everybody likes me as if I were their very own and who think I'm just about perfect. I hope I can live up to all their beliefs in me. I wonder often why they like me and then I know it's because they don't know me, right?

Today I bought myself a nice suit. Dark blue grey, or something. I'll also get myself a beautiful blue dress, the most beautiful one I can find. Just wait to see me in a few years. I'll stop wearing my old black dresses. Will you still like me then?

The next day she wrote again, describing something about her work. She said her office hours were from eight-forty-five in the morning until twelve-thirty, with an hour and a half for lunch, back at two to work until five-forty-five; Saturday mornings she worked from eight forty-five to one. "Not bad, eh?" she commented cheerily.

The next part of the letter gives some indication of Emma Woikin's reservations about Canada's war effort, which were not unnatural in a devout Doukhobor, and her skepticism of official Ottawa, which was expected in someone raised in the west.

All civil servants were X-rayed for TB. Quite a few had it and are of course discharged. The Victory Loan is on. All civil servants were called from work to see a show and hear

speakers in the theatre, and given a day off to encourage
buying bonds. Didn't affect me any. I still didn't buy any.
Every day there is a parade at noon of bands and everything. And cannons and guns stick out at you from every
corner.

She explained that civil servants had an identification card
that enabled them to obtain a ten-percent discount in some
stores. Her new "dark blue grey" suit, for instance, cost her
three dollars less than the price on the label. With a few inches
more of space to fill on the page, she added impulsively,

By the way, I've been to see the Russian Cossacks and were
they wonderful. I never was so thrilled about anything as I
was about that performance they put on. It took all I had
not to just get up and shout I was Russian.
I'm so lonesome. I wish I was home.
I'm well, but I'm losing weight again. Lots of love to
you, my dears, from your Emma.

Only three days later she wrote to Mabel Konkin, one of the
three daughters of Annie and her brother Alex:

Remember that I'm very far away and I live only for the
letters that you people write to me. That's my only contact
with you all. So have a heart, don't wait until you have
nothing in the world to do to write.

For a young woman of twenty-two who had never lived in a
city, Emma showed a considerable degree of enterprise in
finding social groups. She told her niece Mabel that she had
attended a Hallowe'en party in a nearby United Church, where
she enjoyed herself hugely. The previous Sunday she had gone
to a fellowship service in the evening, followed by a spelling
bee, in which contestants had to spell words backwards. Her
team won.

Just before Christmas, the first of her life away from family,
she wrote a letter to Annie and Alex that was drenched in
loneliness:

I'm so alone here, and now during the holiday season I feel

it more than ever. My second Christmas without Bill.
Meaning, the second Christmas that I'm a stranger here in
this world, this war-torn world, where there's hardly any
justice or truth.

With an almost palpable effort of will, she turned to a
favourite subject, the three daughters of Annie and Alex:

Agatha has her way of carrying herself that proves she can
meet with confidence all that life has in store, and she'll
meet it wisely. Here a young woman like Agatha would be
something you could only dream of and never find. But
had she come here she would pass unappreciated because
these people here are quite smug and self-satisfied.

I'm building a little world of books and occasional
shows and the club life of the Young Women's Christian
Association, the Western Girls' Club. My Sundays are
spent in church from morning until night almost because
I go to more than one service. I'm tired of all my dresses
I'm wearing here.

At one point Emma wrote "I can't understand the countless
dirty deals the poor farmers get."

She went on to describe bureaucrats as "only an excuse" for
human beings who "didn't have to strive . . . they don't know
anything. They live secure in themselves." She went on:

Another strange thing is that people here are so very much
afraid of the Russians. They are so sure that England will
be attacked by Russia. They still consider Russia a far
greater enemy and menace than Germany is. I'm going to
see the show *The City that Stopped Hitler: The Great
Stalingrad.* I wouldn't miss seeing it for the world for there
may be at least one Russian word spoken, the sweetest
music to my ears. I often think of talking Russian to
myself, just a few words now and then. Living (for years it
seems) among all English people, not seeing a single one
of your own, is harrowing.

On 4 January, 1944, she wrote Annie and Alex to tell them

how she had spent the holidays and to thank them for a goose they sent her:

> I went Christmas in a Catholic Church at a midnight Mass. I was beautiful. It was English so I understood all. Xmas morning too I was in church and for Xmas dinner.

Despite the isolation conveyed in her letters to Blaine Lake, she clearly was a well-liked person. On 30 December, a Friday, co-workers gave her a surprise birthday party after office hours, complete with a cake, twenty-three candles and ice cream. The next day she was dazzled at the year-end office party, held in the offices after noon closing, because high-ranking civil servants attended. She wrote:

> Strange for me to be one of the "ladies" in attendance at a party of such high and mighty people. New Year's Eve went to a party at the Dominion United Church, service at midnight. We sat with lights low in church in two minutes of silent prayer. For me it was really earnest prayer because I seem to need it.

Emma was promoted only five months after beginning work in the passport office. There wasn't much to do in that branch of External Affairs, since few civilians were travelling, but an opening developed for a bright, quick, accurate person in the cipher division, and Emma Woikin was considered the perfect choice.

Most of the material handled in the cipher office was coded communication between London and Ottawa. All cable traffic passed through Ottawa's telegraph office, and it was considered prudent to convert even routine messages into diplomatic code. It was Emma's responsibility to turn coded messages from abroad into English, and messages that were to be transmitted from Ottawa into code.

A month after her promotion Emma received an automatic raise of five dollars a month; the increase was granted all civil servants of her rank after six months of employment. Her income rose to fifty-seven dollars a month.

The second anniversary of Bill Woikin's suicide found

Emma in pain from reopened grief. Two days after the date she wrote a heart-breaking note to Annie and Alex:

> I guess I am well. These last few days have been especially hard but I guess I've had days that were harder and I will get over these all right.

She quoted the lyrics of a religious song, "The Rosary," which seemed to possess penetrating meaning for her:

> "The hours I've spent with you, dear heart" (my Bill) "are like a string of pearls to me; I count them over every one apart . . ."
> Memories, they bless and they hurt you. I've had gain, but it is barren when there is no one to share it with. There is just bitter loss. A feeling of bitter loss that remains . . . I guess these days being the anniversary of the day when the cross was hung, I strive to learn to kiss the cross.

The mention of the cross was apparently a reference to the approach of Easter. Emma's letter continued on a firmly more cheerful note:

> Yesterday was Sunday and do you know where I was? Well, for the first time I went to the Russian settlement in Ottawa. I knew there was one here somewhere but I didn't know how to approach it. Well, Sunday I went to their Orthodox church. Well, the whole service was in Russian rather than Ukrainian . . . anyway it was great . . . The language spoken was only half the joy. The spirit of the people, it is wonderful. There are no people like ours, that is certain. As Tolstoy said, Truth, Sincerity and Simplicity is the keynote of the people of his country. It is very true.

Emma told Annie and Alex that she was invited after the service to the home of a Mrs. Kachuk, where she had dinner, met the Kachuk daughter Annie and her husband Merron, and listened to a record of the USSR Army chorus. She was greatly impressed by the comforts of the Kachuk home, the most splendid she had ever seen, and described the "lovely house and the lovely furnishings and a car." She added wistfully, "He is working on the CPR and they sure have a nice home."

It was at the home of Annie and Merron that the Soviet Embassy made its first contact with Emma.

Her pleasure and relief to find a Russian environment led her to accept an invitation from a Russian-speaking co-worker in External Affairs, Leo Malania, to take a room in his house at 357 Chapel Street, where he lived with his wife, Anna. The neighbourhood, to Emma's delight, was sprinkled with Russian-speaking families. The new Soviet embassy found the district convivial, and many employees had rented quarters there.

Emma's social life changed. She signed up for night courses in English literature, art and math at the Ottawa technical school. And she began to be part of gatherings of Russian-speaking people in Ottawa, through whom she met another Russian-speaking group who lived in Montreal. Some of the Montrealers sang in a Russian choir, a popular attraction, in those days, at patriotic rallies.

It was a heady time for a Canadian of Russian heritage. The Canadian-Soviet Friendship League had been launched in the summer of 1943 at a packed rally in Toronto's Maple Leaf Gardens. Among the distinguished patrons were Lady Eaton, one of the discoverers of insulin, Dr. Charles Best, and presidents of such ornaments of the capitalist system as the Canadian Pacific Railway, Canada Packers, and Atlas Steel. Prime Minister William Lyon Mackenzie King chaired the opening rally and Raymond Massey, actor son of an authentic Canadian blue-blooded millionaire, was master of ceremonies.

As Soviet troops broke a German Panzer attack in the spring of 1944 and began to roll west through Poland, Canadians rejoiced. There was constant speculation about an Allied landing in Europe to establish a Second Front and distract some of the German resources, but somehow the Allies did not seem quite ready. Instead of a landing in Belgium and France, there was an invasion of the southern tip of Italy. To the dismay of people at home, Canadian, British, and American forces were badly chewed in the grinding advance through Italy's mountain passes. The only good news of the war was coming from the Russian front, and Canadians celebrated each advance gratefully.

Toronto's city council discussed twinning that city with Stalingrad, the Soviet steel centre that withstood a pitiless seige and turned back the German army. No oratorical flight was too fulsome to apply to the gallant Russians. Canadian Communists who had recently been imprisoned for their political views found themselves courted at social gatherings and consulted respectfully by the press and politicians. Some Canadian Communists had dropped out of party activities when Hitler made a pact with Stalin, but those who loyally had survived felt vindicated when the Soviet was invaded. Communists seemed to fall into one of two categories: either they were hard-working and effective organizers with roots in Europe's trade union movement, or else they were intellectuals drawn to the Marxist dream of an equitable society.

In either case, most accepted the dogma that the goal they mutually sought of a better world would be jeopardized if they wrangled among themselves or questioned what Moscow asked them to do.

Reform-minded people struggled to understand the philosophies of Marx and Engels. The climate for exploration of left-wing ideas was so welcoming that the CBC created a hugely popular radio series, "Canadian Forum," produced in Toronto by Neil Morrison. People who thought of themselves as liberals or democratic socialists mingled with Communists to listen to the Forum's lectures on economic and political theory, and afterwards to discuss the ideas presented far into the night. These study groups, as participants thought of them, met in members' homes and were particularly vigorous in such centres as Ottawa, where some of the brightest scientists, economists and writers were clustered.

Emma Woikin, far removed from this stimulating scene, a poorly paid civil servant from a western farm, was being gathered into another set, one in which Canadians of Russian extraction came together in delight that their homeland was for the first time enjoying real popularity in Canada. Pride and patriotism were mixed with a necessary commitment to the political reality of the Soviet; it seemed impossible to rejoice in Soviet victories without adoring Communism as well.

Emma's family has no recollection that she had any political views, left or otherwise, before going to Ottawa but it is difficult to escape the conclusion that she developed a powerful

Chapter Five

Emma Woikin's income, fifty-seven dollars a month, gave no indication of the complexity and importance of her task in the cipher room at External Affairs. She was paid at the level of a simple typist but she did almost no typing at all.

The CNR telegraph office in Ottawa would notify External Affairs when a cable was received from London. A courier went to collect it, often in the middle of the night, and placed it in a basket in the cipher room. It was Emma's responsibility to check in, signing a logbook, soon after the message reached the cipher room. Most communications were between the British secretary of state for dominion affairs and the Canadian secretary of state for external affairs, a portfolio then held by Prime Minister King.

Emma had two tools: the cipher book and the cipher machine, called a "typex." The cipher, or code, was changed regularly to thwart enemy efforts to break it. She would set the message into the machine and tear off the ribbons of decoded material it produced, gluing them on pages for the typist to copy. Codes that required translation with the cipher book were more labourious to convert, but these, too, were typed to provide clean copy for the recipients, who usually included the prime minister, the governor-general (the Earl of Athlone), the minister of national defence, the British high commissioner to Canada, and the Canadian ambassador in Washington.

Messages were kept in an IN basket; Emma removed them in the order in which they were received. When ready for typing they went into the OUT basket. Emma's originals were stored for three months in a filing cabinet locked only at night, then the originals were burned. A carbon copy on flimsy blue paper, was kept for a year and then destroyed.

Emma was required to initial the work of the typists to indicate that there were no errors or omissions from her original deciphering. Typists also initialled their work. There were two kinds of files, "secret" and "top secret." The sender of the message decided upon the designation.

The job was both responsible and demanding, and needed a person with a flair for puzzles and a passion for accuracy. Emma trained first on the typex, coding and decoding under supervision, and mastered the technique in a few weeks rather than the usual six to eight. She learned next to use the cipher book, which was much more difficult; often trainees practised for months before they could work independently. But again Emma was quick and totally reliable. The eager young Doukhobor was a real find for the cipher room.

A few blocks away a sturdy, boyish-faced Russian was performing exactly the same function in the Soviet embassy. Igor Zergevich Gouzenko was twenty-four, a year older than Emma Woikin. He arrived in Ottawa two months before Emma Woikin had, his route a series of leaps from Moscow, over the polar cap to Fairbanks, Alaska, from there to Edmonton, and then by train to the capital.

His training in coding and decoding took place in an intensive ten-month session in Moscow and was conducted by the Soviet secret police, known at that time as the NKVD. Many trainees were eliminated in the process; those who finished were the cream. When Gouzenko graduated, he was sent to the embassy in Ottawa. The embassy said Gouzenko was a secretary, but he was a cipher specialist who handled communications between the Kremlin and the embassy's military attaché, the handsome war hero, Colonel Nicholai Zabotin.

Zabotin's task was to gather information about the secrets the west was concealing from its ally. He investigated the wonderful radar research, the pioneer work in explosives, the new weapons. The Soviet Union didn't believe for a minute in the west's friendship, or in the promises of Churchill and Roosevelt to share their military secrets, or that the alliance would survive any longer than the last shot of the last battle in the war. Accordingly, Zabotin's instructions were to find Canadians within government offices and laboratories who would provide military information during and after the war.

Russia had been denied an embassy in Canada since 1931 and was taking full advantage of the opportunity presented by its sudden elevation as an ally of the west. Zabotin was not the only Russian told to organize a network. The beautiful mansion at 285 Charlotte Street, which housed the Soviet embassy, included at least one other embryo network, run by the NKVD chief; another might have been run by the naval attaché.

Zabotin began cautiously. He was a familiar figure at social events in Ottawa, Montreal, and Toronto, a charming and glamorous figure. One of his social assets was his movie-star good looks, marred only slightly by a front tooth capped in stainless steel. In photographs it appeared black, like a gap, and the *Toronto Star* was not the only newspaper to run photos of Zabotin that had been retouched to give him an all-white smile.

Zabotin's young cipher clerk, Igor Gouzenko, arrived in Ottawa at the height of the city's war-time housing crisis and stayed in the Chateau Laurier until the embassy found him an apartment at 511 Somerset Street. The luxurious Chateau dazzled the young man, fresh from a stark city that had been under Hitler's guns. His salary was enormous by the standard of the day — $275 a month. He had ample disposable income and began to enjoy good wine and fine clothes.

His wife, Svetlana, followed him to Ottawa and together they furnished their new apartment, rented at $50 a month, in time for the birth of their first child, a son. The embassy gave them $150 to buy a dining-room suite, but otherwise they managed the purchases themselves. Both were overwhelmed at the profusion of food in the groceries and the racks of clothing in the department stores. Gouzenko discovered there was something of the dandy in his nature, and he turned himself out in handsome tailoring and bright ties.

Gouzenko and Emma Woikin held parallel jobs, working

with cipher machines and code books, but there the resemblance ended. The security arrangements at external affairs were casual, as suited a country where few people locked their doors. Emma had a key to the main door and signed herself in and out as the work required. During the day the files that contained the decoded messages were not locked, for the sake of convenience, and the staff roamed through the three-room suite of offices freely.

The arrangements in the Soviet embassy were very different. Gouzenko worked in a space sealed off from the other embassy staff, a room with a steel door that opened after a secret bell was rung. The code book was kept in a sealed bag in a safe; messages, wrapped three times and sealed five times, also went into the safe, which Gouzenko fastened with his own secret seal. Colonel Zabotin kept a diary, also sealed in a safe. All this went on inside a locked, guarded embassy building, where even the chauffeur was a NKVD agent and had been trained to kill.

Early in the spring of 1944, just before Emma moved from 63 Frank Street to live with the Malanias on Chapel Street, she learned from another external affairs clerk that transfers to diplomatic offices in other countries were sometimes available. She was swept by an impulse to see Russia, and went immediately to make inquiries. On 28 March, 1944, ten days after the second anniversary of Bill Woikin's suicide, she obtained the necessary application form and filled it out. It became Exhibit 81 in the case before the Royal Commission on Espionage.

DEPARTMENT OF EXTERNAL AFFAIRS
(Please Complete This Form in Triplicate)

APPLICATION FOR POSITION OF: Typist (clerk) abroad
SURNAME: Woikin   CHRISTIAN NAMES: Emma
ADDRESS: 63 Frank Street, Ottawa
TELEPHONE (IF IN OTTAWA): 2-0517
DATE AND PLACE OF BIRTH: December 30, 1920, Blaine
  Lake, Saskatchewan
BRITISH SUBJECT: By birth
PLACE OF BIRTH OF PARENTS: Russia
CONJUGAL STATUS: Widow
PRIMARY SCHOOL: From May 1927 to June 1933
PLACE: Blaine Lake

SUBJECTS SPECIALIZED IN: Art and Literature
SECONDARY SCHOOL: Commercial course in Marcelin,
Saskatchewan, in Bookkeeping, Typing, Shorthand
UNIVERSITY:
LANGUAGES SPOKEN FLUENTLY: English, Russian
LANGUAGES READING KNOWLEDGE: English, Russian
CIVIL SERVICE EXAMINATIONS PASSED (GRADE & YEAR):
Grade 1, 1943
MILITARY SERVICE (IF ANY): Nil
BUSINESS TRAINING: Employed by the Department of
External Affairs from September, 1943 to February 25,
1944, Passport Office Branch; from February 25, 1944,
Cypher Division
WHEN WOULD YOU BE READY TO REPORT FOR DUTY, IF
APPOINTED? WHEN CALLED
ARE YOU WILLING TO SERVE OUTSIDE CANADA? Yes
IF SO, WHERE? Russia

DATE: March 20, 1944   SIGNATURE: Emma Woikin

The application was a long shot. She didn't tell anyone at
Blaine Lake about it.

Two years later, when the application was presented as
evidence before the Royal Commission on Espionage, Emma's
request for a posting to Moscow was a damning document. She
was questioned closely by Mr. Justice R. Kellock of the
Supreme Court of Canada, one of the two Supreme Court
judges on the commission, and by Gerald Fauteux, a lawyer
retained by the federal government to question witnesses.
Fauteux later was appointed to the Supreme Court. The
exchange led nowhere:

FAUTEUX: Did you about that time express a wish to go to
work in Russia?
WOIKIN: About that time?
FAUTEUX: Yes
WOIKIN: Do you mean. . . .
FAUTEUX: About March, 1944?
WOIKIN: Do you mean at work?
FAUTEUX: Yes. Did you express a wish to work in Russia at

that time, in the spring or around the month of March, 1944?

WOIKIN: I had at one time mentioned it at the office. I spoke to some of the employees about it. I cannot remember now when it was when I was speaking.

KELLOCK: What prompted that?

WOIKIN: I do not know. There was not any one thing that prompted it, but I always wanted to. [Pause, indicated by dashes in the transcript] There were many foreign openings and I thought I had a better chance to get that position than any other one because I had the language.

FAUTEUX: You applied, as a matter of fact, as you can see according to this Exhibit No. 81. This is an application for a position as typist or clerk abroad.

WOIKIN: Yes.

KELLOCK: Does it not say in Russia?

WOIKIN: [Apparently looking at the document] Just abroad.

KELLOCK: What exhibit is that?

FAUTEUX: [Looking at the application] Exhibit No. 81. Oh yes, at the end it says: "Are you willing to serve outside of Canada? Where? Russia."

KELLOCK: Is that all in the witness's handwriting?

FAUTEUX: Yes.

WOIKIN: Yes.

FAUTEUX: Did you make this application to work abroad in Russia after the party which preceded that concert?

WOIKIN: No, that was before.

FAUTEUX: That was before?

WOIKIN: Yes.

FAUTEUX: Had you discussed with anyone the idea of going to Russia?

WOIKIN: I discussed it with my co-workers but not with . . .

KELLOCK: Not with?

WOIKIN: Not with anyone outside because I did not know whether I had a chance or not, so I did not discuss it with anyone.

The party to which Fauteux referred took place on the evening of May 1, 1944, May Day in Communist countries. The Royal Canadian Mounted Police informed the tribunal that

Emma Woikin was recruited by the Soviet embassy at the party, where she met a member of the embassy's commercial staff. In 1944, Canada was celebrating with the Soviet. A film called *Song of Russia,* starring Susan Peters and Robert Taylor, was playing at the Capital Theatre in Ottawa, with a Pete Smith comedy short, *Home Maid,* a cartoon, and the news. As an added attraction for May Day, the Glinka choir of Montreal, sponsored by the Federation of Russian-Canadians, would sing Russian folk songs.

An Ottawa woman, Anna Plosenski, whom Emma had met earlier, had friends in the Glinka choir, and she invited them to dinner before the concert. To enhance the occasion, she invited Major Vsevolod Sokolov, a Russian army officer from the Soviet embassy, and his wife, Lida. Rounding out the party she also asked the Doukhobor cipher clerk, Emma Woikin, a friend of some of the people in the choir. Emma prepared herself that evening with her usual meticulous care.

Her income did not permit her to buy other than the cheapest clothes available, but she was fussy about fit, colour, and grooming. She went to the office in the working-girl uniform of the day, a dark suit brightened with a lapel pin and pastel rayon blouse. Suit jackets had wide padded shoulders, a style made popular by movie star Joan Crawford, and narrow skirts with a discreet slit. Only eccentric women appeared hatless on the street; the favourite hat style in 1944 was a pillbox trimmed with veiling and artificial flowers whose components could be purchased in a dime store for less than a dollar. The hats were worn tipped over one eyebrow.

The latest shoes were high heels with ankle straps. The hair-do of the day, which Emma's short, permanented hair did not permit, was called the upsweep. Women with longer hair fastened it on top of their heads with numerous bobby pins.

Emma Woikin dressed the way women do who consider themselves hopelessly plain. She avoided clothes that would make her stand out in a crowd or expose her to ridicule. She shopped carefully so that the colour of her handbag would match perfectly her shoes and hat. She kept her stocking seams straight. Her blouse was always freshly ironed; her suit never had a spot or a wrinkle. She always had one good dress, usually blue, for fancy occasions.

Dustin Hoffman played the role of a woman such as Emma

Woikin in the film *Tootsie*. After the filming he told inter-
viewers what he had learned from the experience of being a
plain woman. Tootsie, he said, was the woman no man wants
to be stuck near at a party. He had been guilty himself of
finding excuses to slip away from a conversation with a plain
woman to fetch up, sighing in relief, beside the prettiest
woman in the room. Playing Tootsie taught him that plain
women expect to be treated with indifference and even rude-
ness, that they protect themselves as best they can by appearing
jolly and kind, and that they bury the hurt.

Emma Woikin may have been prettier than she thought the
night she walked to Anna Plosenski's party in a warm spring
rain. Her ill-proportioned features shone with good health,
intelligence and her friendly disposition. She was twenty-three,
an excited young woman in her best blue dress, walking in
long, easy strides, her short curls bobbing under the sheltering
umbrella.

The party appears to have been a notable social success.
Emma greeted her friends in the choir and they chatted in
Russian as they sipped their beer. She was delighted to meet the
most notable guests, the Sokolovs, the man resplendent in his
Soviet army uniform, the woman shy because she spoke little
English. Emma warmed to them both and was dazzled that they
seemed to find her the most interesting person in the room.
They were cultivated and charming, full of literary references
and stories about life in Moscow; Emma Woikin was won over
in a night.

The Royal Commission on Espionage thought the party was
set up so that Sokolov could recruit Emma as a Soviet spy. The
judges seemed to believe that most of the people there were
involved in espionage; Emma was asked to name all the guests.
She was determined to protect her friends.

She annoyed the tribunal by taking a long time to answer
simple questions, by pausing many times in her replies, and by
giving brief answers, yielding a minimum of information. She
volunteered little. As a technique for withstanding a blistering
cross-examination, it can't be bettered.

KELLOCK: Who was present at the dinner?
WOIKIN: There were quite a few artists that put on the
  concert.

KELLOCK: Whose house?

WOIKIN: Plosenski.

KELLOCK: The first name?

WOIKIN: The lady's name was Anna.

KELLOCK: And the husband's?

WOIKIN: I do not know. We were not very well acquainted.

KELLOCK: The address?

WOIKIN: Broad Street, but I cannot remember the number.
That is the only time I have been there. It was people
who were in the concert who were more acquainted with
me than this place where the dinner was.

KELLOCK: You knew the people who were going to give
the concert better than you knew the Plosenskis?

WOIKIN: Yes. It just happened they were mutual friends of
ours but we hardly knew them.

KELLOCK: You said "friends of ours." Who do you mean
besides yourself?

WOIKIN: Besides myself?

KELLOCK: You said "friends of ours." To whom do you
refer?

WOIKIN: Well, my friends in Montreal.

KELLOCK: And yourself?

WOIKIN: Yes.

There were four questions put to her before the Royal Commission learned that the name of the choir was "Glinka."

FAUTEUX: Who introduced you to Major Sokolov?

WOIKIN: I cannot remember who it was exactly. It was one
of the group from Montreal, I cannot remember who.

FAUTEUX: Whom did you know in the crowd from
Montreal?

WOIKIN: I knew a lot of their first names but I do not know
their last names.

FAUTEUX: Would you tell us what you know?

WOIKIN: There is Savich, I know, and there are many of
them that I know their first names but I do not know....

FAUTEUX: Will you tell us their first names?

WOIKIN: It would be Peter and Nadia.

FAUTEUX: That is only two. We have not reached the stage
of a crowd yet. Have you other names?

WOIKIN: I have not known them long either. I have known some of them, like the Savichs.

KELLOCK: Was there more than one person by that name?

WOIKIN: I am not sure that Mr. Savich was there.

KELLOCK: Do you know her first name?

WOIKIN: Nadia, but her sister-in-law is Nadia, too.

KELLOCK: The sister-in-law's name is also Savich?

WOIKIN: No.

KELLOCK: What is her name?

WOIKIN: I cannot remember her last name.

And so on, for seven long transcript pages. Frequently Emma is asked to repeat what she said or to speak more loudly. Her voice must have been exceedingly faint; she was no more than a table-length away from the judges and lawyers. The frustration the commission felt is best evinced when Mr. Justice Kellock made a flustered, inane remark: "We do not want the names of the people you do not remember," he told Emma Woikin sternly, "but we do want the names of the people you do remember."

By tedious prodding, they learned that Emma knew the hostess, Anna Plosenski, only slightly, was better acquainted with Nadia Savich, though she couldn't remember the name of Nadia's husband, and that someone else at the party was named Peter.

Vsevolod Sokolov lost no time telling his superiors at the Soviet embassy that he had found a Canadian cipher clerk who was young, naïve, romantic and of Russian heritage, and who believed that the Soviet Union was some sort of promised land. Igor Gouzenko happened to be present when Sokolov told Colonel Zabotin about the party. The word he remembers Sokolov using to describe Emma was "impressionable."

The two officers discussed a strategy to enlist Emma's aid. Sokolov said he would cultivate the relationship by inviting Emma to his home. A visiting Kremlin official was present for the discussion and protested. He suggested that they should meet in a restaurant — it would be safer, more casual looking. Zabotin assured him that it was the Canadian way to entertain at home.

They decided not to hurry the process because they did not

want to alarm Emma. First Sokolov was to gain her trust. The decision about what to do with this windfall would come later.

The manoeuvering took place against the background of a war that was approaching a turning point. Canadian casualties at that time were 23,962, of which 11,725 young men were dead. The landing at Dieppe, which some believe was a deliberate massacre designed to show the Kremlin that a second front was impossible, had taken a brutal toll of Canadians, as did the fighting up Italy's long boot and the night bombings of Germany. Civilians were urged to do their share by investing in war bonds; the campaign that spring had a goal of six million dollars, and reached it.

A month after Emma Woikin met Vsevolod Sokolov, D-Day arrived and the allied armies landed on the beaches of Normandy. With Hitler's resources split, the Soviet offensive was unleashed along an eight-hundred mile front that extended south from Leningrad. The news at home was full of Russian and allied victories. In August, seven Panzer divisions were trapped on the killing ground of Falaise; a month later Belgium was liberated.

The final battles began in the winter of 1944. Germany had a prophetic new weapon, rocket bombs called V-2s, which were aimed at London. There was no defense against them. The Russians continued to advance from the east as the allies ground through Holland and approached German soil.

In February 1945, an ailing Franklin Delano Roosevelt met with Joseph Stalin and Winston Churchill at Yalta. One of the best-known photographs of the war is of the three leaders seated together, smiling widely, the best of friends.

Meanwhile, Emma Woikin, had become infatuated with Major Vsevolod Sokolov. People who saw him around Ottawa, where he was a far less conspicuous figure than Colonel Zabotin, describe him as an attractive man with an intelligent face, an easy manner, and a look of coiled energy that suggested sensuality. There is some doubt that he actually seduced Emma sexually. Emma Woikin was a conventional woman, monogamist by nature, and likely to be shocked by an offer to enter into an adulterous relationship, particularly when she was a friend of Lida Sokolov, the major's wife. There is nothing in her history, before or after the events in Ottawa, to suggest that she would be capable of a back-room affair.

Seduction, however, can take other forms than luring someone into bed. Sokolov had no need to compromise Emma Woikin sexually. It was enough that he talked to her about music, literature, and politics, that he introduced her to cultivated conversation, to manners, that he seemed to find her company interesting, stimulating, even thrilling — if only he weren't a married man.

The young woman was flattered out of her sensible mind. She told him the story of her two great losses and how she connected them with poverty. Sokolov, in turn, painted a glowing picture of the Soviet Union, the only country in the world at that time where health services were free to all.

She brought him a shy gift, a painting she had copied from a landscape on a calendar to fill in the long, empty evenings in her room. He gave her, in turn, a bottle of expensive, exotic perfume.

Emma had a Russian-speaking acquaintance, a woman from Saskatchewan who taught English to some of the Soviet embassy staff. This woman told Emma that the embassy had some Canadian employees and that she might find work there as a bilingual typist.

Emma leaped at the opportunity to see Sokolov every day. She hastened to Charlotte Street to apply and was received by someone who gave her a form to fill out. She mailed it promptly but received no reply. After fretting for weeks, she boldly telephoned to ask if the application had arrived safely. She was assured that it had, and was invited to come for an interview.

This time she met V.G. Pavlov, the head of the NKVD in Canada, who chatted pleasantly with her while weighing how useful the eager little cipher clerk might be to the Kremlin. He saw her out, smoothly, promising to let her know when there was a vacancy.

Emma told Sokolov how anxious she was to help him in his work. She thought she could manage a transfer to the department of commercial affairs, which was negotiating with Sokolov's superior to open Canada-Russian trade relations after thirty years. She could work from within to hurry things along, or she could join the commercial staff of the embassy and give them a Canadian perspective.

Sokolov reported to Zabotin, who asked Moscow what they should do about Emma Woikin. Moscow's reply was that she was too valuable where she was; she shouldn't be allowed to move.

Emma was dejected when Sokolov told her that there was no job for her in the embassy. "I really want to help Russia," she told him.

"You can help Russia much better if you remain where you are," Sokolov said. In Hollywood such lines are spoken with a certain intensity in the eyes and a long, meaningful stare. Gouzenko described the scene in subsequent testimony but didn't elaborate on Sokolov's delivery. Emma Woikin certainly must have grasped what he was getting at.

According to Gouzenko, she replied that she understood. Then she added, "Don't tell anybody about this."

Gouzenko thought that Sokolov had developed her much sooner more quickly than the embassy expected. "The result was that she agreed to work as an agent," he commented.

For a while, nothing changed. Emma had a stroke of good luck one day while reading the want advertisements in an Ottawa newspaper: she came across an offer of room and board in exchange for babysitting in the evenings. She went at once to the address, 289 Somerset Street East, and was interviewed by Albert Choquette. He explained that he had been off work for a long time recuperating from an operation, and that his wife had returned to work as a night-shift nurse at Ottawa General Hospital. He had just found employment again, but his job would require him sometimes to make night deliveries. They needed someone to stay with their four children.

Emma saw the children, Jack, who was about eight, Suzanne, six, Peter, four, and the baby, Andrée. She loved them and they responded to her warmth. Albert Choquette told his wife when she returned from her shift that he thought Emma was just what they wanted. Marguerite Choquette wanted to see for herself. When Emma returned that weekend to be inspected, Marguerite pronounced her absolutely perfect.

Forty years later, nothing had changed her mind about Emma Woikin. "She was the loveliest person you would ever want to meet," she said, in a snappy, no-nonsense tone not uncommon among veteran nurses.

Marguerite Choquette was in her seventies when interviewed in the spring of 1983 in her Ottawa apartment in a high-rise set among suburban bungalows. She's a person not easily taken in.

For a while after Emma Woikin moved into the four-bedroom house the Choquettes rented for thirty-five dollars a month, Marguerite arranged with a neighbour to make surprise visits. The neighbour gave enthusiastic reports.

"You don't have a worry in the world about Emma," she told Marguerite. "She's wonderful with your children." One time she found Emma reading the children a story, the baby on her lap. Another time they were singing together; a third visit found her in the kitchen, cooking pies for them, all of them talking a blue streak.

"Jack remembers her best," Marguerite reflected. "She would sing and hum as she cooked for them, goulash and homemade bread. She seemed contented and happy in everything she did. She always left her bedroom door open. I told her that the kids would get in, maybe make a mess, but she said it didn't matter."

Marguerite Choquette gave Emma Woikin her complete confidence and it survived Emma's arrest, the front-page headlines, trials and prison. "I figured Emma was innocent," she said with salty skepticism. "I still figure it was a mistake. She was too nice, too kind, to do anything underhanded. I think she was dragged into it accidentally."

Emma lived in a small upstairs room that was furnished with a single bed, dresser, table, and two chairs. She brought with her no ornaments or family pictures to relieve the bareness. After she had been there a few weeks, Marguerite discovered that she painted in her spare time.

"She was shy about some things," Marguerite explained. "She didn't tell you much about herself. She painted beautifully. One thing I would have liked to have is one of those paintings. She promised me one, but then she left so suddenly . . . ."

The young woman seemed to have no life other than work and the Choquette household. Sometimes, but rarely, she would get dressed up and go out "to see friends," but she came and went alone. Marguerite didn't remember that she received any mail or even a telephone call.

She was seeing a lot of the friendly Sokolovs. She may have cooked a Doukhobor meal for them on occasion. Just before her death, Emma told David Beaubier, a lawyer in the Saskatoon law firm that employed her, that once she served a Russian meal to Lester Pearson, who later became prime minister, Herbert Norman, the Canadian diplomat who committed suicide in Cairo when smeared by Senator Joseph McCarthy's Communist hunters, and one other person whose name Beaubier couldn't recall.

The story may have been a whimsical piece of embroidery. In her later years Emma Woikin was not above sprinkling a few bomb-shells into conversations that seemed in danger of bogging down.

On one occasion, for instance, she casually told a gathering of her kin that she knew Pierre Elliott Trudeau well. "He was one of a crowd of people I saw quite often," she said, off-handedly, and then refused to elaborate.

Former Prime Minister Trudeau, when asked about this, seemed genuinely bewildered; the name meant nothing to him. Told about the Gouzenko connection, he shook his head in puzzlement. "I never knew her," he repeated. "The only one I knew in that group was Boyer."

Doctor Raymond Boyer, one of those named by Gouzenko, received a prison sentence of two years. He has much in com-mon with Trudeau. Both men came from Montreal millionaire families, both are intellectual, bilingual, world-travellers and regarded as leftists. It is obvious that Trudeau would know Boyer, but it would be surprising that he wasn't at least ac-quainted with a few of the others of his own age who were arrested when Gouzenko defected, some of whom skied the same slopes he did.

However, the chance that Emma Woikin moved in the same circles as Pierre Trudeau is almost non-existent. Her only possible contact with Ottawa's brainy young radicals and diplomats was Sokolov, but he was unlikely to spread around the knowledge that he was cultivating the cipher clerk in the department of external affairs.

The story about preparing a Russian meal rings true. Emma loved to cook for her friends, had a genius for cooking, and certainly would want to demonstrate it to her friends, the Sokolovs. It strains credulity, however, that they would have Pearson and Norman as their guests, or that they would allow Emma Woikin to be in the same room if they did.

Because Emma's evenings usually were committed to the Choquette children, Lida Sokolov took the active role in maintaining the relationship with Emma. She formed a habit of having a cup of coffee with Emma at lunch counters near the cipher offices. The two women had much in common: both young, Russian-speaking, and living in a strange city, both thrilled by the exploits of the heroic Russian army, both convinced of the virtues of the Communist system.

Cables between the Kremlin and Zabotin were full of speculation about Emma Woikin. She was assigned a code name, "Nora." In view of his role, the code name assigned Sokolov is intriguing: it was "Devil."

According to Gouzenko, Moscow wondered if Zabotin thought Emma could be approached to produce "practical results." Moscow wanted her to reveal the British diplomatic codes and the workings of the cipher department. Zabotin thought not; maybe later.

In the fall of 1944, Igor Gouzenko was ordered to return to Moscow. The prospect of living in the austerity of a war-ravaged country had no appeal; he was beginning to love the openness and opportunities he saw in Canada. His boss, Zabotin, interceded to protect him, telling Moscow that Gouzenko couldn't be spared.

In the spring of 1945, Benito Mussolini, Italy's dictator, suffered an ignominious death, killed and hung by his heels from the branch of a tree. The war in Italy ended. On 2 May, Berlin fell. Hitler committed suicide. German generals agreed to unconditional surrender on 7 May, and the next day was proclaimed V-E Day, "Victory in Europe."

Though the war with Japan hadn't ended, it seemed to Canada that the worst was over. Ottawa celebrated deliriously with toasts to the gallant Canadians, the gallant British, the gallant Americans, and, of course, the gallant Russians.

A three-paragraph item, which appeared that spring in the Ottawa *Evening Citizen*, drew little attention. Victor A. Kravchenko, of the purchasing commission of the Soviet embassy in Washington, had resigned to protest what he called Russia's "double-faced political manoeuvres" and "concealed policy." He said Russia was violating the spirit of collaboration between allies.

The defection must have rattled the Soviet embassy in Ottawa. Certainly it must have registered on Gouzenko, who again had been ordered to return to Moscow. When the second instruction came, in May 1945, Zabotin temporized by saying he could not allow Gouzenko to leave until a suitable replacement could be found and trained.

The Kremlin also sent Zabotin a list of the military information it required. The items fell into four main categories: explosives and chemical materials produced by the British and Canadians; the naval-affairs branch of the department of defence; United States troops movements; and particulars about something called "the atomic bomb," about which the world at that time had heard nothing. The bomb had not even been tested; that would come in July in the Los Alamos desert.

The Kremlin knew about work on the new weapon from a strategic spy, Alan Nunn May, a British, Cambridge-trained physicist who was loaned to the Manhattan Project as part of a team of British atomic scientists and who had been working in Montreal since 1941. Moscow did not seem to be aware of the apocalyptic force of the new weapon; the inquiry about the atomic bomb had a low priority.

Zabotin's list began with a request for models of the radar sets that had been developed by the National Research Council and were the world's best. Then there were requests for details of the new explosives created at Valcartier; the organization of the National Research Council; progress of the installation at Chalk River, where an atomic reactor was being built; samples of Uranium-235; deployment of returning Canadian troops; and information about depth bombs. The last item on the list, which went from A to Q, was a request for contents of telegrams passing in and out of the department of external affairs.

Efforts to obtain the required information sometimes lacked finesse. Two burly men from the Soviet embassy, both with thick Russian accents, presented themselves at the Canadian patent office and asked for diagrams about secret radar apparatus. The Canadian staff thought the accents of the two were German. The two were arrested. They were released, with apologies, when it was learned they were Russians.

Zabotin's assignment was almost ridiculously easy. He obtained photographs of the Chalk River atomic plant by arranging with an affable Canadian army officer, a lawyer in the armoured corps named James Moffatt Forgie, known to his friends as "Smoot," to take him fishing. Smoot's favourite fishing hole happened to be in the river exactly where the plant was being built. He obligingly sat steady in the canoe while Zabotin took pictures of the lovely scenery.

Smoot Forgie later was compelled to explain all this to the Royal Commission on Espionage. He provided the only entertainment in the entire transcript of the proceedings. He informed the judges that he had taken Zabotin for a "spin up the river" but that Zabotin didn't handle a canoe at all well.

"His hands were the thing that amused me," Smoot went on. "They were long slimy sort of hands. I didn't quite take to him." Besides, the man didn't speak English very well. One of the judges inquired dryly if Forgie happened to notice that Zabotin's command of English improved dramatically after the pictures were taken. Forgie conceded that it had. Didn't Forgie find that rather odd? Forgie pondered. It didn't seem strange at the time, he said.

Chapter Six

V.G. Pavlov, Nicholai Zabotin, and others charged with information-gathering and the recruitment of moles depended, for their initial contacts, on the handful of Canadians who were dedicated Communists. Moscow ruled that Tim Buck, the best known of the Canadians, should not be jeopardized by being involved in espionage. But it had no such compunction about Fred Rose, the first Communist member of parliament in Canadian history, who had just been elected to represent the poverty-riden riding of Montreal-Cartier. Nor did the Kremlin show concern for another loyal party member, Sam Carr, national organizer of the Canadian Communist Party, newly renamed the Labor-Progressive Party.

Both were firm and unswerving in their loyalty to the Communist cause. The pact between Stalin and Hitler had been difficult for most Canadian Communists to swallow but they had accepted the dictum that the party's survival was more important than private despairs. Much had been accomplished, especially within labour unions, in the grim years of the Depression, and much could still be done to build a post-war society where poverty would be eliminated.

The early war years were not conducive to criticism of the party. The time was marked by police surveillance of all suspected Communists, arrests, confiscation of literature, and manhunts. So much energy went into the struggle to avoid annihilation that there was little tolerance for divisions over Moscow's behaviour.

The desperate period of hiding from police and clinging blindly to the faith is eloquently described in Merrily Weisbord's book *The Strangest Dream*, in which, for the first time, the anatomy of Canadian Communists in World War Two is revealed. One group consisted of well-placed intellectuals, men and women who belonged to the few liberal organizations of the day such as the Canadian-Soviet Friendship League, the Federation of Russian-Canadians, civil liberties groups, and followers of the CBC's "Canadian Forum" broadcasts. Some of these believed that the solution to the massive injustices of the capitalist system could best be found in Marxism. These intellectuals were not known by the party members who froze on picket lines and were bludgeoned bloody in demonstrations. It was to these intellectuals that Fred Rose and Sam Carr turned when Zabotin requested their cooperation.

One of the intellectuals was Doctor Raymond Boyer, a brilliant, aristocratic, wealthy professor at McGill University and an explosives expert with the National Research Council. Rose learned from Boyer that a powerful explosive had been developed in Canada. In 1943, a Soviet technical mission visited explosive plants in Canada; the Russians were welcomed warmly by the Canadian government. Through Rose, Boyer told the Russians what to look for when touring the plants.

Gordon Lunan, another member of the group of intellectuals, was asked to provide political analysis to be used in background briefing of embassy staff. The Scottish-born Lunan was an army lieutenant on loan to the Wartime Information Board who sympathized warmly with the Communist cause. He had worked for advertising agencies and was an able writer. What he gave Zabotin was little more than a synthesis of material readily available in the newspapers but he also asked acquaintances and friends to be helpful to the Soviet embassy.

Another person contacted by Rose was James Scotland Benning, known as "Scott," who called himself a one-time "armchair Bolshevist." But his ardour for the cause cooled when Stalin and Hitler signed the non-aggression pact. An official with the Department of Munitions and Supply, he was still sympathetic enough to supply Lunan with an assortment of trivial information.

The network that Zabotin's agents reached into was composed of liberals of varying degrees of commitment to left-wing causes, though almost none had joined the Communist Party.

In 1945, many were in the throes of shifting their lives from war-time occupations. They were cleaning out desks, sorting out documents that they themselves had stamped "secret," and preparing for what all of them hoped would be a post-war world of mutual cooperation and the sharing of knowledge.

Some of the material Zabotin wanted was public — although the Kremlin didn't know it had been published in newspapers and journals — and some was about to be released. The National Research Council, for instance, was anxious to sell its sophisticated radar equipment to airlines and was preparing to describe it fully at a radio and civil-aviation conference in London, England.

A few of the people contacted were puzzled that Russians acted so secretively about the exchange of unimportant information. One person, Ned Mazerall, an outstanding electrical engineer, had helped to develop Canada's spectacular radar technology. A warning bell went off when Gordon Lunan told him he had been assigned a code name. He was careful to give Lunan nothing about radar that wasn't declassified or about to be announced at the London conference.

Others took the paraphernalia of passwords, signals and secret meetings as a good joke, evidence of the peculiarity of the Soviets.

Nikolai Zabotin, however, was in deadly earnest. His career depended on getting results from his network and he was being badgered incessantly by the Kremlin to produce information. He was a frustrated man. For example, Zabotin had been trying for eight months to learn the home address and telephone number of one man, David Shugar, and had not yet succeeded.

Matt Nightingale, a telephone specialist with the Royal Canadian Air Force, produced nothing more valuable than information to be found in a Bell Telephone manual which was available to the public for thirty cents.

Zabotin's major success, however, was exceedingly worthwhile. Alan Nunn May, a physicist recruited by the party during his undergraduate days at Cambridge, had provided the Ottawa embassy with a sample of Uranium-235. He passed it over just before he returned to England. Unaware of the hazards of radiation, Igor Gouzenko stored it in his safe for two weeks, when it was smuggled to Moscow by diplomatic courier.

Gouzenko toiled long hours in his airless office translating the scanty information Zabotin's band of victims and zealots was producing. He had to get code names straight, though some had more than one name and there were others whose identity he did not know. The work was tedious and his replacement was soon to arrive from Moscow. Zabotin could not protect Gouzenko for much longer against the dreaded transfer home.

Kay and C. Brough Macpherson knew almost all the people in the Zabotin net that Gouzenko was recording. Both Macphersons have been awarded the Order of Canada, one of the two husband and wife teams on the list. He is a world-recognized professor of political science, a Marxist scholar and a harsh critic of Stalinism; she is one of the country's most admired and respected feminists, a founder of the Voice of Women and Women for Political Action, a sometimes candidate for the New Democratic Party, and a former president of the National Action Committee on the Status of Women.

The Macphersons believe they themselves would have been assigned code names and lodged in Zabotin's files but for a fortuitous move from Ottawa late in the summer of 1944.

Before they left Ottawa they stayed with Eric and Jo Adams in the top floor of the Adams's house in Rockcliffe. Adams was an economist with a superb education and a well-connected wife. A brilliant man, he was expected to become governor of the Bank of Canada one day. The Adamses saw a lot of Frank Park, a lawyer who, with Brough Macpherson, co-authored New Brunswick's CCF constitution. Fred and Phyllis Poland were also in the group. Poland, a tall, garrulous man who later became one of the country's outstanding science journalists, was an officer in Royal Canadian Air Force intelligence.

They would meet over coffee or beer at the homes of Libby Rutherford, who later married Frank Park, or Agatha Chapman, another economist, to listen to the political lectures on the CBC and to argue theory.

"That group was centre and left of centre," Kay Macpherson

explained, making a pot of tea in the graceful home in central Toronto where she and Brough Macpherson lived in semi-retirement. "It was well sprinkled with CCF people who had a feeling of fellowship. There was good, yeasty talk about creating a better Canada. As I recall, the mood was exploration. Nobody was taking positions very much, especially not Fred Poland. His political views were pretty much those of the last person he talked to."

A lanky woman whose thatch of snow-white hair makes her stand out in any crowd, her face was wistful. "It was an open and hopeful time then. The war had just ended and we were talking about preventing another Depression, how to get something like family allowances and old age pensions, that sort of thing. But all very intellectual."

Asked about Emma Woikin, she put her cup down with a clatter. "Woikin? Never heard of her. That's odd. I thought I knew them all."

The Macphersons left Ottawa for Toronto in 1944 when Brough joined the political-science department of the University of Toronto, where he was to become a star. The study groups in Ottawa continued with their core of regulars. Others would come once or twice, find it boring, and drop out.

Agatha Chapman hosted several of the study groups. The Royal Commission on Espionage issued her a summons to appear, and asked her to give names of people who attended.

She named Fred Poland and Gordon Lunan as among the most dependable in the sessions, though Scott Benning could also be counted on. Benning's brother-in-law, Polish-born Harold Gerson, sometimes joined them. And she knew Raymond Boyer well. With Eugene Forsey, a founder of the CCF and later a senator, she and Boyer worked hard for Montreal's Civil Liberties Union in the era of Duplessis' infamous Padlock Laws.

She knew Eric Adams too, since they were both economists in the National Selective Service. David Shugar, a naval specialist in radar was another friend. Yes, she knew Fred Rose, the member of parliament, and Kathleen Willsher, who was secretary to the British High Commissioner. Kathleen Willsher lived with Islay Johnston, a woman who was a good friend of Agatha's. She also knew Edward W. ("Ned") Mazerall, an electrical engineer with the National Research Council, also a radar specialist, but he was only an acquaintance. And she knew Israel Halperin, the Queen's University mathematics genius.

In her dreamy, vague, patrician style, Agatha Chapman identified photographs of them all, twelve of the thirteen people who were the first to feel the consequences of Igor Gouzenko's defection. Adams was maybe "Ernst" in Zabotin's list of code names; Benning was "Foster;" Boyer was "Professor;" Gerson was "Gray;" Halperin was "Bacon;" Lunan was "Back;" Mazerall was "Bagley;" Nightingale was "Leader." Poland was not assigned a code name because the embassy judged him to be unreliable; Shugar was "Prometheus" or "Promety;" Durnford Smith, a physicist with the National Research Council, was "Badeau;" and Kathleen Willsher was "Ellie."

Agatha Chapman did not know Emma Woikin, the thirteenth person, at all.

Most of the thirteen did not think they were betraying their country or spying on behalf of an enemy nation; indeed, the Soviet Union was still regarded as a friendly nation — as friendly as, say, Australia.

"Let's get away from this habit of calling these people spies," Mazerall's lawyer, Royden Hughes, later complained. "Let us regard them as they really are, the victims of spies. They are all Canadians whose only interests are in Canada."

But one of the few who was clear about the nature of the transactions with the Soviet Embassy was Emma Woikin.

Her involvement began one evening late in the spring of 1945. Emma was visiting the Sokolovs in their home on King Edward Street when Lida excused herself on some pretext and left the room. Vsevolod turned the conversation to Emma's fascinating work in the cipher room. He wondered what kind of information was moving between London and Ottawa. He suggested that she pass along to him whatever might be "of interest" to the Soviet.

Emma, not entirely surprised, told Sokolov that she would have to think over what he was suggesting. He pressed her by saying the embassy would pay for the material. Emma was offended. She replied that if she did it, it would not be for the money.

Sokolov told Zabotin how the exchange had gone. Zabotin

was worried that Emma would refuse. He proposed that she be asked to find someone else in the cipher room who would show more enthusiasm. Sokolov didn't think that would be necessary; he was sure she would come around.

She telephoned two days later to say that she would do it. She would memorize messages she thought would interest the Soviets, write them out as soon as she got back to her room at the Choquettes', and give them to the Sokolovs. Lida was designated as the contact person. The exchanges would take place once a month — there was no need to rush — in such places as theatre line-ups. At each exchange, the two women would fix the date and place of the next rendezvous.

Emma Woikin left no record anywhere of how she made her decision. She did not even tell Louie Sawula, the man to whom she was married for twenty-five years. Her infatuation with Vsevolod Sokolov certainly was a factor. She was a realistic woman and must have suspected she wouldn't see him again if she didn't agree.

The contents of four telegrams in her handwriting, which were used as evidence against her, suggest that Emma Woikin fed the Sokolovs the most innocuous material that crossed her desk, enough to satisfy them that she was cooperating but not anything that compromised her loyalty to her country.

The Royal Commission asked her why she had done it.

WOIKIN: Well, that is a feeling one can't quite express.
KELLOCK: What is that?
WOIKIN: That is a feeling that you cannot quite express.
KELLOCK: I don't understand that. You were born in this country?
WOIKIN: Yes.
KELLOCK: Your parents have been here since 1900?
WOIKIN: Yes.
KELLOCK: Then would you explain why you were willing to do what Sokolov asked you to do?
WOIKIN: Perhaps it is because I have a feeling of love for that country. Perhaps it is because we think that there is — we may be wrong or we may be right — but there is hope for the poor, or something.
KELLOCK: Yes?
WOIKIN: I don't know why I had that, but I did.

KELLOCK: If I understand what you mean, it is that you were sympathetic with the Soviet Union?

WOIKIN: Yes.

KELLOCK: And not so sympathetic with your native country?

WOIKIN: I couldn't exactly say that.

The first batch of messages from Emma was given to Lida Sokolov in late May 1945. In June, when Emma met her to deliver some more, Lida pressed an envelope into her hands. The words "a gift" were written on it in Russian. Inside Emma found fifty dollars in cash, an enormous sum for a government clerk earning sixty-seven dollars a month.

She had grave misgivings and made it clear that she wanted no more money, but she kept the "gift." It bought her a train trip home to Blaine Lake, her first visit since she had moved to Ottawa.

She visited all the Konkins, hugged the children, baked some cookies, and chased Fred when he snitched a few before they cooled, hugged the children some more, had long talks with Annie Konkin in her summer kitchen, helped Lena Konkin in the garden, answered a hundred questions about life in the city, sang the old psalms once more in the Doukhobor prayer home, hugged the children again, and went back to Ottawa.

Her brother John drove her to Saskatoon to catch her train. He wondered if she had found someone to marry. No, she told him. There weren't many Doukhobors or even Ukrainians in Ottawa. She'd met no one who interested her. She mentioned her wonderful Russian friends, the Sokolovs.

While she was away, Igor Gouzenko got a nasty shock. In July, his replacement arrived from Moscow. He was instructed to train the man and leave at once. Zabotin managed to obtain a delay. He said Gouzenko was needed to train the newcomer and the training would take some time, a month perhaps.

The Gouzenkos were distraught. They loved their apartment and the life they were leading in Ottawa's open society, and they loved Canada's plentiful shops. Svetlana Gouzenko was expecting their second child. Some believe that Gouzenko had another reason to dread returning, that he suspected he would be demoted and disciplined on his arrival in the Soviet Union.

On 6 August, 1945, at eight fifteen in the morning Japanese time, the United States Air Force bomber *Enola Gay* dropped an atom bomb on Hiroshima and two hundred thousand people melted. Gouzenko later described the panic that gripped the Soviet Union's Ottawa embassy. The capitalists had the most frightful weapon in human history and Russian paranoia suggested that it would be turned immediately on Moscow.

The importance of the sample of enriched U-235 that Gouzenko casually had kept for two weeks in his safe now assumed world-shaking importance because the Soviet had the key to its own bomb. American scientists would argue that such discoveries could not remain the exclusive property of one country; once a process has succeeded, other scientists can duplicate it. The scientists proposed sharing the knowledge of the atom bomb with the Russians to reduce tension. The scientists were considered fools; many people thought they were Communists.

Washington decided to keep the secret of the bomb from the Soviet Union. (Eventually the policy led to Senator Joseph McCarthy's notorious witch hunts of the 1950s.) The Soviet Union accelerated its efforts to discover what its allies were keeping secret, and where the United States army was going next.

In Ottawa, Zabotin gathered his staff and told them somberly, "Yesterday they were allies, today they are neighbours, tomorrow they will be our enemies."

The alarm created in the Soviet embassy by the bombs on Hiroshima and Nagasaki spawned an obsession for furtiveness verging on the farcical. Zabotin began to collect his information by cloak-and-dagger techniques from the NKVD textbook. His precautions were overly excessive, since Royal Canadian Mounted Police assigned only two men to keep tabs on the Soviets.

Zabotin's contacts were instructed to wait in public phone booths for a double ring. They were asked to stroll Sparks Street with a certain newspaper under a certain arm. They left messages in tree hollows. The material being transferred might be nothing more than locations of training bases of the Commonwealth Air Training Plan that was folding, but it was style that counted.

Emma Woikin entered into the melodrama when she was ready to make her August delivery. Because she had been in Blaine Lake, there had been no contact with Lida Sokolov in

July; their August meeting had not been set up. She was informed by telephone that she was to go to the waiting room of a suite of dentists' offices across from the Lord Elgin Hotel. There she would find a door leading to a small washroom. She was to fasten the material, with adhesive tape, to the underside of the porcelain cover of the toilet tank.

Gouzenko described these arrangements to the Royal Commission on Espionage. Its virtue, he explained, lay in the fact that the embassy chauffeur, Captain Gourshkov, was having dental work done and could retrieve the material without incurring suspicion.

When Emma realized that the Royal Commission knew about the toilet-tank drop, she was shocked. At first she tried to deny that she had gone to the dentists' offices, but eventually the commissioners, Mr. Justice R. Kellock and Mr. Justice R. Taschereau, and the commission lawyer, Gerald Fauteux, wrung the whole story out of her. Fauteux pretended astonishment when Emma began by saying she knew nothing of the dentists' office.

> FAUTEUX: You never met there, you never met anyone there in connection with the transmission of information?
> WOIKIN: Well, seeing that you know, yes.
> FAUTEUX: Pardon?
> WOIKIN: Seeing that you know that, I did.
> KELLOCK: What do you mean by your answer?
> TASCHEREAU: Give the answer.
> KELLOCK: Will you just give your answer and give us all you know, please.
> [no audible reply]
> FAUTEUX: What is the name of the dentist?
> WOIKIN: I do not know.
> FAUTEUX: What is his address?
> WOIKIN: I do not know the actual number, the address. I know it is past the Lord Elgin, that is all.

The commission asked six questions and elicited the information that Emma wasn't being treated by the dentist, but only left a message in the washroom.

KELLOCK: Whereabouts in the washroom?

WOIKIN: Under the cover. I do not know what it is really, what you call it.

KELLOCK: You mean the tank?

WOIKIN: Yes.

KELLOCK: Under the cover of the tank?

WOIKIN: Yes.

TASCHEREAU: You raised the cover of the tank and put it under there?

WOIKIN: Yes.

KELLOCK: How often did you go there?

WOIKIN: Only once.

The Royal Commission had not expected such complexity. They pursued their reluctant witness with peppery questions until they learned that she had gone once to the dental suite to satisfy herself of the layout, then returned the next day to place the material under the toilet-tank lid an hour before the pick-up time, as instructed. The most skilled cross-examiners in the country asked twenty-two questions before they discovered that Emma had not left the waiting room at once. She had stayed to see what would happen.

A man came in, went into the washroom, remained there a few minutes and emerged; then he said something to the dentist in Russian-accented English and left. Emma followed him into the corridor and spoke to him in Russian to be certain he was the man from the embassy. Kellock, who appeared transfixed by all this theatre, continued the dogged questions.

KELLOCK: And you spoke to him and asked him what?

WOIKIN: I can't remember now what I asked him, but just that I wanted to know.

KELLOCK: Wanted to know if he had got the message which you had left?

WOIKIN: I didn't ask him that, actually.

KELLOCK: But what did you ask him?

WOIKIN: I spoke to him in order to know whether he spoke Russian or not, whether it was actually . . . .

FAUTEUX: [breaking in] And in that way you intended to

find whether he was the authorized man to get the message?
WOIKIN: Yes.

The Soviet chauffeur was appalled that Emma had spoken to him after all the elaborate efforts to avoid direct contact. A conference in the embassy following the rendezvous at the dentists' concluded it was safer, all things considered, to go back to the first system: that Lida Sokolov meet Emma and collect the messages.

The September transfer was arranged for either Tuesday, 4 September, or Wednesday, 5 September; the Wednesday is more probable. Emma had spent the scorching Labour Day weekend quietly. The Choquettes were away at a cottage and she had plenty of time to work on the notes she would be giving Lida Sokolov. There were four telegrams she thought would interest the embassy.

They became Exhibits 24-A, 24-B, 24-C and 24-D, the evidence that sent her to prison.

The contents of those telegrams were revealed only to the Royal Canadian Mounted Police, Prime Minister King, the Royal Commission, Emma's two trial judges and the crown prosecutors. Only after a strenuous protest was her defense lawyer allowed to see them. He was not permitted to refer to anything in the notes; he was forbidden to comment on the lack of significance the telegrams might have had in world events.

The contents of the four telegrams did not become public until thirty-five years had passed after Emma's trial and imprisonment. On 10 October, 1981, the transcripts of the Royal Commission finally were released. Emma's telegrams, laid bare, lack the importance that was ascribed to them when they were secret.

The first message, Exhibit 24-A, is dated 24 August, 1945. It was a circular from London, an update on the political situation in eastern Europe. It reads:

FROM: The Secretary of State for Dominion Affairs, London.
TO: The Secretary of State for External Affairs, Ottawa.

The problem of Bulgaria, Yugoslavia, Hungary and Rumania has been brought up and discussed in a piecemeal fashion from time to time but, as a whole (as it really is the same problem), Russia has never agreed to discuss it. They are all under the influence and supervision of Russia. Elections are being planned in all these countries, but they will only result in a totalitarian system and again under the supervision of the Russians.

We have to gain the confidence and attention of these countries and have to show what we have to offer in ways of economics and culture.

Emma decoded that message on 25 August, 1945, between ten minutes after nine in the morning and one in the afternoon, and gave it to a typist, who made copies for Mackenzie King, the prime minister and minister of external affairs; the governor general, the Earl of Athlone; the minister of national defence; the minister of national defence for air; the British High Commissioner, Malcolm MacDonald; Hume Wrong, in external affairs; and Norman Robertson, undersecretary of state for external affairs.

The communication was stamped "top secret cipher" and given file number D-1549.

After work, Emma went back to the Choquette house on Somerset, only a few blocks away from the Gouzenkos' apartment which was on the same street, and wrote down the message as she remembered it. Her memory was so accurate that she made only one error: she omitted the word "recently" from the first sentence.

The second telegram, Exhibit 24-B, is also dated 24 August, 1945, and was decoded the next morning. Marked "top secret cipher" and given file number D-1543, it was also from the secretary of state for dominion affairs in London. Emma summarized the contents of this cable instead of memorizing them. Her notes covered two pages, one of which was lost; the remaining sheet was partially torn. What was left reads:

The present continual differences in regard to these countries will endanger our relations with the Soviet Union. There is not much hope for Yugoslavia having a democratic government. Tito is evidently breaking all agreements of subasia-Tito agreement, but we feel it is too early to step in.

Austria has a better chance of forming a democracy than any

of the other countries because three-quarters of it is occupied by United Kingdom, United States and France, and yet in case of forming a government, it will be the Russians imported from Moscow that will be in the lead.

These differences will eventually bring out different opinions between us and United States, and above all we have to try and prevent that.

Exhibit 24-C is a two-paragraph summary of a message from London dated 28 August. Emma decoded and typed it on 29 August, while working a shift from four-fifty in the afternoon until eleven-thirty at night. The cable reports a discussion about Spain between Gousev, the Soviet ambassador to Britain and Ernest Bevin, British minister of foreign affairs:

Gousev pointed out to the minister for foreign affairs, Mr. Bevin, that Britain was carrying out the agreements of the Potsdam Conference, especially in regard to Spain. Gousev said from Bevin's speech of August 20th Franco could well see that no action was intended against him.

Bevin said that Britain would welcome a change of government in Spain, but would not countenance any action that would bring on civil war. He also added that Britain was carrying out the agreements of Potsdam Conference and asked "was not the Soviet Union asking them to overstep them?" To this Gousev made no reply.

The final document, Exhibit 24-D, is dated 31 August 1945, and was from Bevin to Gousev. Emma worked from nine o'clock to five-forty-five on 1 September and gave it to the typist, who made clean copies and filed the carbon copy, stamped "secret cipher," under file number D-1606. The telegram was a comment on conditions in Hungary:

British political representative advises that municipal elections in Hungary are to be held October 7th. General Miklos says the Russians are hurrying up the elections, but he is afraid to oppose too strenuously as he may be forced to resign and may be replaced by extreme leftists.

British political representative thinks that these elections are to be held as a test. If the outcome will be favourable to the leftists, they [the leftists] and the Russians will rush a general election soon after.

Except for the private conversation about Spain, everything in the four messages appeared in columns written by astute political journalists; there was nothing in the telegrams the Soviet Union did not know. To call Emma a "spy" and a "traitor" for handing on these messages seems excessive.

The notes were in the hands of the Royal Commission on Espionage six months after they were written. Despite her alarming and intimidating situation, Emma made a spunky effort to protect Vselovod Sokolov.

The questioning was, as usual with Emma, exceedingly laboured.

> FAUTEUX: You did not take the information for yourself?
> WOIKIN: I did not.
> FAUTEUX: Why did you copy those telegrams and to whom did you give the copies that you made?
> WOIKIN: Do you want to know the name of the person?
> KELLOCK: Yes.
> WOIKIN: Well, has that got any bearing on it?
> KELLOCK: Yes. You must answer the question put to you.
> WOIKIN: The name of the person or the name of the . . .
> KELLOCK: The name of the person. What did you do with these documents?
> TASCHEREAU: The first person to whom you gave them.
> WOIKIN: I would not like to say the name of the person.
> KELLOCK: You have to.
> TASCHEREAU: You have to.
> KELLOCK: Just answer the question.
> WOIKIN: The foreign power is . . . .
> KELLOCK: That will not do. The *person*.
> WOIKIN: Whoever it is it is not a Canadian.
> KELLOCK: That does not matter. Will you please answer the question.
> WOIKIN: His name is Sokolov.

At one point in the tedious questioning Kellock said

impatiently, "You are making a very bad impression by taking so long to give your answers. You know the answers to these questions. Will you just give the answers?"

Both justices of the Supreme Court were to maintain that they advised witnesses they did not have to answer questions, that they used no pressure to get witnesses to testify, and that the testimony was given freely. The long-awaited transcripts of the Emma Woikin questioning alone refute that claim to probity.

Two weeks after Emma passed the four messages to Lida Sokolov, she received an agitated telephone call from her friend. Lida said something had happened at the embassy; there was a bit of trouble. "We are not meeting any more," she said, and abruptly hung up.

Chapter Seven

The "bit of trouble" in the Soviet Embassy in Ottawa in September, 1945, was to influence world history. Igor Gouzenko had defected, taking with him proof that the Communists were treacherous and were trying to destroy the democracies, proof that contributed significantly to the almost-overnight change in Canada's attitude to the Soviet Union.

Igor and Svetlana Gouzenko had been talking about the defection for weeks, ever since Igor's replacement had arrived. From time to time, Igor slipped a document out of his safe and smuggled it home. Both felt those few slips of paper would not be enough; they would need more evidence to insure that Ottawa would take Gouzenko seriously and give him asylum. So he had been marking documents in his files: he turned down the corners of those he thought would impress the Canadians.

On the afternoon of Wednesday, 5 September, Zabotin entered Room 12, Gouzenko's cipher room, with five sheets of paper written by Emma Woikin — the four messages she had just given Lida Sokolov. Zabotin had translated them to Russian; he gave his translation, together with the originals in Emma's handwriting, to Gouzenko. They were in an envelope, on which Zabotin had written, in Russian, "Material Given by Nora."

Gouzenko set to work with his customary diligence to code Zabotin's translations. He was interrupted by Zabotin's reminder that the staff of the embassy was going to a movie that night. Gouzenko put the work aside and went along. In the line-up outside the theatre he announced he had already seen the film and left the group. Gouzenko returned to Room 12 at the embassy and began looting the safe of the documents he had marked. In the end, frightened he would not have enough, he grabbed papers randomly.

He was lightly dressed for the summer evening; it was difficult to conceal so many documents on his person. He slipped three files under his shirt and put others in his inside coat pocket and in the side pockets of his jacket, worrying about the bulges. He looked around one last time to see if he had forgotten anything. His eye fell on the unfinished Woikin papers. He snatched them up and crammed them into his pocket, locked Room 12 for the last time, struggled for a normal good-night to the guard at the embassy door, and strolled into the warm summer night with a hundred documents on his person.

He waited for a streetcar. At eight in the evening, it was slow to come. He rode to the city's core and got off near the building that housed the Ottawa *Journal*. The quickest way to get attention and protection, he had decided, was to tell the press.

He could only imagine that Canadians would react to such a revelation as the Kremlin would: the appropriate authorities would be alerted immediately and he, Svetlana, and the child would spend the night hidden in a guarded place, perhaps visited by a grateful prime minister.

He found, instead, that Canada was not prepared to deal with Soviet defectors after normal business hours. Chester Frowde, who was working that night in the *Journal* newsroom, could understand little of what the rattled Gouzenko was saying in his thick Russian accent. The young man was on the verge of tears, Frowde later reported, was "frightened and pale." Gouzenko repeated, almost unintelligibly, "It's war. It's war."

Frowde could make nothing of what Gouzenko was about, but he thought someone in the government should see the man. He directed Gouzenko to the department of justice building down the street. A night watchman there advised the Russian to come back the next morning.

By nine that evening, Gouzenko was back in his apartment on Somerset Avenue. The couple spent a sleepless night and set off early the next morning, the documents in a shopping bag and their child in Svetlana's arms. Gouzenko's absence would be noticed at the embassy minutes after he was scheduled to report for work. They went to the justice department and asked to see the minister, Louis St. Laurent. An assistant talked to them, realized something important was afoot and informed St. Laurent.

While the Gouzenkos waited confidently outside his office, St. Laurent conferred with Norman Robertson, undersecretary of state for external affairs and the intellectual jewel of King's civil service. Robertson summoned his assistant, Hume Wrong, and told him that they had a Soviet defector in the building. Both men were horrified. "A terrible thing has happened," Robertson was to tell the prime minister. He didn't mean the revelations about Canadian spies. The disaster as he saw it was the embarrassment Gouzenko would bring on Canada by creating a problem in Canada-Soviet relations.

The Gouzenkos could not have picked a worse day to defect. The sixth of September, 1945, was the opening of the new session of parliament. The Earl of Athlone, the governor-general, was giving his last speech from the throne before retirement. The streets of Ottawa were crowded with people looking forward to the pageantry of the first peace-time opening of parliament since the thirties. There would be a parade of military bands, marching men in glorious uniforms, the governor-general and Princess Alice in a carriage.

In his diary notes of that day, King wrote cryptically, "Met by Robertson and Wrong as arrived at the office, very upset; man from Russian embassy."

The day was hot and humid. The Gouzenkos, waiting in the outer office of the justice ministry, were sweating. The delay was making them frantic. Gouzenko tried to get action by threatening that he would kill himself if he couldn't get help. An officer from the Royal Canadian Mounted Police made note of this and awaited instructions, but no one knew what to do. King was afraid the young defector would create an incident and destroy the efforts at postwar international cooperation that were beginning.

Gouzenko was made to understand that the proper place for

his complaint was a court house. The Gouzenkos were directed down the street to the office of Ottawa's magistrate on Nicholas Street. There they were in luck. They met a bright, assertive woman, Fernande Coulson, the secretary of the crown attorney, Raoul Mercier.

Fernande Coulson is a rightly celebrated figure in Ottawa legal circles. She worked for forty years in the court house, mothering, counselling and scolding law students who became trial lawyers and judges. Though many years past retirement age in 1983, she was still working a few days a week with an Ottawa legal firm, her mind and memory as fresh and her tongue as astringent as ever.

She had a clear recollection of that steamy afternoon the exhausted Gouzenkos came into her office. They looked a nice couple, the woman perhaps seven months pregnant, the man agitated but showing a certain forcefulness and intelligence. He showed her the papers in the shopping bag and Fernande Coulson was impressed. She went into the corridor and found a reporter from the *Journal.*

"Sit down and read these," she ordered him, pushing him into Mercier's vacant office and handing him some of Gouzenko's documents. The reporter did, but he already had heard the story of the strange Russian, and was inclined to dismiss him as another eccentric of a type not infrequently encountered in newspaper offices. Coulson, indignant, telephoned a friend in the RCMP. This friend also knew about Gouzenko, and was reluctant to concern himself, but Coulson insisted he see the documents.

When the RCMP officer emerged from Mercier's office, Coulson asked, "Are they authentic?"

"Yes," he replied wearily, "but my hands are tied."

The RCMP officer told Coulson that orders had come from the prime minister's office to ignore Gouzenko. Coulson, incredulous, activated her network of contacts and reached someone in the prime minister's office, who confirmed what the Mountie had said. The person told her to get rid of Gouzenko.

Instead, Coulson called John Leopold, a Mountie she knew from his frequent visits to the crown attorney's office, and begged that Leopold see Gouzenko. Leopold made an appointment to do so at nine-thirty the next morning, in his office in the Confederation Building, on the corner of Wellington and Bank streets.

Coulson watched the Gouzenkos as they climbed tiredly on a streetcar. She remembered thinking, "My God, he won't be alive tomorrow."

That night Igor and Svetlana Gouzenko hid in the home of a neighbour, a fortunate precaution because men from the Soviet embassy came to get Igor. A member of the RCMP was watching the Gouzenkos' building and called the Ottawa police, who found one of the embassy staff hiding in Gouzenko's closet.

The most mysterious element in the improbable (but true) story of the Gouzenkos' defection involves Sir William Stephenson, the man called "Intrepid" who trained spies for the allies, who happened to be staying at Montebello, a luxurious private club down the Ottawa River from the capital. Stephenson knew all about Gouzenko's defection: Norman Robertson had telephoned him while the Gouzenkos were waiting outside St. Laurent's office.

Stephenson was in the park across the street from the Gouzenko apartment the night the embassy tried to get Gouzenko back. He watched the Ottawa police escort the embassy people back to their car and then, at four in the morning, telephoned Robertson. He told him about the break-in and, in effect, ordered Robertson to give Gouzenko protection.

Robertson agreed that the RCMP would provide a safe house and round-the-clock guards. Stephenson called soon after daylight to remind Robertson of his decision and to inquire dryly if Gouzenko were still alive.

Robertson ordered the RCMP to pick up the Gouzenkos and their child, and to deliver the documents to him. He spent the day going over them, horrified at what might happen if they were made public. The next day a Soviet embassy official asked the Canadian government formally to turn Gouzenko over to Russian authorities; he had stolen some money, the official said. There was an evasive response.

Mackenzie King was worried that the Soviets would find Gouzenko and kill him. He instructed the RCMP to debrief Gouzenko with all speed.

During the debriefing, Gouzenko mentioned many names, some attached to bits of incriminating evidence, some merely names. The most startling was that of Alan Nunn May, the British scientist who had worked on the atom bomb. Mackenzie King notified London and two top agents, Roger Hollis of MI5 and Peter Dwyer of MI6, flew to Ottawa to question Gouzenko. Gouzenko told them that May would be contacted by a Soviet agent in front of the British Museum on a certain day. May was to have a copy of the *Times* under his left arm and await someone who would give one of two passwords, "Best regards from Mikel," or "What is the shortest way to the Strand?"

A vigil was established outside the British Museum but May never appeared. Like Emma Woikin, he had been advised of "a bit of trouble."

The MI6 man, Peter Dwyer, said in a film interview thirty-seven years later that Alan Nunn May was the only significant spy Gouzenko uncovered. "The rest was crap," he observed with a genial smile.

John Le Carré, the novelist whose reputation was built on his portrayal of British upper-class spies, described in a television interview on the United States Public Broadcasting System in 1982 the motivation of men like Alan Nunn May. He thought ideology and greed were only part of the truth, that the thrill of the game was an addiction so compelling that spies would become double agents to increase the danger.

The Canadians named by Gouzenko were of a different breed, Le Carré thought; they were caught in what he called "the seamless transition."

He explained: "We'd gone from the war against Fascism to the war against Communism and we seem scarcely to have drawn breath in between . . . Somehow we were hurried from one war to another without the least choice in between.

"My anger in retrospect is that somehow in the years between 1943 and 1948 or '49, there was the most massive failure in diplomacy on the sides of the east and west which has ever taken place. We are now saddled with the obligation to fight out an ideological war which just possibly need never have been joined."

Igor Gouzenko, the Soviet cipher clerk who gave that "massive failure in diplomacy" a substantial shove, unfolded his story of Alan Nunn May and the Canadian spies in long sessions of sympathetic interrogation by the RCMP. Some of the names he mentioned were not unexpected. Both Sam Carr and

Fred Rose, for example, had been dedicated Communists all their adult lives. But other names were a shock. Eric Adams had a promising career in finance ahead of him. Raymond Boyer's grandfather, one of the first French Canadians on the Montreal stock exchange, was a cousin of Thérèse Casgrain, who fought to get the vote for Quebec women; Boyer was heir to more than a million dollars from his mother's estate, and even more from his father's, and was a brilliant McGill professor. Gordon Lunan, said by Gouzenko to have recruited Ned Mazerall and Dunford Smith of the National Research Council and Israel Halperin of army artillery research, was working in external affairs as a speech-writer and drafter of international documents.

Gouzenko's evidence showed that the Soviet embassy had a vast network of spies who had infiltrated the government and defense establishment. The Canadian government was particularly concerned about the choicely placed women, Emma Woikin in the cipher room of external affairs and Kathleen Willsher, deputy registrar in the office of the British High Commissioner.

Mackenzie King decided to go to Washington to tell President Harry Truman in person that the secrets of his atomic bomb were blown; then, in October, he would travel to London. King was in a dithering state, fussing over travel arrangements, deeply frightened that war would result because Moscow would be furious at Canada for giving Gouzenko asylum.

Paul Martin, Canada's designated representative in the early discussions that led to the founding of the United Nations, remembers that King planned to take a train to New York, change from one station to the other, and finish the journey to Washington by train. He had to be persuaded that the importance of the mission justified the cost of travelling by plane.

In his autobiography *A Very Public Life*, Martin described the opening of the United Nations Assembly reception on 23 October, 1946, when Mackenzie King pursued the Soviet foreign minister, Vyacheslav Mikhailovich Molotov, all around the room, trying get him alone so he could apologize and explain, while the discomfited Soviet diplomat adroitly avoided even meeting King's anxious eyes.

In a meeting in the White House on 30 September, 1945,

Harry Truman listened for two hours to King's account of Gouzenko's defection. The American president from the midwest mistrusted Russia, and King's story of spies confirmed that mistrust. The war had been over for only a few weeks, but already there were indications in eastern Europe, the Middle East and Manchuria that the Soviet Union was a belligerent and territorial-minded power. The story of Soviet spies in North America would jolt the public out of its mood of good-will towards Moscow.

Mackenzie King went next to Britain, and on 11 October told Prime Minister Clement Attlee the details Gouzenko revealed to the RCMP. Attlee didn't like the situation any more than King did. It was his view that a "grave mistake" had been made when Churchill persuaded Roosevelt at the Quebec Conference of August, 1943, that the Soviet Union should not be informed about work on the atomic bomb. "A secret like that can't be kept," Attlee commented to King.

King and Attlee discussed Truman's plan for the Gouzenko information. Truman wanted Ottawa to keep the matter quiet until all the names had been extracted from Gouzenko, after which Britain and the United States would have a show-down meeting with Stalin.

King felt depressed just thinking about the storm that was brewing. He wrote in his diary, "everyone tired out, not ready to tackle new problems."

The intrigue would be exposed when Alan Nunn May made his contact with a Soviet agent in front of the British Museum. King feared that when those Canadians named by Gouzenko read of May's arrest, they would flee the country. He decided to activate the War Measures Act, so that police could act quickly to prevent escapes without waiting to get warrants. King asked St. Laurent to see to it with utmost discretion. St. Laurent issued a secret Order-in-Council, about which even the cabinet was ignorant.

A week passed but Alan Nunn May did not appear in front of the British Museum. Mackenzie King was back at 10 Downing Street on 21 October, full of alarm. He was convinced that when the story broke war would erupt between the Soviet Union and the United States, a war that would be fought on the middle ground of the Canadian prairies. He envisioned American troops occupying a battleground from the Rockies to Rainy

River and wasn't hopeful that the west would stay in Canada in such circumstances.

It would be better, he felt, if the world did not know about Gouzenko. He wrote in his diary, "I am sure that the course of action — secrecy, etc. — is the right one. Direct approach to the Russians is the right thing. I tried to emphasize to Robertson that there would be great difficulty in getting proof. Unless we had entire proof, the thing would backfire in a very serious way."

Norman Robertson, undersecretary of state, and King were appalled that so many of the Canadians named by Gouzenko were in sensitive government positions. Robertson recommended that they be moved so they could do no harm. King agreed. "They can be apprehended later," he said. Robertson suggested that police search their homes for evidence of spying, but King was not anxious to do anything that would draw attention. MI5, the British secret service, concurred; while it might be possible to question secretly a few suspects, it was unlikely that the eighteen people so far mentioned by Gouzenko could be searched and questioned without newspapers learning of it.

The thought of a mass arrest of eighteen Canadian spies made Robertson and King shudder. Negotiations were about to begin to establish the United Nations. It was hard to imagine the talks succeeding if there were stories of Russian espionage on the front page of every newspaper in the country.

The prime minister had another concern: he thought it possible that most of the accused spies would be found innocent. Gouzenko's evidence was by no means complete or conclusively damning; much was vague and unsupported. It would be devastating for Canada to create an international uproar only to have the courts find the accused people not guilty. The fact that an MP, Fred Rose, was named was a particularly sensitive matter. There hadn't been a warrant against a sitting member of parliament since Louis Riel's.

Mackenzie King was pained also by Emma Woikin because she was employed in his own ministry, external affairs. He feared the Conservatives would take political advantage of his embarrassment by using it to charge that King was over-extended in trying to supervise external affairs and be prime minister at the same time. He was beginning to feel, regretfully, that it would be wise to assign the external-affairs portfolio to someone else.

He found some comfort in the presence on Gouzenko's list of Kathleen Willsher of the British High Commission office. Malcolm MacDonald would be as discomfited as he was.

Three weeks after Gouzenko's defection, Emma Woikin was moved out of the cipher room without explanation and sent back to the passport office as a typist. Oblivious to her impending downfall, civil-service bureaucracy a month later promoted her to Class II and gave her a raise.

On 26 October, 1945, Mackenzie King decided to tell Winston Churchill about Gouzenko. The deposed war-time leader of Britain surprised him. Churchill urged King to make an immediate announcement. The Russians were used to double-dealing, he assured the Canadian prime minister, and wouldn't resent exposure.

Six days later, King at last had a private meeting with Gousev, the Soviet ambassador to Britain, at the Soviet embassy. Neither mentioned Gouzenko. The ambassador took the offensive, complaining that Canada had withheld the secret of the atomic bomb from its ally, the Soviet Union. King protested, truthfully, that Canada did not know how the bomb was made, as the United States had concealed the process from its neighbour. Canada's only involvement was to provide the uranium.

Early in November King went to Washington, where he conferred with Attlee and Truman. The British and American leaders agreed that King should arrest the Canadians implicated by Gouzenko two weeks from the date of the meeting. The plan was that Nunn would be arrested simultaneously in London. There would be a round-up of suspected Americans at the same time.

Attlee and Truman were concerned that they didn't have enough evidence to make the arrests. King was in a different position: he had the powerful War Measures Act at his disposal and didn't need evidence to make the arrests.

But King felt the timing was bad. In December, British Foreign Minister Ernest Bevin and the American secretary of state would be in Moscow for delicate tri-partite talks, the prelude to a meeting in London to set up the United Nations organization.

An unaccountable six-week gap in government documents occurs here. A six-week period is missing from Mackenzie King's diary, the only gap in his lifetime of keeping the record. Privy Council papers have vanished. External affairs dispatches, letters, and memoranda were destroyed on the instructions of R.A.J. Phillips, secretary of the cabinet defence committee. There are no references to those six weeks in the papers of Norman Robertson or Arnold Danford Patrick Heeney, clerk of the privy council.

Speculation about the massive cover-up abounds, but as yet no insider has left a trace of what happened in that significant six-week period or of why the documents were destroyed. Many who have studied the Gouzenko defection think that King defied Truman and Attlee and decided to drop the matter, a speculation borne out by the fact that two RCMP officers who had been assigned to watch eighteen suspects returned to normal duty. King may have decided that he didn't want a mess on his doorstep when world peace and understanding seemed within reach. According to the theory, documents were systematically obliterated to hide the pressure Washington was putting on King.

Economist Eric Adams, whose career was destroyed by the Gouzenko affair, made inquiries through the United States Freedom of Information legislation, which is vastly more forthcoming than its Canadian equivalent. Adams discovered that the transcript of the Royal Commission on Espionage hearings in the National Archives has been doctored; the version that went to Washington is not quite the same as the Canadian one. He was unable, however, to find out anything about the missing six weeks.

Frank Park, an Ottawa lawyer and friend of many of the principles in the Gouzenko revelations, did considerable research of the period in preparation for a book he co-authored with his wife, Libby Park. He believes that Gouzenko named prominent Canadians whose identities were never revealed, either because the prime minister wanted to protect them or because the evidence against them was too skimpy to justify exposing them to public disgrace.

"The names had to be suppressed," Park observed, "because the people named were not spies in any sense of the word but rather were friendly to members of the Soviet embassy staff, as many important Canadians were at that time." Park feels, as Adams does, that a major factor in the disappearance of the documents was the attempt by the prime minister's office to conceal the extent of American pressure on Canada to go public on the Gouzenko defection.

King's desire to bury the matter prevailed for many weeks. Gordon Lunan, who had been alerted to possible exposure by Fred Rose the day after Gouzenko defected, began to relax. Lunan's cooperation in any case, had ceased after Hiroshima. He believed then that a time of innocence was ended; if east and west were about to divide into two armed camps, his lot lay with the west.

For six weeks, Gouzenko and his documents sank from view. At Christmas cocktail parties, Ottawa buzzed with the disappointing news that the handsome Nikolai Zabotin had been recalled to Moscow so suddenly that there was no time for farewells. (Zabotin died mysteriously a few weeks later.)

The absence of Vsevolod and Lida Sokolov was not much noticed. Sokolov also had been recalled abruptly, and the couple left without contacting their good friend Emma Woikin. She was crushed and confused by the snub.

Her landlady, Marguerite Choquette, saw only a completely happy, outgoing woman. She had become so attached to Emma that she was moved to write Emma's relatives in Blaine Lake a curious thank-you note for the Christmas gifts they had sent Emma. Dated 7 January, 1946, it read:

Emma was so pleased with her Xmas boxes and the poor girl loves you all so much that I feel I know you and want to thank you too. We are very fortunate in having her here with us . . . .
On 9 January, 1946, Dwight David Eisenhower, supreme commander of the allied forces in Europe, arrived in Ottawa and was given a hero's welcome. Despite the penetrating cold, thousands of people turned out to cheer him. It was all part of the wonderful relief of victory and the end of the war; the troops were coming out of uniform, rationing was easing, consumer goods were beginning to be available at last, and almost everyone had money to buy them.

Emma Woikin went to work each day in a state of shock. The departure of the Sokolovs had been wounding, and she connected it to Lida's warning of trouble in the embassy and her own sudden, humiliating demotion. She had a prevailing sense of imminent disaster.

Marguerite Choquette, who saw her every day, saw no change in the woman who gave the Choquette children such loving care. Emma seemed her usual bright and accommodating self. But she was hatching a wild plan: she would follow the Sokolovs to Moscow.

She telephoned the Soviet embassy and said she wanted to apply for Soviet citizenship. The startled person who took the call asked Emma to come that night and ask for Mrs. Voronina.

The RCMP officer assigned to shadow Emma watched her enter the imposing embassy building. Mrs. Voronina escorted Emma into the office of V.G. Pavlov, the NKVD chief in Ottawa, who had survived the purge that followed Gouzenko's defection. Pavlov gave Emma some papers to fill out. As she slipped them into her bag she asked, "Is there a chance that I will be accepted?"

Pavlov replied blandly, "That remains to be seen."

The embassy, however, had no intention of stirring up additional trouble for itself by allowing Canada's former cipher clerk to become a Soviet citizen.

The application required a birth certificate. Emma wrote to Blaine Lake and told her brother John what she was planning to do. The news came as a thunderclap, but he didn't try to dissuade her. He mailed her the birth certificate. A week after her first visit to Mrs. Voronina, she was back at the embassy with the application.

Two months later, the Royal Commission on Espionage found it incomprehensible that she would want to live in Russia.

> FAUTEUX: You seriously wanted to have Soviet citizenship?
> WOIKIN: Yes.
> FAUTEUX: You were eager to have it?
> WOIKIN: I have applied for it, yes.
> KELLOCK: Does that mean you wanted to go to Russia to live?

WOIKIN: Yes.

FAUTEUX: What prompted you to do so at that time?

WOIKIN: I considered it possibly before.

FAUTEUX: Why did you not make it before? What event took place that prompted you to do it at that time?

WOIKIN: Nothing took place that prompted me to do it at that time.

FAUTEUX: What occurred in your mind? What were the circumstances that made you do it at that time?

WOIKIN: I can't answer that.

FAUTEUX: Why did you come to that decision at that time?

WOIKIN: I can't answer that. Because I just wanted to apply for that citizenship, and I did.

KELLOCK: Did you think perhaps it would be just as well for you to get out of the country?

WOIKIN: No, I didn't do it for that.

KELLOCK: I didn't ask you if you did it on that account. I asked if that occurred to you.

WOIKIN: No, it didn't occur to me.

FAUTEUX: Now you would like to be a Soviet citizen?

WOIKIN: Yes.

FAUTEUX: Why?

WOIKIN: I cannot answer that. I do not know how to answer it.

FAUTEUX: Take your time and tell us what you believe and what you think.

WOIKIN: Maybe it was from the kind of life I had, maybe. [Long pause] Just that I look to that country for security and I would like to live there.

FAUTEUX: Who told you there was security in that country? How do you know that?

WOIKIN: Well . . . .

FAUTEUX: How did you reach that conclusion?

WOIKIN: I do not know how I reached that conclusion.

FAUTEUX: You must have had some reason.

WOIKIN: Well, maybe it was from what I read. What I read, really that is what I mean.

FAUTEUX: What do you mean by security?

WOIKIN: Well, there was a time when I was quite poor, I guess. And my baby died because we had no medical care and nobody seemed to care. My husband was sick and to such a stage where nobody seemed to intervene at all.

KELLOCK: There was no public health service out where you were living?

WOIKIN: No, there was not.

The questioning turned to other matters but at the end of that long day in the witness chair Emma was asked a question that must have cost her dearly to answer. Mr. Justice Taschereau noted that Sokolov approached her and offered friendship soon after she was transferred to the cipher room.

TASCHEREAU: In the other department you could be of no use whatever?

WOIKIN: Yes, that is quite true.

Chapter Eight

On 2 February, 1946, Prime Minister Mackenzie King was lunching in Laurier House with Roland Fairbairn McWilliams, lieutenant-governor of Manitoba, and Stuart Sinclair Garson, Manitoba's Liberal premier. Both guests described the fine qualities of a Winnipeg lawyer, E.K. Williams, KC, and recommended that King name him to a vacancy on the bench of the Manitoba Supreme Court. Williams had been a Conservative but was now a loyal Liberal, they told King, and deserved the appointment. King said he would think it over.

The next day the Gouzenko scandal exploded in King's face. American radio commentator Drew Pearson, acting on a tip from J. Edgar Hoover, chief of the FBI, opened his broadcast that day with a sensational story:

This is Drew Pearson with a flash from Washington. Canada's Prime Minister Mackenzie King has informed President Truman of a very serious situation affecting our relations with Russia. A Soviet agent surrendered some time ago to Canadian authorities and confessed a gigantic Russian espionage network inside the United States . . . .

King wrote a disgusted comment in his diary that the broadcast was "garbled stuff about maps, planes, etc." He added, "I may be wrong but I have a feeling that there is a desire at Washington that this information should get out, that Canada should start the inquiry and that we should have the responsibility for beginning it, and that the way should be paved for it being continued into the US. This may be all wrong but I have that intuition very strong. It is the way in which a certain kind of politics is played by a certain kind of man . . ."

However Machiavellian the manipulation of Drew Pearson, and it appears that he was tipped off by Intrepid, William Stephenson, there was no retreat for Mackenzie King; the genie could not be stuffed back into the bottle. His conversation the day before brought E.K. Williams to mind. He remembered that two months earlier, when Williams was in Ottawa, King had sought the lawyer's advice on the Gouzenko matter. King had wondered what to do because Gouzenko's evidence was skimpy. Williams proposed that King establish a Royal Commission to investigate the matter; there it could be determined if charges could be laid.

On 3 February, following the Drew Pearson broadcast King contacted Williams for suggestions about the composition of a Royal Commission. Go to the top, Williams advised; nothing less than judges from the Supreme Court should be involved in such a delicate matter where credibility was so essential.

On 5 February, two days later, King obtained approval from the privy council to establish a Royal Commission with authority "to inquire into and report upon which public officials and other persons in positions of trust or otherwise have communicated, directly or indirectly, secret and confidential information, the disclosure of which might be inimical to the safety and interests of Canada, to the agents of a Foreign Power, and the facts relating to and the circumstances surrounding such communications."

Under the War Measures Act, which King had activated the previous autumn, the Royal Commission had the same powers that were available to King John before the confrontation with his barons at Runnymede in 1215. The Magna Carta, the most important document of British constitutional history, is the bedrock of civil rights in English common law but in Canada is suspended with a frequency unparalleled in any other functioning democracy to meet whatever situation alarms the prime minister.

King chose two Supreme Court judges for the difficult task ahead, one Francophone and the other Anglophone. The family of Robert Taschereau was descended from a long line of judges. A Taschereau was on the Supreme Council of New France when Wolfe took Quebec. Another served on the first Supreme Court of Canada, in 1875. Another Taschereau was chief justice of the Supreme Court of Canada in 1902. The Taschereaus even produced a rebel, who helped found the French-rights paper *Le Canadien* in 1806. (The rebel succumbed to his Taschereau destiny in his middle years and became a judge on the Quebec bench.)

Roy Lindsay Kellock was considered, in 1946, the flower of the Supreme Court of Canada, the most enlightened and intelligent appointment of his era. He was clear material for promotion to the position of chief justice from the moment of his installation.

To elicit the facts from witnesses, three lawyers were appointed. One was E.K. Williams of Winnipeg, who would later become chief justice of the Supreme Court of Manitoba. Another was Gerald Fauteux, a lawyer frequently retained by the RCMP, who would be appointed to the Supreme Court of Canada. The third was D.W. Mundell, who represented the federal department of justice and who played a quieter role in the hearings.

W.K. Campbell, a dependable civil servant, was named as Royal Commission clerk. His duties included swearing in the witnesses and keeping track of the exhibits. Two shorthand reporters were hired. One, Walter Warren Buskard, was considered the best in the business, with twenty years of experience in court work and Hansard. The other, no less respected, was Edwin Leroy Featherston, a reporter for Hansard in the House of Commons.

Buskard recommended Isobel Hackett, who was accustomed to his shorthand style, to type transcripts. The second typist was Zita Armstrong. Carbon copies of the proceedings were sent almost daily in sealed diplomatic pouches to James Byrnes, American secretary of state, and Ernest Bevin, the British foreign minister. Another copy went to Prime Minister King.

Buskard's widow was living in Ottawa in the spring of 1983 and said she would never forget the day her husband received the call from the RCMP that gave him a ringside seat at the Royal Commission. He was ordered to pack his bags but was not informed where he was going or why; it would take a few days, he was advised. She didn't hear a word of his whereabouts for three days. When he finally was able to call her, he told her nothing more than that he was all right.

A man of discretion, later the editor of Parliament's Hansard, he never did talk much about what he saw and heard, even to her. He took an oath of secrecy and that was that. Sometimes he admitted that the hearings and trials were the most interesting time of his working life, but he offered no other comment.

The Royal Commission on Espionage did not first convene in Ottawa. Arrangements had been made to hide the proceedings at the Seigneury Club at Montebello, about forty miles down the Ottawa River on the way to Montreal. There, on 13 February, 1946, a Wednesday, at ten-thirty in the morning, Igor Gouzenko took an oath to tell the whole truth and began his astounding story.

He was guarded by Mounties, one of whom, Mervyn Black, spoke Russian. Black remained at Gouzenko's side each time he testified to assist with translation as necessary, but the Russian was a stubborn, proud man and preferred to speak for himself in English, however halting and fraught with misconstruction.

The first Canadian he named as a collaborator in Zabotin's spy activities was Fred Rose, the member of parliament for the Labor-Progressive Party. The second was McGill University's elegant aristocrat, Raymond Boyer. The next was Kay Willsher, who worked for the British High Commissioner; then Scott Benning, an official with munitions and supply, then Sam Carr, who was known, as was Fred Rose, as a committed, sometimes jailed, Communist.

The next name, the sixth Gouzenko gave the Royal Commission, was Emma Woikin's.

That period of Gouzenko's life, by the accounts of all who saw him in the witness box, was his finest hour. The wrangles with the RCMP over what he thought to be insufficient respect, the complaints to Ottawa about money, the obsession with secrecy long after history passed him by, the bitter lawsuits, all occurred after the excitement of the spy trials, as they were called, was over. The Royal Commission and subsequent trial judges saw before them a composed, sincere, impressive young man, totally convincing when he declared that the Soviet Union was sowing networks of secret agents all over the world.

Marjorie Earl, an exceptionally fine journalist with the *Toronto Star*, saw him for the first time in March, 1946, when he testified at the preliminary hearing of the case against Fred Rose. She wrote that Gouzenko "looks like a young Canadian workingman dressed up in his Sunday clothes for a special occasion." She judged him to be five foot ten and commented that he had a sturdy build, blonde hair parted at the side and brushed back off a high forehead, and deep blue eyes. Interviewed in Winnipeg in the summer of 1983, Marjorie Earl remembered the young Gouzenko as an attractive, magnetic man with a cherubic face. He was poised, sure of his facts, disarmingly earnest, military of bearing, and shining with honesty.

The Royal Commission was spellbound by Gouzenko's stories of the elaborate security measures within the Soviet embassy, details of how to code messages, code names for agents, and passwords the agents used. They lapped up descriptions of secret meetings and learned the Russian word for "hiding place." Gouzenko was questioned with respect and awe. They had never met anyone like him outside spy fiction.

If Gouzenko had been slimy, shifty-eyed, or sinister, the outcome of his disclosures might have been very different. The experienced lawyers and judges might have been skeptical of the importance of Zabotin's material, might have placed it better as occurring in a period of cooperation with the Soviet. But Gouzenko glowed with goodness. His account became a morality play, with purity of motives all on his side, and only blackness and evil on the other. The commission was seized by righteousness. Their response was much the same as Gouzenko's view of how a modern state should operate against its foes and critics.

Mackenize King's diary refers to "Corby," Gouzenko's code name: "Asking evidence in the Corby case began this morning. It will probably be continued through the week. Arrests will have to follow by the end of the week. I can see where a great cry will be raised, having the Commission sit in secret and men and women arrested and detained under an Order-in-Council passed really under the War Measures Act. I will be held up to the world as the very opposite of a democrat. It is part of the inevitable."

Soon after Gouzenko began his testimony, the Royal Commission decided that everyone named by Gouzenko should be arrested. A period of separation from one another and interrogation by the RCMP was hoped to produce admissions of guilt needed to obtain convictions.

At the end of the second day, the commission had fifteen names. They learned that one of the people named, Sam Carr, had gone into hiding in the United States. The other known Communist, Fred Rose, was a member of parliament, and King resisted subjecting him to arrest. The rest, thirteen in all, however, were going to work every day in a normal manner, although members of the commission feared they would run at the first sign that their activities were known.

In preparation for a swoop on their thirteen targets, the RCMP emptied the barracks at Rockcliffe and drew up a list of instructions for keeping their prisoners on edge. Most of the targets were in Ottawa and Montreal, but Adams was travelling in the west and Lunan wasn't in Canada; he had accompanied Paul Martin, Canada's principal representative at meetings to organize the United Nations, to London. As the RCMP was discussing his arrest, Lunan was preparing a speech for Martin on Canada's contribution of food to hungry nations.

Martin had been informed before leaving Canada that Lunan was under suspicion of espionage and should be watched. Martin wasn't surprised therefore to receive word that Lunan was going to be recalled. The plan was to tell Lunan he was getting a promotion. Martin found the deceit distasteful, but gave the appropriate congratulations when Lunan came to him on 13 February with a cable saying he was needed at once for a new position.

Lunan would arrive at Dorval airport in Montreal on 15 February. That was the day set for rounding up suspects.

Norman Robertson told the prime minister that Gouzenko was being questioned "morning, noon and night." The raids, he said, were scheduled for three in the morning, a time recognized all over the world as advantageous for surprise arrests. King was horrified and insisted that they take place at a more reasonable time, seven in the morning.

Ned Mazerall wakened in the winter darkness to find a policeman standing at the foot of his bed. The shock has remained with him ever since. Gordon Lunan left the plane at Dorval and was looking for his wife, who was meeting him, when he heard his name being called on the loud-speaker. He was directed to a small room with drawn blinds; four Mounties surrounded him.

The two policemen who came for Emma Woikin found her landlady, Marguerite Choquette, downstairs in the kitchen, beginning breakfast preparations. When she answered their knock, they asked brusquely for Emma Woikin.

Astonished, Marguerite said, "She's upstairs asleep. I'll go and get her."

"Never mind," one said, brushing by her.

They went up the stairs quickly, opened Emma's door, went in, and closed it behind them. Marguerite went to her children, still in their beds, and told them to stay in their rooms with the doors shut. She returned downstairs, listening to the sounds of movement in Emma's room, and waited. After a while the police emerged with Emma between them.

"She was in a daze," Marguerite recalled. "They wouldn't tell me what it was all about. I was in just as much of a daze."

Eric Adams was picked up at the Ottawa airport. Lunan was the last to arrive at the RCMP barracks. He was driven from Montreal on the night of 17 February, his arrival so unexpected by sentries that his escort had difficulty getting him inside.

At Rockcliffe barracks, each of the detainees occupied an entire room designed to hold twenty Mountie trainees. The rooms were spartan, with narrow single beds, two to a side, lined along the walls, and a double set of glaring lights in the ceiling. The lights burned day and night.

Guards changed in shifts. None would answer questions.

The men were issued razors once a day, and the razors were taken away when they finished shaving. Meals came three times a day on trays. Before the trays were removed, guards would count the cutlery. Prisoners were not allowed to go near the windows; they could receive no mail.

Something had been overlooked. They were taken out of their rooms without explanation. During their absence, the windows were nailed shut.

One day passed with no human contact, except with silent guards. Another day. And another. Some of the detainees were belligerent, demanding their civil rights in a knowledgeable way; Fred Poland had covered the courts for a Montreal paper. One, David Shugar, tried a hunger strike to force the authorities to allow him to see his wife. He refused to eat for two days, almost three, before he abandoned the attempt.

Others were devastated. The word was that "the women went to pieces," but William H. Kelly, retired deputy commissioner of the RCMP, was staying in one of the nearby barracks at the time and recalled that Kathleen Willsher was composed. It was Emma Woikin who cried all the time, he said. "She was out of her depth from the beginning," he noted sympathetically.

"If they had access to their wives and lawyers in the first few weeks, they wouldn't have talked," explained Arnold Smith, a diplomat who was advising Mackenzie King through the crisis. His comment on the detainment was part of a documentary film, *On Guard for Thee,* produced by Donald Britain for the CBC and the National Film Board. "They would have said nothing," he said. "We wouldn't have been able to learn and disclose, and so on. . . . I thought it was necessary."

The RCMP instructions to the guards, issued under the signature of Assistant Commissioner H.R. Gagnon, were stern:

1. All members of this force detailed for this duty are to be impressed with the fact that the operation is of an extremely secret nature. Not only is it not to be discussed with anyone, but no reference is to be made of it, not even to other members of the force, nor should the member indicate in any way that he is engaged in other than his normal duties.

2. The security of the persons detained is of the utmost importance and constant supervision by day and night is to be given to each and every one of them; particular care to be given to attempts to escape or possible suicide.

3. There must be no conversation between the guards and the prisoners. Should the prisoner make a request or a statement to the guard, it should be promptly transmitted to the N.C.O. in charge.

4. The persons detained are not allowed to communicate with anyone outside. Should they write a letter this will be handed to the N.C.O. in charge.

5. No newspapers or radios will be allowed the detained persons.

6. Guards on duty outside the building will be on continual lookout for any papers thrown from the windows. The N.C.O. in charge will make periodical rounds to make sure that nothing does get out of the windows. If any paper is found it will be turned in to the senior N.C.O. The guards on duty on the grounds will be on the lookout for any possible signalling from the barracks' windows or from neighboring houses or parked cars or any other place. If such a thing should happen, full details of the person concerned must be obtained and the person detained for identification.

7. It must be remembered that the persons detained are not convicted persons and they must be handled with due civility. Attention should be paid to any legitimate requests they may make, for necessities or for their added comfort, provided they do not contravene these instructions.

8. Further instructions will be given later in the matter of exercising the detained persons.

9. IT IS NOTED THAT IN THIS PECULIAR CASE THEY HAVE NOT THE BENEFIT OF SEEING THEIR OWN COUNSEL OR LAWYER.

10. Only one person at a time is to be allowed in the washroom — this under the supervision of the N.C.O.

11. Detained persons must under no circumstances be allowed to speak with one another. As far as possible they should be prevented from seeing one another.

12. Individual guards will keep a minute diary of their watch; including the hour of taking over and the hour of handing over. They will also record every and any incident happening during their turn of duty, the condition of the prisoner, and any peculiar action of his, any remarks he may make, etc. These reports are of the utmost importance and it will be necessary for the guards to keep their eyes and ears highly attuned and observe everything that goes on.

13. Meals will be provided detained persons in their rooms and when empty trays are removed it must definitely be ascertained that all utensils, particularly knives and forks which might be used to inflict self-injury, are returned with the empty tray.

14. Conversations between members of the force detailed for guard duty in hallways or in any other place where there is the

slightest chance of their being overheard, must be conducted in a low tone. Under no circumstances must detained persons be allowed to overhear any instructions regarding their removal, security, or any other thing which common sense indicates to be confidential.

15. N.C.O.s in charge of floors will make frequent check rounds and any incident of an untoward nature is to be immediately reported to the senior N.C.O. in charge.

16. The possibility of sickness must be kept in mind and if medical attention seems required, the matter should at once be referred to the N.C.O. in charge.

17. During the absence of a detained person, either whilst he is in the washroom or is removed for any other purpose, a search should be made of the room in which he is normally detained in order to ascertain if he has secreted anything which he should not have.

18. No written instructions, routine orders or matters dealing with the administration of the force are to be posted on notice boards in the halls where they might be seen by any of the detained persons.

King wrote in his diary unhappily: "There may be some questioning as to this, but this whole matter is so serious that I think there will be disposition by parliament to agree that the right course in the circumstances has been taken. . . . We have now entered upon a situation of world significance."

Since King had been forced to move against those named by Gouzenko, it was critical that the accused people be found guilty. Convictions probably were impossible if the detainees were charged with treason because they had given material to a friendly nation and not to an enemy. It was necessary to look to other avenues. Lawyers scoured the provisions of the Official Secrets Act, an archaic and sweeping piece of legislation that provides penalties, as a wag once observed, for revealing the colour of the rug in a government office. The act had rarely been used to prosecute; its powers had not been explored. They were found however, to be more than adequate to charge the detainees.

H.R. Armstrong reported the first day of the sensational trials in the *Toronto Star*:

The maximum penalty for breach of the Official Secrets Act, a charge now faced by three civil servants and a woman from the British High Commissioner's office here, is seven years "hard labour."

The death penalty could be imposed on persons convicted of treason. There is some question among legal experts here as to whether the alleged acts of those now held, if proven, would constitute treason. People sentenced to death for treason are hanged in Canada, the same method of executing the death sentence as for other capital offences.

One reason for laying charges under the Official Secrets Act is that in the present cases it is believed it will be much easier to prove the Crown's case than it would be in the case of treason.

Secrets given to Russia during the war were divulged to an ally. The war is now over and Russia is not an enemy nation. It would be possible to argue that confidential information given to a friendly nation would not endanger the safety of the state. It would be impossible at this stage to prove that it was Russia's intention to use the information against Canada.

It is believed this constitutes another reason why charges were laid under the Official Secrets Act and not charging treason under the Criminal Code. It is also possible that, knowing the nature of the secrets so far divulged, the Canadian government feels that a penalty up to seven years' imprisonment would meet the situation.

Police with search warrants raided the homes of the thirteen detainees to gather material that might help convict them. Overlooking nothing that might be remotely useful, they took books by Sigmund Freud from Fred Poland's library, and they took Emma Woikin's calendar-like paintings from her room. William H. Kelly, a thirteen-year veteran of the RCMP criminal-investigation branch, was brought from Toronto to sort out what was pertinent to the obtaining of convictions. Such useful objects as letters, telephone numbers, and appointment books linking twelve of the thirteen to one another emerged later as evidence in their trials. There were no such links with anyone to Emma Woikin.

Though the detentions were still not public, Mackenzie King issued a bland press statement. He admitted that Drew Pearson was right, that there were Canadians who had spied for a foreign government. He would not name them or the government; the matter was under investigation, he said.

His distress was increased by the prolonged absence of the Soviet ambassador to Canada, who had been recalled to Moscow soon after Gouzenko defected and had not yet returned to his post. King feared that Moscow was about to break off diplomatic relations with Canada as a prelude to a declaration of war. To demonstrate Canada's friendliness, he called the second-in-command in the Soviet embassy and read him the prepared statement before he released it.

"We are all close friends," he mourned in his diary that night.

It might have been expected that the minister of justice, Louis St. Laurent, would play a prominent role when the statement was issued, but King shrewdly kept him off the stage. He didn't want anyone to suspect that the government was acting punitively against the Soviet as a response to the well-known animosity of the Roman Catholic Church in Quebec to Communism. St. Laurent's religion and Quebec heritage would make his motives suspect in some quarters, King thought.

The Mounties at Rockcliffe were assessing reports from the guards of the behaviour of the detainees during the critical softening-up process. After three days of isolation and confinement, nerves were strung fine. It was a simple matter to identify those who were so shattered they might admit guilt and implicate others.

One by one, the chosen four people were taken into a small office to be questioned by a skilled RCMP officer. The interrogations were tailored to the prisoners. Ned Mazerall, a mild and gentle man, was treated with disarming courtesy. With Gordon Lunan, a tougher man, the officer was belligerent.

According to Lunan's account, Inspector Cliff Harvison, later director of the RCMP secret service, told him that sixty to seventy agents had been arrested. "You cannot get out of this," Harvison told him. "We have mountains of evidence against you. We've wrangled with you Reds before, but this time by God we have got you and we won't let you go."

Kathleen Willsher was informed that the penalty for what she had done was to be put against a wall and executed by a firing squad.

Prisoners were told that there had been suicide attempts, information calculated to increase their despair and terror. Those who were Jewish were subjected to racial taunts. Those who protested the questioning were advised that they wouldn't be allowed to see their families until they cooperated.

The bewildered prisoners were presented with the evidence Gouzenko had taken from the safe in the Soviet embassy cipher room. The shock of seeing the documents must have been staggering. The police position had the added advantage of clarity. The Mounties had no interest in such ambiguities as whether the material was useful to an enemy or even secret, or whether the detainee was a patriotic Canadian, or whether there was a sincere belief that the cause of peace is advanced by international cooperation. The interrogation had to answer one simple question: had the prisoner given anything to the Russians? And the answer, in Lunan's case, was yes.

Gordon Lunan, thirty, a six-footer, bald about the temples, explained at his trial that he provided information to Zabotin because "I felt it was perhaps that we were making a slight contribution or giving a little push to this international cooperation which was the basis of my political ideology."

The Mounties were not interested in motives. When Lunan was questioned, he was horrified to learn that the RCMP knew his code name, "Back," and had details of his meetings with Zabotin's assistant, Lieutenant-Colonel Vassili Rogov. Harvison smoothly told Lunan that others had implicated him and that Lunan should tell his side of the story to protect himself. Lunan, badly rattled, provided Harvison with descriptions of his contacts with three others, Ned Mazerall, Durnford Smith, and Israel Halperin. It was to earn Lunan the title of "head of a spy ring" in accounts of his trial.

Ned Mazerall was questioned next. A small, handsome man of twenty-nine with a Clark Gable moustache, he came from New Brunswick. His family had suffered tragedies in both world wars. His father was shell-shocked in the trenches in World War One, and his younger brother was killed in a Royal Canadian Air Force training accident at the age of twenty.

Harvison showed Mazerall the newspaper headline that accompanied Mackenzie King's press release about spy activities: "FIFTH COLUMN UNCOVERED IN CANADA." He told the radar engineer the location and time of each of his meetings with Lunan. Mazerall could only conclude that Lunan had been a police under-cover agent and that he had been set up. Crushed by the enormity of the mess he was in, he lost sight of the fact that what he had given Lunan was a National Research Council library card, a telephone directory, and declassified information. Mazerall, consumed by despair, seemed a picture of guilt.

When a weeping Emma Woikin was brought into the interrogation room, she was confronted with the five pages, in her own writing, that she last had seen almost six months earlier in the hands of Lida Sokolov. She admitted she had written the notes and told the RCMP officer everything of her involvement with Sokolov. When she had concluded, he called in a stenographer and she dictated her confession.

While the detainees were in Rockcliffe barracks, the public attitude towards Russia was changing. Stories about the courage of the Russian army and the valour of the Russian people had given way, in the newspapers and news-reels, to stories of Russian intransigence in Manchuria, Iran, and Eastern Europe.

The United Nations organization was having a rocky start, apparently, because the Soviet Union was being suspicious and difficult. There were disquieting stories that suggested the Kremlin was ruthless. For the first time, people learned that Stalin had extracted a promise from Roosevelt and Churchill at Yalta that all Soviet deserters would be returned to him; it had an ominous ring.

The United States president and the State department complained daily of the Soviet Union. North Americans were dismayed when the former United States ambassador to Moscow, W. Averell Harriman, reported that war between the United States and the Soviet Union wasn't inevitable, as some seemed to believe. Wasn't inevitable! Harriman recommended that the United States stay well armed to meet the threat of Soviet hegemony, a warning that increased alarm.

The Konkins of Blaine Lake were unaware that Emma Woikin was in custody. She was the only one in the barracks who did not have relatives and friends trying to make contact. Phyllis Poland, roused before dawn when Fred was taken away, called Kay and Brough Macpherson in Toronto to tell them what had happened and to seek advice. Phyllis Lunan spent days on the telephone trying to find out what had happened to her husband between his airplane and the waiting room at Dorval. Frank Park, a lawyer they all knew, fielded calls from tearful women and put together a pattern: most of those who had vanished had backgrounds in civil-liberties and leftist causes.

The Macphersons, who fit the profile, wondered if they would be next. They spent an anxious few days waiting for the police to knock on their door. In some places people who belonged to causes destroyed their membership cards. One organization's executive took its entire membership list to the country and burned it.

The interrogations went on. Kathleen Willsher, forty years old, a cultivated, British-born woman with a bachelor of science degree from the University of London, was questioned three times, two hours each time. She agreed to everything the police put to her and implicated others, notably Eric Adams; she told the RCMP that she gave him documents from the High Commissioner's office.

The RCMP recommended that the state proceed against Ned Mazerall, Gordon Lunan, Kathleen Willsher, and Emma Woikin. They thought it probable that all four would plead guilty. The four would be brought before the Royal Commission, which had finished with Gouzenko and was preparing to question the prisoners in a room in the Justice Building.

The RCMP provided transcripts of the four confessions for Fauteux and Williams, who would conduct the questioning. Mr. Justice Kellock, one of the two presiding judges, had developed an appetite for the colorful details of spying and fumed with indignation directed against the detainees, so his participation in the cross-examination was considerable. There are long stretches in the transcript of the Royal Commission hearings where Kellock is the only questioner and his examination bristles with unconcealed hostility.

For the hearings, two long tables were placed parallel to each other but some distance apart. The two judges sat at one, the lawyers at the other. Witnesses were seated at a small table between the two, across from the clerk and shorthand reporter, so they had the sensation of being surrounded.

Ned Mazerall's involvement began in the fall of 1943, when he was approached by a CBC announcer who invited him to

join a group discussing Marxism and other ideologies. Mazerall
went to meetings for about a year and then dropped out
through disinterest. Lunan must have obtained his name
through this connection because as the war ended in 1945
Lunan made a contact. He said the editor of an army newspaper
wanted to know what was going on in radar development.
Mazerall gave Lunan documents marked "confidential,"
knowing they were about to be released by the head of his
section at a press conference in London.

Ned Mazerall was the first to be questioned by the Royal
Commission.

"The Royal Commission, from my point of view, was a
disaster," Mazerall said when interviewed in his University of
Manitoba lab in Winnipeg in April, 1983. He was retiring after
ten years with the health sciences faculty of the university. The
lab in which he sat was testament of his ingenuity. The walls
were lined with modular shelves and counters of his own
design, allowing such flexibility that the entire lab could be
moved in a matter of hours.

Mazerall, a precise, soft-spoken man, beautifully dressed in a
camel jacket, a vest and cocoa-colored trousers, could not
discuss what had happened to him almost forty years earlier
without weeping. There were times in his account when he
found it difficult to speak.

His voice was broken as he described his appearance before
the Royal Commission. "I was taken from the barracks and I
wasn't told where I was going or what was happening. Guards
brought me into a room full of people. One of the first questions was an attack on my patriotism, a charge that I had been
involved with an unpatriotic group."

He paused, then continued quietly. "There were two justices
of the supreme court, who didn't come off well. Williams and
Fauteux, the lawyers, seemed to be a little bit fairer, as I recall.

"The very first thing that was said to me was, 'You are under
oath and you will answer all questions.' I wasn't given any
indication that I had any right whatsoever not to answer
questions. Those of us who appeared before them in the first
group had no knowledge that we had a right to counsel, or that
we were in any danger because we had no counsel."

He steadied his voice. "There was no doubt that they started
with the four they thought would be easiest. I guess I was

cooperative about explaining what I had done, which was essentially nothing. When Lunan told me that I had a cover name, this immediately got my back up and probably was the cause of my not actually ever giving him anything. It immediately gave it a conspiratorial aspect which was completely unnecessary. Our own people at National Research Council had just delivered our latest version of radar to the Russians, so it was difficult for me under those circumstances to think that I was aiding an enemy state. We were switching to peacetime aviation and we were anxious to get publicity because our radar was well in advance of anything in the world at that time."

Arnold Smith, one of the leading hawks around Mackenzie King at the time of the Gouzenko defection, confessed on the CBC-NFB film *On Guard for Thee* that he regretted what happened to Ned Mazerall.

"Well, I felt he was a confused little man," Smith commented. "I felt rather sorry for him. When he was asked to hand over some secret information he handed over some pretty innocuous information that was confidential and that he expected or knew was going to be declassified in a matter of months. And he didn't hand over top-secret information. He didn't know what to do."

"Mazerall spilled his guts in that Commission hearing," Mazerall's lawyer, Roydon Hughes recently recalled. "The judges were skilled cross-examiners and scared him out of his wits. He was a loyal British subject, there was never any question of that. His whole family was very patriotic. What they did to him was wholly unfair. I never dreamed that justice was as they administered it. The witnesses weren't told in advance of testifying that they had the right to refuse to answer, that they could have the protection of the Canada Evidence Act. The basis of the case against Mazerall wasn't his true story at all, but the cross-examination tying him to the others. That's what hurt him."

Hughes paused heavily. "I always thought it was unfair that some were convicted on the basis of their testimony before the Royal Commission, but I decided in my own mind that the end justifies the means." He sighed with regret and spread his hands. "What other way could they have convicted those people if they hadn't resorted to unfair tactics?"

The Konkin family collection contains this photograph of Doukhobor women harnessed to a plough in the spring of 1900.

Mary Konkin, thirteen, and her sister Emma, five. Mary already had taught Emma to read and write in two languages.

Pearl Konkin with her youngest child, Emma, on her lap. Emma was one year old and her mother was forty-three.
(MARY PERVERSEFF'S COLLECTION)

A proud Konkin family gathered around the tractor. Emma is at far left, her father and mother beside her.
(MARY PERVERSEFF'S COLLECTION)

Emma and Bill Woikin, deeply in love, the summer of their first year of marriage.

(MASHA KALESNIKOFF'S COLLECTION)

Emma and Bill Woikin's wedding picture taken soon after the event in April, 1937. She was sixteen.

(DOREEN AND FRED KONKIN'S COLLECTION)

Emma and Bill Woikin, all dressed up in their wedding clothes, squinting into the spring sun.

(MARY PERVERSEFF'S COLLECTION)

Doukhobor funerals used to be homemade, the coffin built on the spot. This is Pearl Konkin in her coffin. Emma, fifteen, has her hands on the coffin.
(DOREEN AND FRED KONKIN'S COLLECTION)

Bill Konkin, Emma's young husband, a suicide at the age of twenty-seven. Emma's brother Bill stands at right.
(DOREEN AND FRED KONKIN'S COLLECTION)

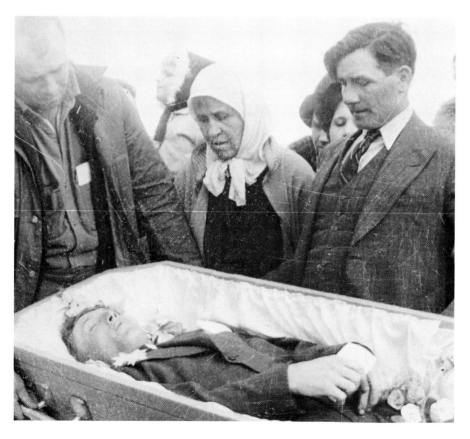

Emma at the door of the home she shared with Bill Woikin at the height of the Saskatchewan depression.

(MARY PERVERSEFF'S COLLECTION)

Emma and Louie Sawula pose for their wedding picture in March, 1949. She had only recently been released from prison.

(DOREEN AND FRED KONKIN'S COLLECTION)

INDEX
Amusements—11 Radio—16
Births, Deaths—22 Sports—18-21
Comics—29-30 Want Ads—22-28
Markets—12-13 Women's—18-19

TORONTO DAILY STAR

THE WEATHER
Toronto and vicinity: Tuesday.—
Generally fair and a little colder.
Low tonight 12, high tomorrow 31.

54TH YEAR TORONTO, MONDAY, MARCH 4, 1946—32 PAGES 3c PER COPY, 18c PER WEEK

MOSCOW ORDERED SPYING--KING
4 CANADIANS APPEAR IN COURT

TWO WOMEN, TWO MEN AIDED SOVIET-OTTAWA

HOME AND SPORT EDITION

BRITAIN ASKS RUSSIA EXPLAIN TROOPS IN IRAN

Three Were Employees of Canada and Fourth in Office of British High Commissioner—Atom Bomb and Radar Were Objects of Spies

By H. R. ARMSTRONG

2 MEN, 2 WOMEN APPEAR IN COURT
WOIKIN GUILTY

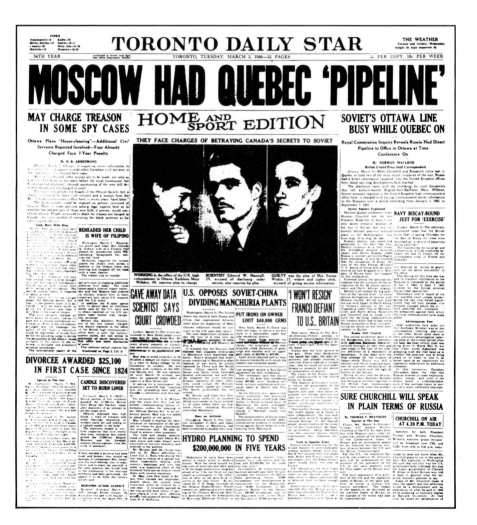

INDEX
Amusements—11 Radio—16
Births, Deaths—22 Sports—18-21
Comics—29-30 Want Ads—22-28
Markets—12-13 Women's—18-19

TORONTO DAILY STAR

THE WEATHER
Toronto and vicinity: Wednesday.
Fair, tonight 24, high tomorrow 36.

54TH YEAR TORONTO, TUESDAY, MARCH 5, 1946—32 PAGES 3c PER COPY, 18c PER WEEK

MOSCOW HAD QUEBEC 'PIPELINE'

MAY CHARGE TREASON IN SOME SPY CASES

HOME AND SPORT EDITION

SOVIET'S OTTAWA LINE BUSY WHILE QUEBEC ON

Ottawa Plans "House-cleaning"—Additional Civil Servants Reported Involved—Four Already Charged Face 7-Year Penalty

By H. R. ARMSTRONG

THEY FACE CHARGES OF BETRAYING CANADA'S SECRETS TO SOVIET

Royal Commission Inquiry Reveals Russia Had Direct Pipeline to Office in Ottawa at Time Conference On

By NORMAN MacLEOD
British United Press Staff Correspondent

Link Went With Ring

BEHEADED HER CHILD
IS WIFE OF FILIPINO

Soviet Absence Explained

NAVY BISCAY-BOUND
JUST FOR 'EXERCISE'

WORKING in the office of the U.K. high commissioner in Ottawa, Kathleen Mary Willsher, 40, reserves plea to charge

SCIENTIST Edward W. Mazerall, 29, accused of disclosing radar secrets, also reserves his plea

GUILTY was the plea of Mrs. Emma Woikin, 25, widow and cipher clerk, accused of giving secrets information

GAVE AWAY DATA
SCIENTIST SAYS
COURT CROWDED

U.S. OPPOSES SOVIET-CHINA
DIVIDING MANCHURIA PLANTS

PUT IRONS ON OWNER
LOOT $40,000 GEMS

'I WON'T RESIGN'
FRANCO DEFIANT
TO U.S., BRITAIN

DIVORCEE AWARDED $25,100
IN FIRST CASE SINCE 1824

CANDLE DISCOVERED
SET TO BURN LINER

SURE CHURCHILL WILL SPEAK
IN PLAIN TERMS OF RUSSIA

By THOMAS F. REYNOLDS
Special to The Star

CHURCHILL ON AIR
AT 4.30 P.M. TODAY

REMANDS AUSSIE SUSPECT

HYDRO PLANNING TO SPEND
$200,000,000 IN FIVE YEARS

The Standard

VOL. XLII No. 11.   MONTREAL, SATURDAY, MARCH 16, 1946.   **TEN CENTS**

MRS. EMMA WOIKIN, blond Doukhobor, who has pleaded guilty to conspiracy to provide the Soviet with secret information.

Spy Ring Folk Unassuming

First Four Accused Were Average Wage-Earners

The Ottawa espionage trials are proving one thing. Average citizens whose friends thought them quiet and unassuming suddenly can be catapulted to notoriety, their names on every tongue, their insignificant lives questioned and ripped apart, their acts and words used to condemn them.

Take the cases of the four people who were first identified by the Government. They are not spectacular. They are not suave or sinister. They are ordinary wage-earners. But they have been accused of selling their country's secrets to another power.

Captain Gordon Lunan, accused of being an intermediary between a group of Canadian scientists and Lt.-Col. Rogov, former military attache in the Soviet Embassy, was born in Kirkcaldy, Scotland, December 31, 1916. He attended public school in Britain. His family is well-to-do middle class and his father is an official of a British linoleum company.

"Lunan came to Canada in 1937," a friend of his explained. "He had started out on a world trip, but he never made it. His idea was to work for different newspapers and pay his way. He hadn't had a chance to be a reporter when he reached Canada. He had been trained in advertising work in Britain, though, and he was able to get a job as a copywriter with a Montreal advertising agency.

"On the whole, he was an average guy. He liked to play golf and to fish. He was an idealist, bull-headed Scotsman.

"He left his first job and went to another Montreal agency as a copywriter. He was very well liked by the staff and advanced rapidly. When public opinion was all for the opening of a second front, Lunan was asked to join the Quebec committee. His advertising knowledge was used to push the committee's work.

Loses Job

"One day he went to a Montreal newspaper with a bulletin from the committee. An editor on the paper knew who he was and phoned some of the larger accounts of his firm to tell them Lunan was a member of the Committee for a Second Front.

"These firms phoned the agency and told them that if they didn't get rid of Lunan, they would drop their accounts.

"Gordie was fired. He then worked full time for the committee and made arrangements to enlist in the army. He joined as a private in 1943 and took his officer's training course. He came second out of a cadet class of 600 and entered the Signals Corps."

Lunan was seconded to the War—

Continued on Page Two

Living Cost To Be Higher At Year's End

Price Boosts Will Be Allowed to Increase Index 5 to 10 Points

(Special to The Standard.)

Ottawa — Prices in Canada are to be allowed to increase so that the cost of living index will stand between five and 10 points higher than the present level by the end of 1946.

Reliable sources here state that the government's program of dismantling wartime controls is geared to produce this result. If it does so, it will mean that this year the cost of living in Canada will rise one-quarter to half as much as it has done since 1939.

The decision to allow prices to increase are said to have followed recent trade conferences. Representatives of other nations, all of which have experienced a greater degree of inflation than Canada, stated that they could not sell at the Dominion's low prices and make a profit. And if they could not sell, they could not in turn buy Canadian goods.

May Restore Ceilings

In announcing plans for relaxing controls, Prime Minister King warned that price increases would probably take place. "It is even conceivable," he said, "that widespread and significant advances may occur." If such happens price ceilings will be reimposed, he stated.

There is some concern among officials who administer the program, however, as to how far it is possible to let inflation go and still be in a position to clamp on the lid if it goes too far.

Already the unions of the Cana—

Continued on Page Two

Soviet Scientists Know How To Produce Atomic Bombs

Four Groups Were Engaged On Uranium Fission During War

By THOMAS R. HENRY
North American Newspaper Alliance

Washington — Russia has all the "brains" necessary to produce atomic bombs, regardless of whether any information is obtained outside the country. Four groups of Russian nuclear physicists worked on the problem of uranium fission during the war and presumably still are engaged on such research.

Some of the essential early discoveries which were basic to the Manhattan project have been made independently in the Soviet Union. This is the picture presented by the atomic scientists of Chicago, composed of men who worked on the Manhattan project at the University of Chicago, who have assembled all available data on the progress of this work in Russian laboratories.

A few weeks ago it was announced that Professors G. N. Flerov and K. A. Petrazhak of the Physics-Technical Institute at Leningrad had been awarded the Stalin prize of the Soviet Academy of Scientists for discovering "spontaneous fission of the uranium atom." They actually did the work in 1940 for which the prize was awarded, according to the Chicago group, and published their results for all the world. They received, in fact, only second prize, indicating that in the opinion of the Russians themselves, their work had no very great practical importance.

It was, however, "an interesting discovery," according to the Chicago scientists, although it has not even the remotest connection with atomic bombs. They had found that uranium and thorium atoms sometimes split naturally without the necessity of any outside bombardment, either by man-made neutrons or cosmic rays.

"An analogous discovery," says the Chicago report, "would be to have found in the field of ordinary chemistry that out of a nuclear shells in an ordnance storehouse, one will explode, all by itself, once in a million years, without any detonating mechanism being put into action.

"What the achievement did prove is the high level of research in nuclear physics in Russia, because of the extreme weakness of the spontaneous fission effect it could have been discovered only by extraordinarily skilful experimentation."

Flerov and Petrazhak belonged

to the Leningrad group, nuclear physicists working in three institutes, all constituent parts of the Soviet Academy of Sciences. These are State Radiation Institute and the Institute of Chemical Physics. At the latter in 1939 were made the possibility of an atom-breaking chain reaction, which is the basis of the atomic bomb.

At Moscow work in nuclear physics has been concentrated at the Lebedev Institute of Physics. There, in 1943, Prof. V. I. Veksler suggested a method of producing super-speed electrons which was rediscovered independently in the United States in 1945. It was this group, working in cooperation with the celebrated Russian physicist, Peter Kapitza, which recently discovered a negative cosmic particle, looking to the possible assumption of "negative matter" somewhere in the universe.

Another group of nuclear physicists was at work in 1940—they presumably are continuing their researches although nothing has been heard from them at the Ukrainian Physico-Technical Institute at Kharkov. There Prof. A. I. Leipunsky was one of the first investigators to analyze the fission of uranium for neutron emission.

At Sverdlovsk a considerable group of nuclear physicists was working at the state university before America entered the war and

Continued on Page Two

Emma Woikin with two unidentified friends in Ottawa during the summer before her arrest.

Emma had this picture taken just before she accepted a job in Ottawa's civil service in the fall of 1943.

A mysterious photograph taken during Emma's trip to the Soviet. Emma is the woman on the left, the others are unknown.

Emma and Louie Sawula during one of their motoring vacations in 1964. Emma, on the left, strolling with a friend on the streets of Saskatoon.

Emma and Louie Sawula on their twenty-fifth wedding anniversary.

(MARY PERVERSEFF'S COLLECTION)

Louie Sawula standing beside Emma in her coffin, May 1974.

(MARY PERVERSEFF'S COLLECTION)

Sam Kalesnikoff, a skilled amateur archivist, who has exhaustive records of early Doukhobor history.
(AUTHOR)

Masha Kalesnikoff, a sister of Bill Woikin, seated in the cheerful clutter of her Blaine Lake home.
(AUTHOR)

Bill Konkin, Emma's only surviving brother, and an active farmer in his eighties. (AUTHOR)

The Konkin homestead where Emma was raised and married Bill Woikin. (AUTHOR)

Bill Konkin standing beside a well digger with which he used to eke out his family's survival in the Depression. (AUTHOR)

The snug bungalow in Saskatoon where Emma and Louie Sawula lived almost all their married life. (AUTHOR)

Bill Woikin's grave on a sweep of Saskatchewan prairie. Until recently, it was unmarked. (AUTHOR)

Louie Sawula standing beside Emma's gravestone. He bought her the best one he could find. (AUTHOR)

Chapter Nine

Emma Woikin appeared before the Royal Commission on Espionage on 22 February, 1946, eight days after she had been locked in the barracks. The session began at ten-thirty in the morning. Emma, her hand on the worn cover of a Bible, swore to tell the truth, and that she would never divulge to anyone what transpired in that room.

Like the other detainees, she was not informed that her testimony could be used against her in a subsequent trial, that she was likely to face criminal charges, or that she had a right to claim protection under the rules of the Canada Evidence Act from having her testimony used against her in a trial. The two Supreme Court judges later claimed that they gave such assurances; the transcript shows they did so only *after* Emma testified.

The morning session contained questions about the procedures within the external-affairs department's cipher room, then moved to the sensitive matters of Emma's relationship with Sokolov and her application for Soviet citizenship. Judging by the notations of the shorthand reporter, Emma spoke slowly and in an extremely low voice. Kellock appears, in the transcript, to be furious with her.

At the end of the morning, the police matron who accompanied

Emma, Sadie E. Halcro, was also sworn not to reveal anything that transpired in the hearing room. Emma was taken out of the Justice Building by a route different from the one she followed in the morning and was driven back to her barracks room for lunch, a rushed affair since transportation took up most of the break time.

The hearing convened again at two-thirty. Emma was required to go over some of the morning's testimony. Much time was spent on her story of leaving the notes in the toilet tank of the dentists' office and her application for a transfer to Canada's embassy in Moscow. The judges asked if she belonged to the Communist party; the answer was no. What did she know about Communism? Only what she read in the papers.

She was dismissed at ten minutes after three and was returned to the barracks.

Prime Minister King and his justice minister, Louis St. Laurent, were uncomfortable with the mail they were receiving from wives of the men imprisoned in the barracks. King's distress was so acute that his staff thought it wise not to tell him about all the letters. When he found out, he felt even worse.

"It is all very upsetting," he confided in his diary. "People will not stand for individual liberty being curtailed or men being detained and denied counsel and fair trial before being kept in prison. The whole proceedings are far too much like those of Russia itself."

The Royal Commission's obsession for details irritated him; he had anticipated that the people in the barracks would be detailed for only a few days, but two weeks had passed and many of the detainees had not yet been examined. Transcripts were being delivered to him as quickly as they were typed, the trivia they contained fuelling his impatience.

Just after his morning devotionals on 25 February, King settled himself to read the transcripts of the questioning of Emma Woikin. He told Norman Robertson later that he thought "it was wrong that those who are suspected should be detained indefinitely, and that some way should be found to shorten the inquiry and give them the full rights of protection which the law allows them."

King was particularly concerned that the detainees were not told of their right to have a lawyer. The judges told him that no one who testified to that point wanted a lawyer. But David

Shugar, for only one example, made six written requests to the Royal Commission for a lawyer and thirteen written protests to the prime minister and the minister of justice asking to be allowed counsel.

King's anxiety bore fruit, however. On Thursday, 28 February, Emma Woikin was recalled before the Royal Commission to be advised pleasantly by Taschereau, in obscure legal language, that she was entitled to have a lawyer and that the evidence she had given might lead to charges being laid against her.

TASCHEREAU: Do you understand what I have just said to you?

WOIKIN: I think so.

TASCHEREAU: Have you anything to say or anything else to add to the evidence that you have already given?

WOIKIN: No.

TASCHEREAU: Before we make our recommendation to the Governor in Council, do you wish to be represented by counsel?

WOIKIN: By that you mean I should have an attorney?

TASCHEREAU: This Commission is not a criminal court. We just report to the government.

WOIKIN: Yes.

TASCHEREAU: But before we make that report we want to tell you that you are entitled to have counsel appear before us.

WOIKIN: No.

TASCHEREAU: You do not wish to have counsel appear before us?

WOIKIN: No.

TASCHEREAU: That will be all, thank you.

Satisfied that they had protected their judicial rears, the judges of the Royal Commission continued with the inquiry as before. They did not tell detainees their rights until after the detainees had been questioned.

Ned Mazerall said his impression of the Royal Commission was that it seemed to be a private discussion. Inspector Harvison, who seemed to him a decent man, told Mazerall things would go better for him if he told the Royal Commission everything. Mazerall believed him. He wondered about the observers in the room who were not introduced; he believed they were Americans. The harshness of the judges, especially Kellock, took him aback but he didn't think it mattered; he never sensed that he was in any personal jeopardy.

The most self-damaging remark he made, one that sent him to Kingston Penitentiary for four years, was that he was sorry for what had occurred. The comment was read to a jury; jury members assumed that Mazerall was remorseful because he had betrayed his country. His statement was taken as an admission of guilt. What he meant was that he regretted that he had been drawn into the debacle.

Prime Minister King continued to grumble as one day of slow questioning followed another. He sent a message through the government's lawyers to the judges, urging them to act quickly. The judges produced an interim report describing the four best prospects for conviction: Emma Woikin, Ned Mazerall, Kathleen Willsher and Gordon Lunan.

King observed in his diary that he was sorry "that examinations have only proceeded far enough this far to justify the arrest of four persons. That one of them, the first one on the list, should be a woman in the department of external affairs. The worst feature about her is that she should never have been employed, seeing she is of Russian descent, but of course she was sent by the Civil Service Commission to the department. It will, however, afford room for an attack upon the department and the Opposition will say that I have been taking on too much to give supervision needed to the department. I am glad along with her is an employee of the British government, which brings the British into the picture."

The next day, 3 March, 1946, a Sunday, King telephoned Winston Churchill, who had just arrived in the United States to receive an honourary degree and to give a convocation address. Mike Pearson, of Canada's external-affairs department, was helping him with his speech, and Churchill told King he was grateful for the assistance. King told Churchill that the first report of the Royal Commission would be ready the following day. Churchill was delighted.

"You are completely right," he told King. "Do not hold anything back. Go ahead." Exposing the Soviet Union could prevent a war, Churchill continued. If the world had known that Germany was re-arming, he thought the war in Europe might not have happened. A stiff challenge might make Stalin back down.

The two men discussed a concern raised by United States Secretary of State James Byrnes, who wondered if it would seem that Washington had manipulated Canada into the spy exposures to suit America's anti-Soviet policy. To avoid the look of puppetry, Byrnes wanted Alan Nunn May arrested in London at the same time the Royal Commission report was released.

The first report of the Royal Commission on Espionage was issued on 4 March, 1946. In the account of the activities of Woikin, Mazerall, Willsher and Lunan, there is no suggestion that they might not be guilty of conspiring against their country.

The report reads, in part:

The evidence establishes that a network of undercover agents has been organized and developed for the purpose of obtaining secret and confidential information, particularly from employees of departments and agencies of the Dominion Government and from an employee in the office of the High Commission for the United Kingdom in Canada.

The evidence reveals that these operations were carried out by certain members of the staff of the Soviet Embassy in Ottawa under direct instructions from Moscow. The person directly in charge of these operations was Col. Nicholai Zabotin . . . .

We have noticed that each of the dossiers compiled by the staff of the military attaché with respect to Canadian agents contained this significant question: "Length of time in the net." We think that the word "net" well describes the organization set up and under development by Col. Zabotin . . . . The evidence heard so far, however, establishes that four persons, namely Mrs. Emma Woikin, Captain Gordon Lunan, Edward Wilfred Mazerall and Miss Kathleen Mary Willsher . . . have communicated directly or indirectly secret and confidential information to representatives of the U.S.S.R. in violation of the provisions of the Official Secrets Act 1939 3 Geo. VI Cap. 49.

The first of the four persons the judges considered guilty of espionage was Emma Woikin:

This person was employed as a cipher clerk in the Department of External Affairs, having taken the usual oath of secrecy required in such cases. Taking advantage of the position she occupied, she communicated to Major Sokolov the contents of secret telegrams to which she had access in the course of her duties . . . .

Each of the persons has given evidence before us and has admitted the substance of the above. To each in accordance with the provisions of Sections 12 and 13 of the Inquiries Act RSC Cap 99, an opportunity was given to have counsel but none desired to be represented by counsel or to adduce any evidence in addition to his or her own testimony.

On Monday, 4 March, the prime minister read the report to his stunned cabinet, whose members were learning about Gouzenko for the first time. There was a silence when he finished. James L. Ilsley, a lawyer who was minister of finance, was the first to question King. He asked uneasily if publication of the report was not prejudicial to a fair trial of the accused. King assured him there was no problem. All four, he said, would plead guilty.

Joseph Sedgwick, a crusty, brilliant Toronto lawyer who successfully defended Eric Adams a few months later, complained of the Royal Commission's report during the documentary film *On Guard for Thee*. The trials were greatly prejudiced, he declared. "After that, how could you get a fair, an unprejudiced jury? How could you get a judge who would be prepared to say two justices of the Supreme Court of Canada are talking through their hats?"

Another defence lawyer who acted for the detainees was H.L. Cartwright of Kingston. He appeared in the same documentary to ponder the dilemma he faced: the most outrageous contempt of court of its time was committed by two judges of the highest court in the land. He commented, "If the CBC or newspapers or anyone publishes anything that is likely to prejudice the fair trial of an action that is contempt of court."

The Royal Commission report created a sensation around the world and brought reporters flocking to Ottawa to witness the most exciting spy drama since Mata Hari's execution in France in 1917. Front pages bore pictures of a smiling Zabotin, this time with the blank space of his steel tooth unretouched.

The lead editorial in the *New York Times* congratulated Canada for its "judicial and restrained" handling of the matter. "The facts may condemn the Soviet government," the editorial declared. "The Canadian government does not."

The final paragraph of the *Times* report had a more dubious tone:

The information sought was what any military service would like to know about its opposite number in any foreign country, either friendly or hostile. Some of the information on radar given to the Russians later was made public. Movement and strength of army units generally is easy to obtain, especially in a country like Canada or the U.S.

The editorial concluded to the point at issue: the improper transfer of information:

This information could not properly be given away by any Canadian or British subject. The Russian government itself guards far more closely than does any country in the world military information of even less importance. Any of its subjects detected giving information to other countries is quickly purged.

The four people in the barracks whose names were being flashed around the world had good news the morning of 4 March: they were told they could pack their things. They were leaving.

When Mazerall stepped out of the barracks, his mood was one of elation and glorious relief. Two policemen were waiting. They told him he was under arrest and snapped handcuffs on his wrists. He could not recall anything that happened to him during that black year that devastated him more.

The press was notified that the four spies would be brought into an Ottawa courtroom to be arraigned. They would appear before Magistrate Glenn Elford Strike.

The thirteen people detained in the barracks could have done a lot worse than to come before Strike. In 1946, magistrates were not required to have legal training. But Strike, then forty-seven, was a superbly trained lawyer who had graduated at the age of twenty-two after valorous service in the trenches during World War One. The war left his lungs permanently weakened from the effects of poison gas. Strike set up legal practice in Ottawa, but found so little work at the beginning of the Depression that he was grateful to accept an appointment to the bench at the adequate salary, then, of five thousand dollars a year.

Glenn Strike died of a stroke in his winter home in Florida in 1976, leaving a wife and daughter. The quality of his mind and his ability to distill legal argument were such that he would not have been out of place on the Supreme Court, his associates say. After forty years on the bench he ended his career as the senior judge in charge of administration of the courts of Eastern Ontario. He received a standing ovation when the Carleton County Law Association honoured him with a testimonial dinner. For many years he was president of the Ottawa Boys' Club and in 1961 he was named B'nai B'rith Citizen of the year.

His widow, Helen Strike, a slim, vigorous, well-groomed and charming woman in her eighties, was interviewed in the spring of 1983. She said her husband left no notes or diaries about that momentous period of his life when his courtroom was thronged with the thirteen detainees from the barracks and the reporters and curious public who wanted to see them. She recalled that he was stimulated by the interruption of his usual calendar of drunks and traffic violators. Some of the most famous lawyers in the country came to defend the accused spies.

"My husband found it a real pleasure to deal with first-class minds and expertise," Helen Strike said fondly.

The first of the four detainees brought before Magistrate Strike on 4 March, 1946, was Emma Woikin. She entered the room between two guards, her head down, and was placed in the prisoner's box while reporters craned to see the first of the notorious traitors. She was a disappointment, a drained, mousey woman in a cheap black coat, hatless, dull-eyed from weeping, and looking much older than her twenty-five years. Strike, a severe-looking man with a military moustache, firm eyes and a cleft chin, listened stiffly as the charges were read by Lee A. Kelley, KC, an experienced Ottawa lawyer, retained by the federal government to act for the crown.

The long delay caused by the protracted deliberations of the Royal Commission had given Ottawa sufficient time to realize that it would be difficult to decide what charges would stick in this unprecedented situation. The justice department wanted a federal trial, but the crimes had been committed in Ontario. The provincial attorney-general might feel his department should be in charge. However, Ontario's attorney-general realized how expensive the trials might be; he was happy to yield the stage.

In the end it was agreed to lay multiple charges. Emma Woikin was charged with conspiracy to provide information to the Soviet Union, in violation of the Criminal Code, and with obtaining secret information prejudicial to the safety of the state, contrary to the Official Secrets Act.

Both charges brought with them the same penalty: up to seven years in prison on each charge for a total of fourteen years, and a fine of up to two thousand dollars on each charge. In 1946, two thousand dollars was more than most people earned in a year.

Kelley read the charges and Magistrate Strike asked Emma, "How do you plead?"

Emma looked about her in confusion. "I did it," she said faintly. "Yes, I did it."

"You have to answer either 'guilty' or 'not guilty,'" he instructed her.

She nodded that she understood. "Guilty," she said in a voice so weak that reporters at the press table six feet away weren't certain of her answer.

Strike made a note of her plea and informed her that she could be tried by a magistrate, by a judge, or by a judge and jury. Emma stared at him without speaking. Strike patiently explained what each meant. Emma grasped that the quickest process was to be tried by a magistrate, and asked for that.

Strike was uncomfortable that she was facing grave charges and was making crucial decisions without the help of a lawyer. He asked her if she was sure she wouldn't prefer trial by a judge or trial by judge and jury. Emma shook her head. Strike said she would have to give her answer verbally for the court record. She drew a breath and whispered, "No."

Her guards moved to her side and escorted her back to jail. Of all the detainees, only Emma Woikin appeared in court without a lawyer. All the others had help, some of them the best that money could buy, immediately after their arrests. Despite the Royal Commission's promise to Mackenzie King that the first four detainees would plead guilty, Emma Woikin was the only one to do so.

The day Emma appeared before Magistrate Strike, Winston Churchill received an honourary degree at Fulton, Missouri, and made a speech that helped polarize western nations. "From Stetin in the Baltic to Trieste in the Adriatic, an iron curtain has descended across the continent," he said. He urged the democracies to beware of the evil Soviet Union. The bluntness of his speech owed much to the fact that Churchill was out of office, and had no obligation to be diplomatic. Churchill knew his speech would be heard along with the shattering news of Russian spies in Ottawa. The speech played a powerful role in reshaping the Canadian view of the Soviet Union. People were afraid that a new war was brewing. It was a short step from a sense of jeopardy to turning on alleged traitors with loathing.

Some time during the day of her arrest and appearance in Magistrate Strike's courtroom, Emma Woikin was allowed two telephone calls. One was to the Choquettes. Marguerite's alarm had been growing during the seventeen days her babysitter had been held incommunicado in the barracks. When RCMP officers came to search Emma's room and take away her paintings she begged for an explanation. "You'll know in good time," they told her curtly. She was frightened even more when one of them said that the police knew every move she and her husband had made during the previous month or so.

Bert Choquette had the newspaper front page in his hand when he answered Emma's telephone call. She looked wan in the newspaper photograph; her eyes, huge in her narrow face. Neither referred to the newspaper story. Emma asked a favour, that he bring her her schoolbooks. Albert gathered up some textbooks and loose-leaf binders and delivered them to the jail. He returned home in a state of depression. "How could she have made such a fool of us?" he asked his wife.

"Maybe there is more to it than we know," she replied loyally.

Emma's second telephone call was to Blaine Lake. She spoke to her brother John. John's son Fred was there when Emma called.

"Dad was holding the receiver, standing there," Fred

recalled, "and then he just sat down like his legs had folded under him."

When he hung up, John said, "Emma's in jail."

The family collected in the homestead where John and Lena were living with their half-grown sons and a new daughter, Lily, only four months old. Emma's father, Alex E., drove from Blaine Lake with his wife Natasha; Alex A. and Annie came from their farm close by; and Bill and Hannah arrived from Marcelin.

Emma's sister Mary, recovering from a long illness, wasn't present. She heard a radio bulletin that described her sister as a "spy" and called John to verify it. He replied heavily that it was true; he had talked to Emma and it looked very bad. She thought she could go to prison for seven years, maybe more.

"When I heard that, geez, I was ready to die," Mary recalled. She stayed at the farm she and Pete had rented near Marcelin but kept in touch with the paralyzing developments.

Lena Konkin stood over the stove in the homestead, cooking for the clan, wiping tears from her cheeks. The men sat around the kitchen table, talking. The Konkins asked the advice of John Boyd, their lawyer in Blaine Lake. Not certain of the charges, he was pessimistic. Emma might be kept in prison for the rest of her life, he thought. He recommended that they seek the help of John Diefenbaker, the riding's member in the House of Commons.

Diefenbaker's partner, John Cuelenaere, was keeping the practice together in Prince Albert, with occasional visits from Diefenbaker. Diefenbaker denied in the House of Commons that he had anything to do with Emma Woikin, but several of the Konkins have a clear recollection that it was Diefenbaker himself, and not Cuelenaere, who told them what Ottawa lawyer to get for her and assured them that Emma wasn't in serious trouble. Her sentence would be two years at the most, probably less.

"As soon as I heard that," Mary said cheerfully, "I didn't worry no more."

Examination of Diefenbaker's legal appointment book for that period wasn't helpful. Most of the pages are blank. His clients simply dropped by without appointments when they knew he was in town. He appears to have been in Prince Albert the first week of March, 1946, however, because there is a reminder on 7 March: "I sent to Chinese laundry opposite Royal Bank 5 handkerchiefs, 2 collars, 1 shirt."

The Konkins were new to the ways of criminal charges. When they were informed that a magistrate would set the amount of Emma's bail so that she could be free until her trial, the kitchen conference made several decisions. In spite of Emma's protests to John that she didn't want them to do anything, they would hire the lawyer Diefenbaker recommended. Someone would have to go to Ottawa to put up the bail money. They looked from one to another. That would be John, the "good-neighbour" Konkin.

Bill Konkin recalled that they put together what cash the family had, which was just enough to pay for John's trip to Ottawa. Fred watched, big-eyed, as his father stuffed the bills in his money belt. He still thinks there was ten thousand dollars on the kitchen table that day. His uncle and aunt scoffed at the figure.

"We didn't have anything like that kind of money," Bill said flatly. "I think my dad, Alex E., put in the most. He might have borrowed it from the bank and put up his farm as collateral. He had two quarter sections then. Anyway, that came later. We didn't send the bail money until John wrote us from Ottawa. When he left Blaine Lake he had a few hundred dollars, no more."

John placed a call to J.P. Erichsen-Brown, the Ottawa lawyer Diefenbaker had suggested. Erichsen-Brown accepted the case and the two men arranged to meet as soon as John arrived in Ottawa. Meanwhile, Erichsen-Brown would contact Emma in the Ottawa jail.

Erichsen-Brown had the bearing of a guardsman and an austere expression to match. He may have been an excellent choice as Emma's legal representative, but he had no courtroom experience.

Roydon A. Hughes, then and now one of the best-regarded lawyers in Ottawa, defended Ned Mazerall and Matt Nightingale. Hughes observed during an interview in his Ottawa office in April, 1983, that he had never met Erichsen-Brown, either in criminal or civil court. Fernande Coulson, with almost half a century of legal experience behind her, would say only, "He was not a well-known man."

When the Royal Commission released the names of the first four traitors, it was not immediately clear that one of them was from the prairies. The Canadian Press story of Emma's appearance on 4 March before Magistrate Strike identifies her only as "an Ottawa civil servant." It was two days before the Saskatoon *Star Phoenix* discovered that one of the central figures in a worldwide news story was a Doukhobor from Blaine Lake. A reporter made inquiries about her in Langham, where Emma and Bill Woikin had lived for five years, and met the members of the family who spelled the name "Voykin." News reports from coast to coast called her Emma Woikin, but in Saskatoon, in the *Star Phoenix*, her last name was always spelled "Voykin."

The *Phoenix* skimmed the highlights of her life: the death of her mother when she was in her teens, her marriage at sixteen, the death of her only child, the suicide of her husband which, the paper said, was the result of a "clot on his brain" that produced unendurable pain. The reporter noted that Bill "Voykin" had left a note saying he was sorry.

The picture accompanying the story was one taken in Saskatoon two years earlier in a photography studio. It shows Emma with a demure smile, her short hair in a tight new permanent. She is wearing a dark dress with a lace collar.

As Mackenzie King had predicted dolefully in his diary, the Opposition was not kind to abridgements of civil rights. M.J. Coldwell, leader of the CCF in the House of Commons, prefaced his remarks with a declaration of disgust for "treachery or the betrayal of confidential information vital to our country's welfare," but then denounced the government's methods. "The war was fought to destroy states which made such police activities a general practice," Coldwell said. "To say that it was necessary to resort to totalitarian methods in order to secure evidence is no valid excuse for abrogating the elementary principles of Canadian justice."

After a week in the Ottawa Jail, Emma was brought before Magistrate Strike a second time, on Monday, 11 March, 1946. She was represented by Erichsen-Brown.

"I have been retained by her family in the west," the lawyer explained to Magistrate Strike. "The distance makes it difficult to discuss the defence with them. I would like a remand without a plea or election."

He was asking Strike to disregard what happened at Emma's first appearance in his court.

When the clerk called her name Emma stepped forward. Ross Harkness wrote in the *Toronto Star* that she stood timidly, with her hands clasped in front of her and her eyes downcast, as Erichsen-Brown asked Strike to withdraw her plea of guilty. His client did not have "complete comprehension" of all that was involved in the charges, he explained.

Strike listened, drumming his fingers, and nodded. He said he had planned to permit Emma Woikin to change her plea.

Judge Robert Hutton, Senior Judge of the Criminal Division of the Ottawa Provincial Courts and a life-long friend of Strike's, said that this would be typical of the man. Strike would have been unhappy to accept a plea of guilty from someone without a lawyer, Judge Hutton thought.

Harkness wrote that Emma was crying as she took her seat "on the hard worn bench in the Victorian courtroom."

Crown Attorney Lee Kelley told Emma's lawyer that he was not in a position to discuss bail. There would be more charges laid against Emma Woikin, he said, probably on the following day.

The four detainees went before Magistrate Strike again on 12 March to learn that the Crown had heaped more charges on all of them. The new charges resembled the old ones and referred to the same offences. Lunan faced five more charges, Mazerall three more, Willsher two more, and Woikin four more.

The new charges against Emma were: that she made confidential notes useful to the Russians; that she communicated confidential documents to unauthorized persons; that she used information for the benefit of the Russians; and that she retained confidential notes in her control, which should not have been retained.

Kelley informed the magistrate that he was proceeding by way of indictment on all twenty-two charges, each of which carried the penalty of a maximum of seven years and a fine of two thousand dollars. He opposed releasing any of the prisoners before the trial. "There is some doubt as to the safety of these people if they are released on bail," he declared. "There is just a vague possibility that these people, through no fault of their own, would be unable to appear for trial if they are released." He plainly meant that the Russians would kill them to keep them from testifying.

The ominous suggestion of assassination and the bewildering number of new charges left an impression — quickly seized by the press — that the four defendants were extremely dangerous people and that the crimes of which they were accused were volatile.

Magistrate Strike, however, was not impressed by the mysterious warning or the new charges. "No court should refuse bail as a matter of punishment," he told Kelley curtly. He announced he would allow bail for each defendant.

Ned Mazerall, through his lawyer, Roydon Hughes, then pleaded innocent and elected trial by judge and jury. Rowell Laishley, a young lawyer in Hughes's firm who had been retained by Kathleen Willsher, also entered a plea of innocence and asked for a jury trial. Lunan and Woikin remained silent.

Harkness wrote a fine description of that day in Magistrate Strike's court. In 1946, newspapers printed many editions in one day; stories of news events appeared only hours after they occurred. Reporters worked big assignments in teams, taking what was called "running copy" in their notebooks in relays. While one reporter stayed at the scene, the other telephoned notes to a rewrite editor in the newsroom. Journalists had to take down information quickly; they needed an eye for detail, and some skill at on-the-spot oral composition.

Harkness wrote in the noon edition of the *Toronto Star* that day:

The women were ushered in at 9:55 and sat down quietly in a corner of the court. They were dressed almost identically in Hudson seal coats, silk stockings and short rubber boots. Miss Willsher wore a small fur hat. Mrs. Woikin was bare-headed. Neither wore any make-up. They strolled into court like a couple of spectators, the shepherding constable about six feet behind them. Mrs. Woikin looked around and then sat down by the door.

There were no visitors for Miss Willsher or Mrs. Woikin during the adjournment, but Woikin, whose parents live in western Canada, exchanged signals of recognition with friends among the spectators.

John Konkin arrived in Ottawa later that day. There is evidence to indicate he stayed with Doukhobor friends, but their name has been lost. The coat Emma was wearing in the courtroom that day must have been borrowed from this friend because she didn't possess such a luxury. The same generous friend not only accommodated John Konkin and Emma Woikin over the following three weeks but also loaned them $1,000 of the bail money. On his arrival, John consulted Erichsen-Brown in the handsome Central Chambers Building at 46 Elgin Street, where the lawyer had his office.

On 14 March, a Thursday, Magistrate Strike was ready to set bail. Bail for Lunan, consistently described as "a master spy," was $6,000. Ned Mazerall was freed on bail of $2,500. Bail for the women was $1,500. John Konkin borrowed enough to pay.

Emma was photographed with her brother leaving the jail, small and sad-faced, some books tucked under her arm. They stood for a moment in the sunshine of a spring-like day. Reporters surrounded Emma and asked a good warm-up question, "How do you feel?"

She replied sensibly, "As anybody would feel."

Photographers asked them to pose together. They suggested that John put his arm around her and John, embarrassed, obliged. The photographer asked them both to smile for the camera. John did; Emma did not.

What were their plans?

"We're going to get a good meal," John answered for both. "She hasn't had any oranges in a month. She wants an orange."

A reporter tried to get a response from Emma. He asked, "Were you scared when you were arrested."

"No," she told him. "I was startled but I wasn't scared."

John Konkin volunteered an observation. He didn't want to say too much in front of his sister, he said, but conditions in the jail were "pretty bad."

They were crossing the jailyard as they spoke. Emma asked her brother where they were going. John said he didn't really know. "Let's go anywhere," Emma suggested desperately. "Let's go see . . ."

Another reporter breathlessly joined the moving group and asked, "How do you feel?"

Emma replied shakily, "If I had another pair of strong feet to stand on, I would feel perfectly fine."

With that, the press let them go, walking down Elgin Street on a lovely day.

Willsher and Mazerall posted bail the same day and were released. Lunan took a day more. Ross Harkness, studying the charges against Kathleen Willsher, wrote that they were "less serious than . . . shopbreaking . . . . The truth is, she is charged with a technical breach of the Official Secrets Act." He observed that the seven charges laid by the Crown against Willsher were part of a strategy to impress the judge with her guilt. The same analysis could have been applied to Emma Woikin and Ned Mazerall.

As the *Montreal Star* noted on 16 March, the "spies" were far from glamorous:

The Ottawa espionage trials are proving one thing. Average citizens whose friends thought them quiet and unassuming suddenly can be catapulted to notoriety, their names on every tongue, their insignificant lives questioned and ripped apart, their acts and words used to condemn them.

Take the case of the four people who were first identified by the government. They are not spectacular. They are ordinary wage-earners. But they have been accused of selling their country's secrets to another power.

The day after the four detainees were released on bail, the Royal Commission on Espionage was ready with another interim report. The second report named Dr. Raymond Boyer, assistant professor of chemistry at McGill, whose contribution to war-time research had been significant; Harold Gerson, who worked in a crown company that produced chemicals and explosives; Dr. David Shugar, a radar specialist with the Royal Canadian Navy's submarine-detection research; and Squadron Leader Matt Nightingale, a telephone expert.

Once more Kellock and Taschereau discussed the people as though they had been already convicted. Of Boyer, for instance, the report says:

His name, and the fact that he had disclosed information with regard to [a] secret project appear in documents in the Russian Embassy produced before us by witness Gouzenko. We have now heard Dr. Boyer and he has told us that, commencing in 1943 and continuing into 1944, he gave for transmission to the

Soviet Union full information with regard to his work which he himself admits was secret . . .

Although the two Supreme Court judges were confident that he would plead guilty, Boyer pleaded innocent and elected trial by jury. His jury could not agree on a decision, and the judge sentenced Boyer to two years in prison, commenting that he was being lenient because of Boyer's excellent war record.

Of Gerson, Kellock and Taschereau wrote:

"Gray" is the cover name used by the embassy for Gerson. The material Gerson supplied [to the embassy] was not . . . limited to photos. Gouzenko also produced a document from the embassy in the handwriting of Gerson, as he admits to be a fact, which is a copy of part of a report dealing with the testing of certain projectiles in England by the United Kingdom authorities . . .

Gerson was sentenced by a jury to five years in prison.

The two judges said of Matt Nightingale that they were "unable to accept" his association with Vassili Rogov of the Soviet Embassy, although Nightingale insisted he was innocent. "If he did not in fact give the USSR secret and confidential information, he may very well have conspired to furnish such information," the judges wrote. On 7 November, 1946, Nightingale was acquitted in a jury trial. His lawyer, Roydon Hughes, said, "Nightingale was the most satisfying case I ever had. He was just a big farm boy from a Quebec farm. He was married to a girl with great ambitions to become a socialite and because of her took part in meetings with friends of Russia. He was at those meetings all right, but he didn't tell anyone anything. I had no doubt that he would be acquitted. He was a very refreshing man."

The Royal Commission report on David Shugar stated:

Shugar denies having given, or having agreed to give, any secret information but has no explanation for the existence in the documents [supplied by Gouzenko] of the references to himself. We are not impressed by the demeanor of Shugar, or by his denials, which we do not accept.

In our view we think he knows more than he was prepared to

disclose. Therefore there would seem to be no answer on the evidence before us to a charge of conspiring to communicate secret information to an agent of the USSR.

Shugar was acquitted of the charges against him on 7 December, 1946.

Stung by criticism that they were acting as a Star Chamber, the members of the Royal Commission defended themselves in their second interim report:

In cases of this nature, where the evidence has revealed the existence of an organization constituting at least a threat to the safety and interests of the state, as evidenced by the fact that some witnesses holding strategic positions have made the significant statement under oath that they had a loyalty which took priority over the loyalty owed by them to their country and for that reason acted as they did, and would unquestionably have continued so to act had they not been detected, we are of the opinion that should these persons be allowed communications with outsiders or between themselves until their activities have been fully investigated, some of the basic purposes of this inquiry would be entirely defeated.

The Commission's second report coincided with a sensational development in the spy cases, a development that almost drove Boyer, Gerson, Shugar and Nightingale from the front pages: Fred Rose, Labor-Progressive Member of Parliament for Montreal-Cartier, had been arrested. He was picked up by the RCMP, who went to his Ottawa apartment on the evening of the first day of a new sitting of the House of Commons. Prime Minister King marvelled at Rose's cool in the House: he looked relaxed and confident though it was no secret that Gouzenko had named Rose and that his arrest was imminent. Newspaper reporters were waiting outside his home to see the arrest.

The next day, 15 March, 1946, John Bracken, former premier of Manitoba and leader of the Progressive Conservative Party, rose in the House of Commons and for two hours gave what King described in his diary a "tiresome" speech about civil rights.

In reply, King asserted that curtailing the liberty of the detainees was necessary because the safety of the state was in peril. "The matters with which the inquiry was concerned appeared to us to be of so serious a nature from the national standpoint that we believed the course advised [by the Commission] should be pursued in the exceptional circumstances existing."

King promised the House a full statement on the matter on Monday of the following week. He ordered that copies of the Royal Commission's reports be printed, twenty-five hundred in English and one thousand in French; they were distributed to members of parliament and other interested persons.

"I would ask the honourable members to remember reading these reports that they have been prepared by two justices of the Supreme Court of Canada," King declared. He added that the judges were "gentlemen who, above all, would be anxious to maintain in every possible way the full freedom and liberty of individuals in our country."

Only a few days earlier, one of those gentlemen judges concerned for freedom and liberty of individuals had shaken his fist in the face of David Shugar, a stubborn witness, and shouted, "I'll punish you."

The day of Bracken's speech in the House of Commons, John Konkin wrote his wife to ask that money be sent to cover the loan for Emma's bail. Thirty-seven years later, on a sharp May morning in 1983, John's son Fred embarked on a search for that letter. He borrowed a Honda with four-wheel drive and bounced it across newly cultivated fields southeast of the village of Blaine Lake, on what had been Konkin land and now belonged to his cousin Agatha and her husband Bill Kardash.

Wet furrows the colour of dark chocolate combed the rolling land and parted gracefully around abandoned buildings and clumps of bush. Brume grass tossed in the hard, stinging wind, which that night brought six inches of snow to that part of Saskatchewan.

Fred Konkin parked in the lee of a collapsed shack, silvered by the weather, which he said had been his mother's summer kitchen, the only building still standing where there once had been a house, a barn and some sheds. Head down against the wind, he plunged through a gaping space where the door had been, rummaged around inside for a few minutes and emerged grinning with some torn pieces of paper.

"The cows got in and most of the stuff is trampled," he said, slamming the car door, "but I found this."

He held a page of a letter and two envelopes, both empty. One was post-marked Ottawa, 18 March, 1946, and was addressed to Mrs. John A. Konkin, Box 153, Blaine Lake, Saskatchewan. The other, which bore the same address and a seven-cent airmail stamp, was dated 12 April. The partially torn page was in the first envelope, Fred explained. The letter is in his father's handwriting:

I am well and hope you are the same. Hoping to here [sic] from you soon on account of your condition [this is a reference to Lena's rheumatism] and on account of bail. We are well and well respected by the people of Ottawa. In side of another week we will be known to every child of the city. I am sending you the clipping and you people send me $1,000.00 for her bail. So this is all I will [torn] you late this [torn] is to all of Konkin.

The clipping, which Fred could not find in the debris in the summer house, might have been the picture of John posed with Emma when they left the jail. It appeared on front pages across Canada.

The Royal Commission had completed forty-four sittings since its opening hearing in Montebello. After a month of hard work, five and a half days a week, forty-eight witnesses had been heard, most of them associates and employers of the detainees; there were still five anonymous people confined in the barracks. The five had been identified by the RCMP as the most stubborn of the detainees. Isolation had not weakened them; if anything, they were growing angrier with each passing day.

Allowed a half-hour visit from their wives, they learned for the first time that eight who testified before the Royal Commission without lawyers had subsequently been denounced by the Commission and arrested. Taschereau and Kellock no longer faced meek witnesses whom they could bully. The last five in the barracks were fire-breathers.

A typical exchange took place when Eric Adams was summoned by the Commission and asked to take the oath:

ADAMS: Does this mean I have to answer questions without a legal counsel?

TASCHEREAU: We will let you know, we will give you the necessary information about that, Mr. Adams.

ADAMS: Well, I will not answer a question until I have legal counsel then . . .

KELLOCK: Under the statute, the Inquiries Act, you are under obligation as a witness here to answer questions, just as you would be if you were in court.

ADAMS: But in court I have counsel and here I have not.

Adams was acquitted in a jury trial on 22 October, 1946.

When Scott Benning appeared before the Commission, he also refused to take the oath.

KELLOCK: What is troubling you?

BENNING: Well, I think it should be rather obvious. Five weeks plus two days and the abrogation of all civil rights.

KELLOCK: We are not going to discuss anything of that kind.

Benning subsequently was freed.

Israel Halperin, recalled by the Commission for a second visit, came with a lawyer:

HALPERIN: I was shown a couple of documents but given no opportunity to speak about them, and then the questions proceeded to be of the same type of questions which did not particularly seek information but were of a prosecutional type, which tried to get me by trickery to commit myself . . .

KELLOCK: You can stop right now. Do not use that kind of language here. I will not put up with it, personally.

HALPERIN: I am sorry. I withdraw those words.

KELLOCK: All right. You are here as a witness, you have counsel here. You will listen to the questions. If your counsel thinks any question is improper, he will object and we will rule on it.

HALPERIN: In that case I will have to ask my counsel to

withdraw and stand on my own because I refuse to go on
with this kind of thing. . . . Am I here by compulsion?
TASCHEREAU: You are not here by compulsion.
HALPERIN: Then I'll walk out of the room.
TASCHEREAU: No, you will stay here.
HALPERIN: Unless I am held by compulsion, I will leave
the room [witness got up and went to the door].
TASCHEREAU: No, you are not leaving the room.

Halperin returned to his seat but said he would not open his
mouth again, and he didn't. He was charged and tried. On 24
March, 1947, Israel Halperin was acquitted of all charges
against him.

Phyllis Poland, Fred Poland's wife, filed an application to
have her husband released on the ancient and venerable
grounds of *habeas corpus.* Her furious husband was firing off
special-delivery letters to Prime Minister King and Justice
Minister St. Laurent. In one, dated 12 March, 1946, he complained hotly that he had been held for four weeks "without
any charge being laid against me and without being allowed to
consult counsel."

He went on, "I have been refused access to the Order in
Council under which I was arrested and even the terms of
reference of the Royal Commission, which I am told has been
appointed to investigate a 'plot,' the details of which have been
withheld from me. I am not allowed to see any newspapers.
Someone even cut out of the *New Yorker* magazine what was
apparently a reference to the case.

"This is on a par with the search of my apartment during
which the police seized such books as *The Basic Writings of
Sigmund Freud* and a thesis my wife was preparing for her
course at McGill University . . .

"Sir, I want my freedom or a speedy, fair trial . . . . I have seen
injustice, and it works."

On 16 January, 1947, Fred Poland was acquitted of all
charges against him.

The final tally demonstrated that the technique of detention
and isolation served its purpose best with the most vulnerable
of the accused, the first four, Woikin, Lunan, Mazerall and
Willsher. All four went to prison. Of the next four, two were

acquitted; three were acquitted of the final five. Detainees' score: eight guilty, five innocent.

The Civil Rights Union of Toronto noted during the summer of 1946, "The first groups interrogated got off the worst," and added, "It seems as if the purpose of the Commission had been to intimidate those whom it was examining."

The union charged that Mounties "bluffed, cajoled and frightened [the detainees] into making statements . . . It has been stated in court that extreme political and racial bias was shown by the examining officers of the special branch of the RCMP in the espionage cases."

Mackenzie King made a reference to racism in one of his diary entries. On 21 March, 1946, he was visited by two clergymen. He noted that they discussed the prevalence of Jewish people in the Communist party. "It is a rather extraordinary thing," King observed, "that most of those caught in this present net are Jews or have Jewish wives, or are of Jewish descent." He added sanctimoniously that he and the clergymen agreed there are also "many fine Jews."

"The excuse given for ignoring the legal rights of suspects is that it was for the good of Canada because it made conviction more certain," commented the *Toronto Star* in an editorial on 19 March, 1946. "That, of course, is exactly what totalitarian governments have said in attempted justifications of their own gross disregard of civil liberties."

The Honourable C.G. Power, known as "Chubby," popular war-time minister of defence for air, observed that the Order in Council was "a revocation of the Magna Carta after 731 years of existence." He added:

If this is to be the funeral of Liberalism, I do not wish to be even an honorary pallbearer . . . Some of these very people who applaud today what is going on might find that they cheered today but wept tomorrow . . . I freely admit in the popular mind the government is doing the right thing. I do not controvert or deny that. I only regret.

As Power said, most Canadians supported the measures the government had used against the detainees.

A Gallup poll was taken in 1946 to measure the public's response to the confinement of the thirteen detainees under the

War Measures Act. Eighty-four percent of Canadians favoured the government's action. This was the single most approved government action to that date, a record not exceeded until October, 1970, the next time the War Measures Act was used, when almost five hundred Canadians went to jail without being charged. That time eighty-seven percent of the public applauded.

In the summer of 1946, Arthur W. Roebuck, a distinguished Toronto lawyer who ended his stellar career in the senate, told the *Toronto Star* his opinion of the Royal Commission. "Notwithstanding they were eminent jurists, they walked over the civil rights of accused persons as no experienced police officer would dream of doing, and they did things which no good crown attorney would for one moment permit. They became part of the proceedings which, if brought before them on the bench under normal circumstances, I am confident they would soundly denounce."

David Shugar wrote from the barracks to Louis St. Laurent, minister of justice, to complain about the Royal Commission. He said, "I have been completely stripped of all my rights before the law." He demanded to be permitted to consult a lawyer. St. Laurent replied that it was "not proper" for him to intervene.

In desperation, Shugar turned to John Diefenbaker, who was noted as a fiery protector of civil liberties. He told Diefenbaker that the RCMP officer who interrogated him had called him a spy. When Shugar indignantly denied it, saying the charge was ridiculous, the officer responded, "If you think this is ridiculous, I can assure you it is not. I am a very busy man. If you think this is ridiculous you go back to your quarters and wait until you change your mind."

But the crown attorney at Shugar's trial agreed there was no case against him. The attorney declared, "I concede what my friend [Shugar's lawyer, A.W. Beament] has said, namely that there is no evidence to show that Dr. Shugar ever gave information improperly to anyone."

Chapter Ten

Mackenzie King made his eagerly awaited speech about espionage on 19 March, 1946, after the six o'clock dinner break in the House of Commons. He wrote in his diary that he was so tired he couldn't raise his voice; his body felt heavy and his mind was clouded. The purpose of the speech, he noted, was "to prepare the ground for the future by separating any knowledge of this business from Stalin and expressing a certain confidence in him . . . an opposite course, one of antagonism and fight, would very soon provoke an appalling situation."

Guided by his concern that to expose the spying would create a hostile environment in which World War Three might erupt, King opened his speech that evening by saying:

I intend to devote my time for the remainder of my life in trying in every possible way to see that the greatest amount of friendship and harmony and goodwill is promoted between all peoples and between the Russian people and Canada in particular.

One of his first impulses when Gouzenko defected, King said, was to visit Stalin and clear the air. It was his conviction that the spying had taken place without Stalin's knowledge, he declared, and that Stalin "would not countenance action of this kind on the part of his country. I believe when these facts are known to him we shall find that a change will come that will make a vast difference indeed."

King then turned to the prickly matter of the suspension of civil rights. He explained why he concluded that a Royal Commission was advisable, giving credit to E.K. Williams of Winnipeg for the idea. He spoke of Gouzenko in glowing terms; his voice became sorrowful when he turned to the Canadians whose espionage activities had been revealed.

King delivered the ninety-minute speech without notes and with great sincerity. When he finished, the packed galleries exploded in wild applause.

Emma Woikin again appeared before Magistrate Strike on 20 March, 1946. In Blaine Lake, her sister-in-law, Lena Konkin, gave her first and only press interview to someone from the *Free Press Weekly Prairie Farmer*. She was quoted as saying that Emma was "a good girl, a very good girl . . . untaught . . . what she knew she picked up herself . . . she just knew enough to get by."

Ross Harkness of the *Toronto Star* was outside the courthouse on 20 March when Emma appeared.

All dressed up in her Easter best, sunny blue from tip to toe, with a pert little bonnet perched on her blonde crown, Mrs. Woikin was as usual the most at ease of the accused. Smiling cheerily, she entered the courtroom with her brother from Blaine Lake, Saskatchewan, and sat beside a worried-looking little Miss Willsher. Her cheery chatter failed to brighten her friend, and Miss Willsher spent most of the time talking in a low voice with Rev. H.S. Clugston, United Church chaplain of the county jail.

Mrs. Woikin elected in a low voice as each of the six charges was read to her and left the courtroom after her remand to March 28 with every evidence of carefree self-possession.

One of the charges against Mrs. Woikin, who is of Russian-Doukhobor ancestry, is that she conspired with Mrs. Sokolov, wife of the Soviet commercial attaché, with whom she was acquainted.

At the reading of the charges, Emma's lawyer, Erichsen-Brown, asked for a copy of Emma's testimony before the Royal Commission. This testimony would be used by the Crown in the case against Emma, and he needed access to it to prepare his defence.

Lee Kelley, the crown prosecutor, snapped, "I suggest you apply to the Royal Commission counsel."

Erichsen-Brown appealed to Magistrate Strike. "Your worship," he said patiently, "I have been in contact with the Commission counsel. I have given the usual oath of secrecy and I think have convinced them that I am a person to be trusted, but have received no assurance that the evidence will be available to the defence."

Throughout the espionage trials, the Royal Commission was unwilling to allow defence attorneys to see the transcripts that would be used against their clients. The attorneys' protests became part of the press coverage of preliminary trials. The public could only conclude that the material passed to the Russians by the accused was of such earth-shaking magnitude that it was too sensitive for even the defense lawyers to see.

Jimmy Nichol of the *Toronto Star*, who covered the preliminary trial in Montreal of Fred Rose and Raymond Boyer, observed, "Perhaps never before in Canadian history has the fate of an accused person been determined on secret testimony."

On 20 March, newspapers published photographs of Emma Woikin leaving the courthouse after another appearance before Magistrate Strike. Her lawyer, Erichsen-Brown, is on her right, an austere, gaunt, well-tailored man wearing rimless glasses. On her left is her brother John, clad in a dark three-piece suit, a watch-chain visible across the solid girth of the vest, his shoes protected from Ottawa's slush by rubbers, and a wide-brimmed fedora in his hand. The newspapers, seeing something bucolic in his attire, described his hat as a stetson.

It became increasingly difficult for even avid followers of the trials to keep track of what was going on. There were nine people involved so far, counting Fred Rose, and each was at a different stage — preliminary hearing, hearing to add more charges, hearing to set bail, or remand. Some accused were changing lawyers and changing their minds about what kind of trial they wanted. The early enthusiasm for juries had subsided because the press was describing the accused as "spies," "traitors" and "secret agents," rendering the likelihood of finding impartial jurors difficult.

Magistrate Strike was hard put to deal with this torrent of activity on top of his normal court load. There were logistic problems, as well: for example, the shorthand reporters, Buskard and Featherston, had to be in court to identify the Royal Commission transcripts used in evidence as the true ones, but both Buskard and Featherston were required also to be in the House of Commons to report for Hansard. The availability of Buskard, in particular, became one of the determining factors when lawyers and the judge conferred about remands.

Lunan had recovered his poise and emerged as the angriest of the nine. He complained in court of the "psychological torture" to which he had been submitted in the RCMP barracks. He mentioned in particular the bright lights that burned all night, making sleep difficult. His lawyer, H.L. Cartwright of Kingston, questioned him about the conditions he faced as a detainee. Cartwright wanted to cast doubt on the admissability of testimony before the Royal Commission.

CARTWRIGHT: How long was it before you were taken before the Commission?

LUNAN: Under the circumstances, I lost track of time and date, but I think it was about the second week . . . .

CARTWRIGHT: What was this interrogation [by Inspector Harvison of the RCMP]?

LUNAN: The same as before the Royal Commission.

CARTWRIGHT: Did Inspector Harvison give you any warning?

LUNAN: No.

CARTWRIGHT: Did they let you obtain counsel?

LUNAN: No.

CARTWRIGHT: Did you ask for any?

LUNAN: Yes.

KELLEY: We are not submitting any evidence taken at the police barracks at Rockcliffe.

STRIKE: No, but Mr. Cartwright is leading up to the evidence taken before the Commission.

KELLEY: Mr. Cartwright is drawing a mighty long bow.

CARTWRIGHT: Oh, is it drawing a mighty long bow to refer to the fact that a man is interrogated half a dozen times and given no warning that he does not need to answer questions?

LUNAN: When I asked for counsel, Inspector Harvison said the proceedings were extraordinary but I could do nothing about it.

CARTWRIGHT: Was suicide ever mentioned?

LUNAN: Yes . . . . One guard in particular frequently mentioned suicide attempts by others detained in the barracks, but all these rumors proved completely false.

M.J. Coldwell, the leader of the CCF party, made a furious speech in the House of Commons protesting the all-night lights. Commissioner S.T. Wood of the RCMP denied that there had been any "third degree." He issued a statement that said the lights in the barracks were of "ordinary" wattage and that special bulbs had not been inserted. In any case, he added, a few days after the detainees complained, the overhead lights were replaced with soft reading lights.

John Diefenbaker declared that the handling of the detainees made it clear that Canada needed "a bill of rights." He appealed to Canadians to uphold the principle of a fair trial over what he called "administrative lawlessness."

He added sternly, "I do not believe the minds of liberty-loving Canadians, however much they hate Communism, have become so apathetic during six years of domination by the state that they are not interested in civil liberties." Diefenbaker described approvingly the manner in which Britain proceeded against Alan Nunn May, the physicist who gave the Soviet Embassy a sample of U-235 and secrets of the atomic bomb. He contrasted May's treatment with the treatment of the thirteen detainees. May had been arrested in London the day the Royal Commission issued its first sensational report in Ottawa.

Diefenbaker observed that May "was proceeded against after he appeared in court fully represented by counsel," and asked, "Why was not that procedure adopted here?"

The prairie lawyer had more information to embarrass the government. While the detainees were sitting in the RCMP barracks because they allegedly gave military information to Zabotin, the Canadian army had invited Zabotin's replacement, Major Peter Domishev, to witness military manoeuvres in the Arctic to demonstrate its readiness to fight a polar war.

The information came to Diefenbaker in a letter from George Drew, premier of Ontario. Drew added, "Either the whole [Gouzenko] investigation which started months ago was not taken seriously — and that I cannot believe — or the presence of Russian observers even if they were only at the beginning of the expedition is stupidity beyond belief."

On 27 March, 1946, Emma Woikin was back before Magistrate Strike with her brother, who applied to have responsibility for the entire bail bond shifted to him; the money had arrived from Blaine Lake.

On 29 March the temperature soared to eighty degrees and Ottawa's streets were thronged with delighted residents freed from the bondage of mufflers and boots. The Royal Commission released its third interim report, naming Eric Adams, Fred Poland, Israel Halperin, Durnford Smith and Scott Benning. Like the other detainees, they were released from the barracks, arrested on the doorstep and driven to the county jail to appear before Magistrate Strike.

Kellock and Taschereau, unrepentent despite criticism, continued to assert that all the suspects were guilty. Of Smith, for example, the judges wrote:

Smith, as the evidence shows, was one of a group of agents reporting through Lunan to Lieut.-Col. Rogov . . . Smith did not admit participation, but a great deal of the evidence he would not deny . . ."

Prime Minister King was anxious to revoke the Order in Council, passed secretly on 6 October, 1945, that had activated the War Measures Act. He saw no reason the order should not be revoked at once, since everyone in the barracks had been arrested, but St. Laurent advised caution. He said there was a forged passport to be investigated, and reminded King that Sam Carr was still in hiding. The RCMP wanted the powers continued.

King protested that the investigation could be completed without the powers of the War Measures Act. St. Laurent offered to consult with the Royal Commission, which informed him that the extraordinary powers of the act no longer were needed. With the consent of the judges King announced in the House on 31 March, 1946, that the Order in Council was revoked.

"It is an immense relief to have that Order in Council cancelled," he noted in his diary that night. "I feel the Commissioners have thought more of themselves and doing a fine bit and of the report they are making than of the position in which they have placed the government and our party. It will always be held against us and the Liberal party that we sanctioned anything that meant so much in the way of depredation of liberty for a number of people."

He observed that public opinion was beginning to be critical of the government's actions. The evidence of wrong-doing was not convincing editorial writers. King had to agree that the detainees didn't appear very dangerous. He wrote, "Some will be freed altogether or get trifling sentences."

After King spoke in the House about the War Measures Act, John Diefenbaker asked how Emma Woikin happened to get a position in the civil service. King replied that she was hired as a grade-one civil servant after a "normal investigation" of her past, and that she came of "a good family" and had a satisfactory work record. What happened was lamentable, he added, but the department of external affairs could not be held responsible.

The government, considerably embarrassed, was anxious for results and was pressing its lawyers to bring the first four people — the most likely to be convicted — to trial quickly. The press had dubbed Lunan, one of the four, a "master spy." A picture of him in the *Globe & Mail* on 2 April, 1946, was labelled "Spy cell head."

"They took the view that Lunan was a more hardened individual, for some strange reason," Mazerall commented recently. "I don't see how he could have been because he wouldn't have given way so early in the barracks if he had been an experienced person."

Roydon Hughes, Mazerall's lawyer, thought Mazerall had a good point. He observed that Lunan "sang and sang and sang."

The lawyers were jockeying to avoid being the first into court, since none of them had any experience with defending actions brought under the Official Secrets Act and all were loath to undertake the burden of pathfinding. Both women, however, were determined to plead guilty. Hughes had the impression, when he recalled that period of his career, that his legal partner, Rowell Laishley, who was Kathleen Willsher's counsel, had some assurance that Willsher would get a sentence of only six months if she pleaded guilty. As Hughes remembered it, Laishley was "inveigled" by the Crown during a time when Hughes, a senior lawyer, was absent on vacation.

"When I got back I asked Laishley why the hell he was such a sacrificial lamb," Hughes related in an interview in the spring of 1983 in his office. "I said she was sure to get a stiff sentence from any judge, given the mood of the times."

Laishley denied it. Questioned in November, 1983, he said he wasn't a green young lawyer at the time. He was thirty-three, newly discharged from the artillery with the rank of major, and had experience in criminal-court work. "There was no plea bargaining in those days," he stated firmly. "Willsher insisted on pleading guilty."

A number of people believe, however, that Emma Woikin and Kathleen Willsher were given reason to believe that their sentences would be light in return for a guilty plea, a confidence that might explain the perky mood that marked Emma's later courtroom appearances.

Emma appeared before Magistrate Strike on 4 April for her preliminary hearing. Lee Kelley filed the Crown's exhibits: the four telegrams and the oath of secrecy she had signed, the oath of office, and attendance sheets showing her working hours. Kelley notified Strike that the Crown was dropping four of the six charges; the first two charges were enough. He asked that evidence about the four telegrams be given *in camera* because of their sensitive nature. Erichsen-Brown had no choice but to agree.

He advised the judge that Emma wanted a speedy trial. She didn't wish to wait until the fall assizes because her brother was anxious to return to his farm. Erichsen-Brown observed that Emma Woikin's case was "rather different" from the others, giving the impression that he knew Magistrate Strike would agree that it didn't amount to much.

When the cabinet met on 8 April, 1946, there were three items on the agenda. One was labelled "World Food Situation" and concerned shipments of Canadian wheat to the United Nations relief organization. Another was a discussion of a subsidy to permit the Canadian National Railway to build an ocean-going freighter. The third addressed the problems of the government's employees who were still on the payroll despite being suspected of espionage.

It was decided unanimously that they would all be suspended, and the suspensions would be retroactive to the date they were named by the Royal Commission as conspirators.

On 10 April, a week after it was requested, Emma got her trial. She was brought to the Carleton County Court House to face Judge A. Gordon McDougall and a formidable Crown attorney, John R. Cartwright, KC, of Toronto. (Cartwright, regarded as one of the country's best lawyers, later became chief justice of the Supreme Court of Canada.)

Fernande Coulson, who watched the proceedings from the vantage point of the office where the paperwork for the Crown was done, observed with merry irreverence, "All the lawyers who worked for the government on the Gouzenko trials got fat appointments out of it. They were all Liberals and they all got promoted."

Emma stood steadily in the prisoner's box and pleaded guilty to both charges.

A great deal of effort has gone into a determined search for Emma Woikin's court records in order to have a more authoritative account than newspaper stories of what happened. Nothing is available; possibly, nothing exists. There are files in the National Archives about many of the detainees and the lawyers who represented them, but no files on Emma Woikin. Robert Hutton, senior judge of the Criminal Division, Provincial Court, in Ottawa, located the reference number for a box in the files held by the Ontario attorney-general. A search of this box produced nothing about Emma Woikin.

Perhaps her files have been lost. Government archives were in a primitive state in 1946. Perhaps her files have been distributed, without being indexed, somewhere with session papers in the attorney-general's file. Her files may have been pulled out and sent to Montreal when Emma later was called to testify at the trial of Fred Rose; maybe they were misplaced in Montreal.

The fourth floor of 2 Daley Street, the Ottawa courthouse, is said to be filled with dusty boxes of material that are not indexed, labelled or sorted. The Woikin file may be there. (There was a fire at 2 Daley Street some years ago, though, and some files were burned.)

Catherine Sheppard, an archivist in the Ontario Archives in Toronto who specializes in government documents, examined four file boxes sent from Ottawa for information about Emma Woikin. Some papers were scorched, she noted, but the only material relating to Emma Woikin were copies of two of the charges against her. These were not available for publication without special permission.

Sheppard suggested asking Judge Hutton if Judge McDougall left a case book in which he made notes about the Emma Woikin trial. Hutton replied that judges do keep such notebooks, called "bench books," during a trial, to jot down reminders of testimony and such matters, but that these personal aids usually are destroyed when a case is settled.

"The Woikin case was disposed of so quickly that it's not likely there is much documentation around," Judge Hutton commented.

Sheppard found it curious that an important case like Emma Woikin's, the first one of the thirteen detainees whose case was settled, has not been preserved.

"It's interesting that when we get to that period prior to the 1950s there are many gaps in the records," she mused. "What happened in cities where the courts are very busy, cities like Windsor, Toronto, Hamilton and Ottawa — there used to be applications to the judge for permission to destroy old records to make room for the new."

But it seemed odd to her that permission would have been given to destroy Emma Woikin's files. Unfortunately, the applications to destroy files are themselves lost.

Sheppard telephoned an Ottawa archivist, Graham Pinos, who appeared intrigued by the mystery. He explained that the files he works with are marked "secret" but that if Emma Woikin's folder was among them, perhaps permission to see it could be gained. A later call to Pinos found him even more caught in the treasure hunt. He said he had searched the secret files out of curiosity and found a folder labelled "Emma Woikin." Inside there was nothing but a newspaper clipping, a picture of Emma.

James M. Whalen, an esteemed archivist in the National

Archives, suggested another route, the Attorney General File 4G4 Series C-3 #345: Rex versus Emma Woikin, 24 April, 1946.

Access to this file required a letter of permission from Archie Campbell, deputy attorney-general of Ontario. Permission was secured. A few weeks later, the file was produced in the office of the Government Records Section of the Ontario Archives, under the eyes of the staff.

The room where the material was examined was large but crowded with shoulder-high metal filing cabinets, stacks of cardboard boxes, shelves holding plastic-covered looseleaf binders, and sturdy government-issue desks covered with books and papers. A notice on the bulletin board reminded the staff that the softball season had begun. Across the room was a sepia reproduction of a 1792 map of Upper Canada.

File #345 was labelled "Rex versus Emma Woikin." Inside were a great many papers; not one of them referred to Emma Woikin.

The file was an attorney-general's version of the shoebox in which many people keep their household receipts. It included documents appointing John R. Cartwright to act with Lee Kelley for the Crown in the Ottawa espionage cases, fees to be paid by the federal government. A letter from the deputy minister of justice in Ottawa noted that, on 14 June, 1947, court costs for the espionage trials amounted to $12,283.22. One of the itemized entries was for constables who guarded the accused: they were paid four dollars a day.

Gerson's trial cost the state $2,732.62. The jury for the Adams trial ate twelve dollars worth of meals. Shorthand costs for transcribing a page of testimony were thirty cents, five cents extra for the carbon.

Much correspondence dealt with the need to find a second courtroom to accommodate the extra work. A vacant room was found in the southwest corner of the new Supreme Court building.

But there was nothing about Emma Woikin.

The archivist who received the file back wasn't surprised. He said casually, "It probably was culled before the file was sent here. What you're looking for is gone."

An appeal for information was sent to the Royal Canadian Mounted Police at the suggestion of Chief Superintendent Patrick E.J. Banning, the departmental privacy coordinator, who seemed, on the telephone, an affable and urbane man. Banning gave the impression that the RCMP is anxious to cooperate with historians and is open about documents that had been withheld in the past.

"The security service didn't exist in 1946," he explained. "The material might be in the Criminal Investigative Branch files, in which case it is possible to get it."

Once material has been lodged in the secret-service files, though, the public absolutely is denied access to it.

Banning advised that the request for material should be accompanied by a letter of authority signed by Emma Woikin's husband, together with a copy of her will establishing that her husband is her executor.

This was done on 6 June, 1983. On 13 July, Banning, no longer in the least affable, replied:

Your request has been reviewed in light of the provisions of the recently proclaimed Access to Information and Privacy Acts. As set out in the Privacy Act Regulations, Section 10 (b), access to a deceased individual's personal information may be granted by the executor of the individual's estate, but only for the purpose of administering the estate. The purpose for which you are requesting this information is not in keeping with this provision and therefore, access to any records pertaining to Emma Woikin cannot be granted.

Further to the aforementioned, the material you are requesting is personal information concerning a third party who has been deceased for a period of less than twenty years. For this reason, disclosure cannot be made at this time, regardless of an application under either the Privacy or Access to Information Acts. In addition, such information would be maintained within the Security Service Records Bank. The Governor-in-Council has designated our Security Service Records, described in the Index of Personal Information Banks, as exempt from the access under Section 18 of the Privacy Act. We cannot comply with your request nor can we confirm whether or not such information exists concerning Emma Woikin.

I regret that I am not able to provide you with a more favourable reply. Yours truly, P.E.J. Banning, c/Supt., Departmental Privacy and Access to Information Coordinator.

Informed that the RCMP had refused to divulge information about Emma Woikin — for example, a report on her emotional state in the barracks and the name of the person who interrogated her — retired deputy commissioner of the RCMP William Kelly, a former director of the security and intelligence directorate, commented, "Isn't that stupid. They shouldn't be so arbitrary."

Emma Woikin never saw herself as anything other than guilty. From the beginning she was anxious to get her trial out of the way and serve her sentence. She must have been frantic with concern that her brother, John Konkin, was obliged to stay in Ottawa at a time when other Blaine Lake farmers were preparing their land for seeding.

The charges to which Emma pleaded guilty on 10 April concerned violations of the Official Secrets Act. The maximum penalty — seven years for each charge — could be served concurrently or sequentially, as the judge wished.

Judge McDougall, according to all accounts, was a sympathetic man. "Gordie McDougall was a good judge, not tough at all," said Roydon Hughes, who should know. "He would listen to both sides of the case. He was very hard on the two women but later on his ideas changed a bit. I appeared before him with Arthur Martin in defense of Fred Poland, despite what happened to the women. Poland got off."

Mention of Poland reminded Hughes of something. Poland had refused to talk to the Royal Commission. Williams and Fauteux, the Commission lawyers, approached Hughes and "tried to soft-soap me." They wanted him to recommend to Poland that he should answer questions. Hughes replied, properly, that he would discuss the matter with his client but he would not instruct him to talk. Hughes recalled that Poland was adamant. "I've done nothing and I'm not going to talk to them," he told his lawyer. "They are abusing my civil liberties."

Hughes grinned at the memory, marvelling. "Poland wasn't afraid of the judges. He said he wouldn't talk to them, and he didn't."

All fifteen trials arising from Gouzenko's defection — the thirteen barracks detainees, plus Fred Rose and Alan Nunn May — were in progress. Emma Woikin was the first to be tried. Judge McDougall's sentence for Emma Woikin would set a

precedent. If he imposed the maximum, as perhaps the government hoped, he would leave no room for himself to move in the
cases to follow. If her sentence was very light, he would be
implying the transgressions were all of a trivial nature.

John R. Cartwright, the crown prosecutor, strove to impress
upon McDougall the necessity of making a severe example of
Emma Woikin.

Cartwright produced a single witness, Stanley C. Daley,
assistant chief of the cipher division in external affairs, Emma's
boss. Daley testified, as he had before the Royal Commission,
and identified the exhibits that showed Emma Woikin's
signature on an oath of office and an oath of secrecy.

Erichsen-Brown asked Judge McDougall to read Emma's
testimony at the Royal Commission before he called character
witnesses. McDougall agreed, declared that the trial would
reconvene on 12 April, two days later, and snapped his gavel to
adjourn.

It was late on Friday afternoon, 12 April, before the the trial
of Emma Woikin resumed. The streets of Ottawa had been
packed all that bright cold day to welcome Canada's new
governor-general, a war hero, Viscount Alexander of Tunis,
who arrived at Union Station with his wife and three young
children.

There had been a parade to Parliament Hill with marching
bands, Union Jacks everywhere and a double salute of nine
guns. Paul Martin, secretary of state, gave an address. It wasn't
until the festivities were over that Prime Minister King realized,
to his horror, that not a word of French had been spoken. As he
expected, John Bracken, Leader of the Opposition, pounced on
the omission.

The courtroom was quiet as Emma Woikin slipped into the
prisoner's box. Her gaiety was gone. She seemed shocked and
depressed, her voice a whisper, her expression dazed. Reporters,
crowded at the press table a few feet away, were free to stare;
Emma sat with her head bent. Marjorie Earl, who was there for
the *Toronto Star,* was moved to pity her. "She looked small and
mousey," Earl remembered.

John Konkin was the first character witness. He told the story
of the hardships of his sister's life. She was the baby of the
family, he related, and was married at sixteen. During the
Depression, conditions in Saskatchewan were very bad. She

had a child who died shortly after birth because of malnourishment, (which had become Emma's diagnosis of the stillbirth.) Two years later her husband, who was suffering from a brain tumour and had no money for an operation, committed suicide. For six months after that, Emma was too weak to work. When she regained her strength she went to Marcelin and lived in a convent while attending commercial school.

He added that his sister had always shown an exceptional willingness to help others, despite her own troubles. During the war she was a volunteer with the Canadian Red Cross and she also raised money for the Milk-for-Britain fund.

Erichsen-Brown rounded out the picture of a tragic, unselfish life by drawing from John Konkin some information about the family to show that they were solid people, respected in the community.

John Cartwright had no questions to put, so it was Emma Woikin's turn.

She went through the same grim story, beginning with leaving school at the age of twelve. Her baby died because of lack of food and care, she explained, and her husband's suicide was the result of poverty. He left her an estate of seventy-five cents. Because she was "too weak for farm work," her family chipped in to send her to school in Marcelin, she said, where she was much older than the other pupils.

Erichsen-Brown asked if she tried to continue her education and she answered that she had enrolled in night classes at the Ottawa Technical School.

Her lawyer then raised the delicate matter of her relationship with Major Vsevolod Sokolov. Emma brightened and smiled for the first time.

Did she find him attractive?

"He was a very handsome man," she replied, her face transformed. She had been flattered that he invited her many times to his home. "They were very intelligent people," she added proudly.

She described the gifts she had exchanged with the Sokolovs, a water-colour painting from her, a bottle of perfume from him.

Marjorie Earl found this part of the testimony very touching. "I had seen Sokolov," she related. "He was not of the same calibre of handsomeness as Zabotin but he was a very attractive man. It ran through my mind as she was talking about him that he'd probably seduced her. Someone who looked like that, who was in Ottawa at that time, was ripe for seduction. That was all my imagination, of course. I really don't know if that was the kind of relationship it was or not. It just looked like it on the surface."

She paused and considered. "What the hell would a man like that be doing with a little mouse like Emma Woikin?" she wondered. "Who just happened to be a cipher clerk?"

Emma testified that she had known Sokolov for a year before she gave him any information. Asked why she wanted to become a Soviet citizen, she explained that her knowledge of the Soviet Union was gained entirely from reading and she "wanted the facts."

"Is it true that anything you did in this case came from a desire to assist the Soviet Union and not a desire to hurt Canada?" asked Erichsen-Brown.

"That is true," Emma nodded. "I didn't want to hurt Canada."

"Would you elaborate on your feelings towards the Soviet?" Erichsen-Brown continued.

There was a long silence. "What I was trying to say was that I have a feeling of love for that country," Emma replied slowly. "We may be wrong or we may be right, but there is hope for the poor there."

John Cartwright, in cross examination, opened sharply by asking her why she had betrayed her country.

She had difficulty with the question. At last she mumbled something about having a "great feeling" for Russia.

"Are you sympathetic also to Canada?" Cartwright asked.

She hesitated. "I couldn't exactly say that," she replied honestly.

John Cartwright presented the Crown's argument for imposing a stiff prison sentence. He said "a very serious breach of the law" had been committed. It was true that Mrs. Woikin hadn't acted as a mercenary, he conceded, since "she gave information both before and after money was paid her."

He reminded the judge that there was a war going on when the revisions of the Official Secrets Act were passed in 1939, and that breaches of security were "much more serious" than in peace-time. He didn't want to make a recommendation as to sentence, he said, but he pointedly mentioned that the sentence given to Emma Woikin would set a precedent for other trials.

"What is important in this case, as a deterrent to future offences of this nature," he continued, "is the impression the sentence will make with the public at large."

Erichsen-Brown rose to sum up the defence's argument for a light sentence. Emma Woikin was not part of the network of spies the newspapers had been describing, he told Judge McDougall. She was the only one of the detainees who didn't know any of the others; she never had dealings with any of them.

When her offence was compared to the offences of the others, Erichsen-Brown went on, all of whom were intellectuals closely associated with war-time research, it could be seen that what she did was of a minor nature. He quoted sections of the Official Secrets Act, which he said supported his contention that the two charges against her were redundant, since they stemmed from the same offence. He was surprised, he said, that his learned friend Mr. Cartwright took such a serious view of the charges.

"In the general picture of all these cases," he argued, "this one is small, unimportant, and in some ways trivial."

He also said that Emma Woikin had made a favourable impression on the Royal Commission. "At least a partial reason for her acts," he added significantly, "was that she was flattered by the attention paid her by Major Sokolov, who was what might be termed an attractive, good-looking man."

Emma's lawyer concluded by saying that he thought a fine was all that was indicated in the case.

Judge McDougall studied his notes and began his decision, directing his remarks to Emma:

I have listened very carefully to the excellent address by counsel for the accused, and also to the Crown counsel.

It has been suggested that the charges brought against you are not nearly so serious as some charges that have been brought against other parties. As to that I have no knowledge, I do not know the charges against the other parties, nor do I know what the evidence will be. There is no evidence against you of any communication between yourself and the other parties who are charged.

As to yours not being a serious offence, I cannot agree with your counsel, excellent as his argument has been.

You are a person of some education, you were brought to Ottawa and given a good opportunity. You took an oath of office, and an oath of secrecy, and you violated those oaths in a deliberate manner which shows careful planning.

You were fully aware of what you were doing, which is apparent from the methods in which you conveyed the information and from the fact that the messages which were divulged were marked *secret* and *top secret*.

Moreover you were placed in the supply office of the Department of External Affairs where matters of a very secret nature are discussed and it would be a matter of great danger to the country if these secrets became known to the public. Just what serious consequences might result from the information you took from there might be, I do not know.

I have considered the matter very carefully and I cannot accede to the suggestions of your counsel that a fine would be satisfactory in this case. However, considering all the evidence which has been submitted to me, and all that has been pleaded, I have come to the conclusion that in the interests of justice which has to be served I will sentence you to a term of two years and six months in the Kingston penitentiary on each of the charges, the sentences to run concurrently.

In the Criminal Reports, an annotation to the judgement immediately follows the transcript. A.E. Popple comments that the Emma Woikin case settled a problem the Crown had been facing, namely which of the provisions of the bewildering Official Secrets Act had been violated by the detainees.

Canada's Official Secrets Act is patterned on the British act of 1889; the Canadian version was amended in 1911 and in 1920. In 1939 it was redrafted to smooth out certain ambiguities and contradictions, but no effort was made to alter its nineteenth-century severity. It remains a fearful weapon of great complexity and power which Canadian courts rarely see exercised. The onus is not on the state to bring evidence of guilt, but on the defendant to prove innocence. This is not a negligible difference in a court of law. Under the Official Secrets Act, defendants come into court guilty as charged.

Popple wrote of the Woikin verdict: "It will be noticed in the

Woikin case now decided that the prosecution was under s. 4(1) (a) and 4(1) (b) of the Official Secrets Act, 1939."

John Konkin went sadly around to the house on Somerset Avenue where Emma had lived with the Choquettes. He introduced himself and explained to Marguerite that he had come for Emma's belongings. Marguerite was surprised when he said he was Emma's brother. She looked for a family resemblance, but could see none.

"You don't look like Emma," she blurted out. John grinned, taking no offence. She asked him what was going on.

He shrugged. "I don't know any more than you do," he answered.

Marguerite Choquette felt badly that none of Emma's paintings were available. She couldn't get over what an accomplished artist Emma Woikin was.

The Choquette children still asked about Emma every day. Mrs. Choquette had put them off in the beginning with excuses, but now she decided to tell them that Emma had returned to Saskatchewan to be with her family. Her son Jack was in his teens before he learned that the woman who made him goulash and home-made bread, who sang to him and made him laugh, was one of the people who went to prison as a spy.

Marguerite changed her shift so she could be home those evenings that Bert worked. She didn't feel like advertising for another tenant. Her friends were full of curiosity about her baby-sitter, but the Choquettes put them off by saying they knew nothing; it was, after all, the truth. After a while, people grew tired of speculating.

Chapter Eleven

The day Emma Woikin was taken to the prison for women in Kingston, Bob Hope and Dorothy Lamour were starring in a movie called *The Road to Utopia*. A temperance organization in Toronto was urging City Hall to hold a plebiscite to determine whether women should be permitted to drink beer in beverage rooms. Thousands of war brides and their babies were being brought to Canada in troopships that had their war-time fittings modified for new duty as passenger ships.

There was an acute housing shortage. People complained that houses that sold for $4,200 during the war were going for the inflated price of $7,200. Newspapers carried pictures of veterans and their families living in tents and abandoned streetcars. One alarmist predicted that people earning less than two thousand dollars a year would never be able to afford housing. Some white-collar workers were not earning this much.

Lana Turner announced that she was thinking of taking a third husband but "didn't want to rush impulsively into another marriage." Easter suits for men were advertised at thirty-five dollars. The trials of Nazi war criminals in Nuremberg dragged on; most people had lost interest. President Harry Truman was ending his first year in office; the press noted that he hadn't amounted to much. Lieutenant-General Lucius Clay, head of the American army of occupation in Germany, thought United States troops might have to stay for "at least ten years."

A headline in the Women's Section of the *Toronto Star* declared: "Tomorrow's hot dinner will come from the freezer." Chinese Communists, led by Mao Tse Tung, were falling back towards Changchun. The Ontario Education Association demanded that sex education be taught in high schools. A Gallup poll reported that twenty-seven percent of Canadians favoured prohibition. Despite the poll, Toronto's first two cocktail lounges opened and both were packed.

Raymond B. Fosdick, president of the Rockefeller Foundation, said in New York that the idea that Russia and the United States were incompatible was "a counsel of despair." A survey in the United States revealed that seventy-one percent of Americans disapproved of Russian foreign policy in Iran and Manchuria.

George Drew's salary as premier of Ontario was $13,995 a year. Porterhouse steak cost thirty-nine cents a pound, coffee forty-three cents a pound; grapefruits were a nickel apiece, and a four-cent stamp would send a letter anywhere in Canada.

The Winnipeg Monarchs arrived in Toronto for the first game of the Memorial Cup against St. Michael's, to be played in Maple Leaf Gardens. Trans Canada Airlines had four flights a week to Britain for $675 a seat; the plane was borne on four engines with propellors. Lieutenant-Colonel Cecil Merritt, Victoria Cross, a newly elected Conservative member of parliament from the riding of Vancouver-Burrard, said that Japanese-Canadians should not be allowed to stay in Canada. British Columbia, he said, didn't want "the Japanese problem."

The Supreme Court of Canada ruled that it was legal to deport Canadians of Japanese heritage, whether they were naturalized citizens or born in Canada. The decision was later overruled by the British Privy Council.

On the first anniversary of the death of Franklin Delano Roosevelt, the *Globe & Mail* speculated that if he were alive "misunderstandings which have darkened this year of victory could have been swept away before they clouded the vision of peoples."

In Britain, the new minister of health, Aneurin Bevan, introduced nationalized health services. *Maclean's* magazine ran an article that asked the question, "Should nice girls neck?" Tommy Douglas, premier of Saskatchewan, was alarming financiers with his speeches about socializing industry.

William Arthur Deacon, book editor of the *Globe & Mail*, announced that Hugh McLennan's *Two Solitudes* was the winner of the governor-general's literary prize for fiction. Ross Munro, war correspondent for *Canadian Press,* won the non-fiction award with *Gauntlet To Overlord.*

Women wearing slacks were not admitted to the gallery of the House of Commons if the slacks were "too tight or displayed curves too prominently." Tailored slacks were permissable only if covered by a topcoat.

Nylon stockings made their first post-war appearance on store shelves in Saskatoon and there was a near-riot of buyers. Canadians were disappointed to learn that butter rationing would continue for another month. A subscription to the *Toronto Star* cost eighteen cents a week. The Canadian Broadcasting Corporation reported its first deficit, $35,000. The Dominion Bureau of Statistics said that Canada's population had reached 11,490,000, and daringly predicted that by the year 1990 there would be fifteen million people in Canada.

Dr. C.J. Mackenzie, president of the National Research Council, was one of dozens of scientists who was ignored when he insisted that the secrets of atomic power were unkeepable. He asked that information about the new reactor at Chalk River be made available to universities and industries across Canada.

The spy trials continued to be confusing. Some papers were publishing daily updates, styled much like the box scores in the sports pages, so people could follow the two trials in Montreal, those of Fred Rose and Raymond Boyer, and the twelve in Ottawa. Most of the trials were slipping from news pages because something more gripping had happened. In Hamilton, a beautiful woman, Evelyn Dick, had chopped up her husband with a meat cleaver, leaving his torso to be found on the side of Hamilton mountain.

John Konkin was back in the homestead near Blaine Lake, facing neighbours who were shocked to hear that Emma was in prison. For a while he stuck close to the farm, getting his spring seeding done, and avoided them. People came to visit, their tones hushed and their faces as full of sympathy as if there had been a death. The Konkins were rarely seen on the streets of Blaine Lake. Doreen Konkin, who married into the clan much later, could understand that.

"In small communities people are inquisitive," she explained. "They really are nosey, you could even say. They want you to answer their questions. If they can't figure out what's happening, rumours fly around, inflated rumours. That just builds up more questions and you could spend three hours downtown just getting a quart of milk."

John met with his brothers and his sister Mary to report on Emma's condition. She had lost a great deal of weight, as she always did under stress, and her hair was turning grey. Annie Konkin wept at John's report, but Alex and Bill reacted to their sister's plight with indignation. She had been a fool, they said, and she was paying for it, as well she should.

Emma's sentence was two years and six months. Because the sentence exceeded two years, it had to be served in a federal penitentiary. The only federal prison for women in the country was in Kingston. Since a mere handful of women receive long sentences, it had never seemed economical to house the women in their own communities. Most of the inmates in the Kingston prison for women were a long way from home.

Emma faced her ordeal with her customary fortitude. Her first letter from prison was written little more than a week after she arrived in the grim institution, and was written to her brother Alex. Dated 24 April, 1946, it reads:

Dear Alex: In years to come it shall be a memory that in 1946 I wrote my first letter home from penitentiary in Kingston. Right now it is a cold hard fact; then as a memory it will present itself to us in a far different form. Yet, even now, I can see that this time spent here will not be a waste of time but shall be a great school of character. I'll see how different people react under different circumstances; most important, I want to know how I myself will react. . . .

To everyone of you in my family, I know it is heart-breaking. Because no one else in our family has ever seen the inside of a jail, I am well aware of the fact that my plight will be harder by far for you all to take than it will be for me. I will be lonesome for you all terribly. I'll want to see the children growing. I would want them to love me, to be proud of their aunt, but Pearl might even forget me. . . .

Please remember that I am quite comfortable, well fed — therefore, you see I am physically imprisoned yet all my physical needs are well looked after . . . feelings of either love or hate cannot be imprisoned; from Dostoevsky and countless others we have learned that these feelings flourished and bear fruit . . . an unexpected pleasure awaited me here, that of meeting Lucy Voykin of Riverhill and Helen Padavelnikoff of Riverhill too. They are here with five others. . . .

I made the mistake of sending everything home when I could have taken a few more things so [John, I presume, brought these things home] please send me some snapshots. You will know which ones are dearest to me. I want two Exercise Books for notes in my studies, also Anglo-Russian Dictionary and the Bible. I want my oil paints too; pack them well in tissue paper, also a bottle of turpentine, a little bottle of linseed oil. . . .

Remember I am still your sister, and that I am quite the same girl I always was. . . .

Penitentiary, the dictionary tells us, has something to do with "penance" or "reformatory treatment." Penance I don't feel; reform maybe. In my case I would have to "reform" my ideals, love feelings.

The archives of Kingston Penitentiary are in a wretched state. Some are infested with termites, others rat-chewed, most are mouldy, and they reek. Much material is missing and the classification system is haphazard. Still, it is possible to draw a picture of life in the women's prison at the time Emma Woikin was there.

For instance, there is the report of a Royal Commission on Penitentiaries, which described conditions as "harsh" and "bleak." All prisoners were in barrier cells without windows, the Commission protested, "a very unnecessary form of construction for an institution for women prisoners."

The grounds were neglected, the report continued. The area enclosed by a high stone wall where the women were allowed their only time in the open air was "in disgraceful condition, the surface rough and infested with weeds, no grading and practically no trees, shrubs, flowers or vegetables . . . not even a cinder or board walk and no provision for outdoor exercise of any kind."

Further, "there is no school, and no teacher . . . the 'library' is contained in a small bookcase and consists of about 100 books . . . female prisoners' correspondence is censored by the women's prison and again by the male censor at Kingston Penitentiary. The duplication would appear to be unnecessary."

Inmates were allowed only one bath a week. Hobbies were not permitted. Mail was restricted; gifts were allowed only at Christmas. The Royal Commission said that there was too much punishment for minor offences, but did not elaborate on the form that punishment took. There is a strange comment that "not all chaplains are adequate" and a complaint that the clothing provided women upon discharge was of poor quality and did not fit.

All the walls within the prison were painted the same institutional colour, known as "Imperial green." There were cockroaches in the kitchen and bedbugs and rats in the cells. In a report to her superior, the warden of the men's prison, the matron complained that a mixture of DDT and kerosene had been tried but proved ineffective against the vermin. She said, "Cockroaches are found in drawers, on tables, and sometimes in the cooked food."

Few of the cells had toilets. Women used chamber pots, which were kept in plywood commodes.

Women were not allowed to mount anything on the walls of their cells to interrupt the starkness. Cells were poorly lit; a single bulb high in the ceiling did little to illuminate the windowless space. Once a week a small package of tobacco and another of cigarette papers were distributed to smokers. (One prisoner was dying of cancer in Kingston General Hospital; she was permitted a double ration.)

Toilet paper was rationed; women received the same ration as men.

Once a month a film from the National Film Board was shown. During the time Emma Woikin was there, a radio was introduced; the dial was controlled by the matron.

Inmates could receive cards from relatives and friends only on their birthdays and at Easter and Christmas.

The food ration was fixed at 29½¢ a day per convict, augmented in summer by some vegetables grown on the prison grounds.

The environment was devoid of stimulation, distraction or comfort of the most basic kind. Most of the women were far from home. Many never saw family or friends the entire time they were in Kingston.

The Royal Commission recommended that the women's prison at Kingston be closed and "the women transferred to institutions in the provinces in which they live." Forty years and many such Royal Commissions later, the Kingston prison for women still stands.

The Commission apparently expected that its recommendation to close the prison would be ignored. It also recommended that the grounds inside the stone walls be landscaped, outdoor exercise and recreational activities be provided the women, and suitable educational and vocational facilities be made available. The reports that passed between the matron at Portsmouth and the warden at Kingston do not indicate that any of these recommendations were carried out during the more than two years Emma Woikin was there.

When Emma arrived, the prison population was thirty-nine and did not strain the facility, which had been built for fifty. Emma was stripped and searched crudely before receiving her prison clothes, which consisted of a coarse grey cotton dress, heavy bloomers, lisle stockings and black Oxfords. She was assigned a number: 8535.

The staff of the Kingston Portsmouth Prison consisted of six women who were responsible for providing round-the-clock supervision of the prisoners seven days a week. The women on night duty, for instance, worked thirteen-hour shifts; sometimes only two were available for duty during the day.

Because there were not enough guards to watch the women, prisoners were locked in solitary cells as much as possible. Prisoners were confined for thirteen hours of every twenty-four. They were let out at eight in the morning to eat, then to work (in the kitchen, laundry or sewing room), then returned to the cells at noon for an hour. They emerged to eat lunch, to work and have a brief recreation period; after supper they were locked up again at eight. Lights were turned off at ten.

Emma Woikin had three weeks to adjust to the routine before Kathleen Willsher arrived. Willsher, the second of the thirteen detainees to be tried, the second and last to plead guilty, the second and last of the women kept in the barracks, appeared before Judge McDougall on 3 May. He sentenced her to three years in prison.

Roydon Hughes defended Ned Mazerall, whose case was heard next before Judge J.C. McRuer and jury in Toronto. Hughes questioned each of one hundred men summoned to make up the jury and declared that none of them was acceptable because none was unaware of the Royal Commission report. McRuer then exercised an almost-never used power of the bench: he sent someone on the street to impanel twelve passers-by at random.

During the trial, McRuer would not accept Hughes's argument that Mazerall's testimony before the Royal Commission should be excluded. On 22 May, 1946, he sentenced Mazerall to four years in the penitentiary. An appeal was filed, but Mazerall was taken to prison anyway. (His appeal was denied later.)

Gordon Lunan, the last of the first four to be arrested, was a bitter and fearless man on the witness stand. Mazerall suspects that Lunan was sickened to find that his testimony during the RCMP interrogation had implicated three men, Mazerall, Smith and Halperin, far beyond anything their deeds justified. He became a choleric witness; no court reporter had ever seen anything like it.

When he was required to testify against Fred Rose, he protested. He was charged with contempt and taken to the cells so speedily that he wasn't allowed time to collect his overcoat.

His own trial, which lasted four days, began on 13 November, 1946, before Judge McDougall. Lunan had hoped to be represented by a celebrated Quebec lawyer, Lucien Gendron of Montreal, but the Law Society of Upper Canada refused to permit it. Instead he retained H.L. Cartwright of Kingston, who agreed with Lunan that he needed someone more senior. Only a week before the trial was scheduled to begin, Lunan was able to retain J.L. Cohen, a Toronto lawyer celebrated for his brilliance and his sympathy for underdogs.

Cohen, a chubby man who smoked cigars and wore his hat square on top of his head, was the first lawyer to be disrespectful to Igor Gouzenko. When he asked how Gouzenko, an atheist, could take an oath on a Bible, the young Russian lost his customary poise and became excited, waving his hands in outrage as Judge McDougall glowered at Cohen.

Cohen's brash tactics continued. He had subpoenas served on Prime Minister King, Mr. Justice Kellock of the Supreme Court of Canada and C.D. Howe, Canadian's much-admired cabinet minister who turned Canada into an almost-first-rank industrial nation during the war.

No prime minister had ever been compelled to testify in court. The press was full of speculation about Cohen's intentions and the sheer nerve of putting a judge of the Supreme Court on the stand. Cohen apparently was hoping to discredit the Royal Commission, but the strategy was not carried out. None of the sensational witnesses he subpoenaed ever appeared in court.

McDougall found Lunan guilty and sentenced him to five years in prison. Lunan appealed, and remained free while awaiting the result of the appeal. The conviction and sentence were upheld. The colourful Cohen was not Lunan's lawyer for the appeal. The two argued over fees and the relationship ended in acrimony.

The pillar of the Civil Liberties Association of the period was B.K. Sandwell, a man of ethereal courtesy and editor of *Saturday Night* magazine. Mackenzie King took care to keep Sandwell informed of the reasons the government required the War Measures Act, and why he thought the detentions in the barracks were necessary. Sandwell, flattered and sympathetic, influenced the decision of the Civil Liberties Association to support the government and disapprove of protesters.

"The atmosphere was such that good middle-of-the-road liberals were completely sold on the government's view that all kinds of unusual measures were necessary to get rid of the spy menace," Kay Macpherson commented dryly almost forty years later.

Among those who did not believe the imprisonment of the suspects was necessary were Brough Macpherson, artist A.Y. Jackson, Allan Ashley, senior professor of political economy at the University of Toronto, Sam Beatty, dean of arts and science at the same university, and a well-to-do Rosedale woman,

Margaret Spaulding, who supported the newspaper advertisements placed by the group, which called itself the Emergency Committee for Civil Rights.

In October, 1946, the Emergency Committee issued an edition of its publication, *Civil Rights*, in which it denounced the government for continuing to distribute the Royal Commission's prejudicial report while many of the detainees were still being tried. In response, the government ordered another printing of the Commission's report.

The trials proceeded in Montreal, Toronto and Ottawa in the summer and autumn of 1946. The people already in prison were frequently taken to the Kingston train station to be delivered, handcuffed to a guard, at one trial site or another. The purpose of the exercise was to link a convicted "spy" to someone not yet convicted.

Kay Willsher, the most obliging of the detainees, was most frequently called upon to perform this service for the Crown. Willsher knew almost all the defendants socially or from discussion groups in Ottawa or from skiing weekends in the Laurentians; she spent a good deal of time away from Kingston, and became a connoisseur of regional prison conditions. In Montreal, she learned, she could expect head lice.

Emma Woikin was summonsed less frequently; it is puzzling that she was asked to testify at all. She was taken to Ottawa and held in the county jail there for twenty-six days in June, four days in September and nine days in October, but she did not appear at any trials. On 17 May, 1946, as Fred Rose's trial began, Emma spent two weeks in a Montreal jail. She was returned to Kingston without being asked to testify.

Fred Rose's trial dragged on for three weeks. At the end of it, Emma was taken to Montreal again. The increasingly frustrated Crown had to contend with witnesses who would not cooperate. Eric Adams, one of those asked to testify against Rose, answered every question about spying by saying, "I decline to answer on the grounds that it might incriminate me at my own trial." Adams was charged with being in contempt of court.

One after another, Gordon Lunan, Matt Nightingale and Harold Gerson were asked to describe their relationship with Fred Rose; all refused.

Joseph Cohen, the flamboyant Toronto lawyer who had defended Lunan, was one of three counsel retained by Rose.

Rose's trial became the focus of public attention and of the government's efforts to demonstrate that Gouzenko had indeed flushed out a major spy network. Rose, the best known of all the defendants, was thirty-eight years old, a small man of five foot three, a compelling orator on such topics as poverty and the bitter lot of non-unionized workers, and a duly elected member of parliament. Crowds lined up early every day to gain admission to the spectacle, but seats were scarce: sometimes there were fifty reporters claiming seats in the small spectators' gallery.

Emma Woikin was a surprise witness near the end of Rose's trial. The press described her sympathetically as "the little widow from Blaine Lake." She was shown some handwritten papers and asked if she knew the writing. She scarcely gave them a glance. Her eyes fixed in middle distance above the heads of the audience, she declared in a firm clear voice, "I don't want to answer any more questions."

The judge, Wilfred Lazure, declared her a hostile witness, cited her for contempt, and ordered her taken back to her cell.

Rose took the stand and spoke movingly in his own defence. "I have done nothing against the people of Canada," he said. "I still insist I am innocent."

Joseph Cohen summed up his client's case and the crown prosecutor, F. Philippe Brais, used the words "treason" and "traitor" a good deal in his address to the jury. After thirty-four minutes of deliberation, the jury decided Rose was guilty.

Two days later, on 20 June, 1946, the courtroom was only half full to hear Rose's sentence. Among the spectators were Lunan, Gerson, Nightingale and Adams, all immaculately dressed, summonsed to hear their sentences on the charge of contempt of court.

Judge Lazure sentenced Rose to six years in prison, one year less than the maximum. He explained that he had dropped a year off the sentence because Rose's behaviour while free on bail had been exemplary. (Rose had been told not to give interviews or appear at any rally or benefit staged on his behalf while he was free on bail; he had obeyed.)

As Rose was led away he asked if he could kiss his wife good-bye. His request was refused.

After Rose had been escorted out of the room, Judge Lazure turned his attention to the recalcitrant witnesses. The four men lined up in the prisoners' box just vacated by Rose and were told they would each serve three months in prison for the offence.

A court attendant called Emma Woikin. A door at the rear of the courtroom opened and Emma was led to the prisoners' box by two guards.

"As for you, Mrs. Woikin," Lazure began, "you have less excuse than the others because you have been sentenced. I am sending you to jail for six months and the term will be served in a Quebec jail at the expiration of your present sentence."

Emma Woikin showed no expression. Nudged by her guards, she turned obediently and went back through the rear door.

Ned Mazerall remembered when he was one of those shuttled between Kingston penitentiary and the various trials.

"The feeling is as if all your insides were removed from you," he recalled thirty-seven years later in his University of Manitoba laboratory. "I never hope to ever go through anything in my life again that was so dehumanizing. It was beyond description."

One of the trials for which he was summoned was that of Durnford Smith. Mazerall, a dazed man, was asked about a conversation between himself and Smith. He thought his response was innocuous: he remembered that Smith one time had cautioned him, saying something like "Be careful what you say," or "Watch out." He testified that it meant nothing to him at the time.

The Crown used that testimony to argue that Smith knew he was acting furtively. Taken with other evidence against Smith, Mazerall's statement was not helpful to the defense. Smith drew a sentence of five years, almost as severe as the one meted out to Fred Rose.

When Mazerall was returned to Kingston penitentiary he was shunned. "They [prisoners] have a strange set of values," he reflected. "It was the worst thing I could do, in their eyes. I didn't really think I had said anything too serious, and that was the only thing I said against Smith, but news of it travelled ahead of me and it was a while before I was forgiven."

With Rose's trial completed, the best crime news in the country was coming from Hamilton, where the trial of Evelyn Dick had begun in October. In an article in *New World* magazine, journalist Eva-Lis Wuorio described Dick as a woman who would have been at home in pulp fiction. She seemed to have gangster connections who provided her with money to dress with flashy style; she aspired to be part of Hamilton's social set. She had at least one child before she married John Dick. The child's corpse was found in her attic.

Evelyn Dick was found guilty and sentenced to be hanged. She appealed the verdict and was granted a new trial. She was found guilty of the lesser offence of manslaughter during the appeal and was sentenced to life imprisonment. She arrived in Kingston Portsmouth penitentiary the next day, was assigned number 1726, got her bearings, and set her heart on seducing Emma Woikin.

At first Emma made no mention of Evelyn Dick in her determinedly bright letters home. She wrote to Annie and Alex on 8 September, 1946:

Today I had been painting all day. I was doing the scene we could see from the upstairs window here, the lake [Lake Ontario], its islands, and a mental hospital which is a very beautiful building. . . .

Thanks for your kind words, Alex, and I shall be brave, as you said I should be, and it isn't hard. When I know that there are people like you in the world and they are behind me, I should say I only feel humbly grateful. . . .

She mentioned that she was taking some correspondence courses. One, ancient history, had impressed upon her the sophistication of the Greeks and "how far behind we are in thought and culture." She told Alex where, in Shakespeare's *Richard II,* he could read for himself a passage that had deep meaning for her. It is John of Gaunt's famous speech:

All places that the eye of heaven visits
Are to a wise man ports and happy havens.
Teach thy necessity to reason thus;
There is no virtue like necessity . . .
Look, what thy soul holds dear, imagine it
To lie the way thou go'st, not whence thou comest . . .

The trials of the detainees were not proceeding as the government had hoped. Eric Adams was acquitted on 22 October; Matt Nightingale was acquitted on 7 November; David Shugar was acquitted on 7 December. Protests against the Royal Commission's public declarations that those on trial were guilty were increasing. The Commission's final report, a document 733 pages long, released in July, bore statement after statement that Adams, Nightingale and Shugar were traitors.

On 27 December, 1946, the cabinet met to discuss what should be done. Frank Park, writing in the *Canadian Forum* of March, 1983, commented on that discussion. He wrote that the cabinet decided "in view of the acquittals to date, further distribution of the report should be suspended until an 'appropriate insertion' had been made, setting out 'the existing position with respect to related criminal proceedings'." In other words, a disclaimer — for those who would read the document thoroughly — that several people the judges declared to be guilty had been found not guilty in a court of law.

In January 1947 the cabinet agreed on the wording of the insert and distribution of the report resumed. In the spring the cabinet again was troubled by what had been done. There was concern about the "propriety" of the report, but it was not withdrawn from distribution.

Emma's letters to her sister Mary and others in the family sometimes failed the standard of cheerfulness she sought to maintain. She was finding prison a place of terror, full of women who were edgy and mean, their tempers on a short leash; their inclination, when angered, was to attack. The most frightening woman of all, she wrote, was Evelyn Dick, who followed her everywhere.

"That Evelyn Dick was always after Emma," Mary Perverseff, Emma's sister, recalled, adding meaningfully, "*you* know." Louie Sawula, Emma's second husband, confirmed this. "She used to ask Emma if she could wash her back, things like that," he said. "Emma was very afraid of her."

On at least one occasion, Emma Woikin was beaten by another convict. A description of one incident was found in prison records in the National Archives:

Convict 8535 Woikin went to Mrs. Cherry, a matron, advising

her that she thought the matrons were becoming careless . . . .
On occasions other than regular lockup at the close of prison
[day] when the convicts were placed in their cells, the matrons
had a habit of standing at the end of the range giving the order
for the convicts to go to their cells.

After they entered they merely put on the locking bar without
taking any count or checking the cells. She further stated that
at these times she desired to study but was unable to do so owing
to the actions of women in the next cells. It appears that not
being checked too closely, two women would enter one cell and
if the matron happened to come along, one would get under the
bed.

Mrs. Cherry stated further that she advised Miss Burke,
matron, of this situation and that she called the women
together, advising them that such actions must be stopped. As a
result of this, Mrs. Cherry inferred that Woikin was attacked
and struck over the head, indicating that the woman who
struck her is not known. At the time Woikin would give no
information concerning the incident of the attack.

Louie Sawula was puzzled when he heard this account. Emma
had never mentioned such an episode to him, he said. She said
she was attacked and beaten on the head by a man who hid
himself behind a pillar in the sewing room and sprang at her
when she was alone there.

Emma wrote to Alex Konkin again on 14 October, 1946:

Dear Brother Alex: Today was Thanksgiving Day. Holidays,
even great ones like Xmas and New Year's, come even to prison
but a holiday comes to prison garbed differently. . . .

Today I had a visit from Mary and Al Conkin from Toronto.
It was quite a surprise. One is quite at a loss, what to say, what
to do, like one confined in darkness for long is startled by a ray
of sunshine. . . .

I can't help feeling there is something unnatural in a visit to
a prison. It's not as if Mary and Al came to see Emma but as if
they came to see her grave. . . .

By all that, I mean I would not wish you to come at all; not
any of you. . . .

She concluded by saying she was reading H.G. Wells' *Outline of History*.

Reports in the archives contain several references to the vexatious problem of education in the women's prison. There were no professional teachers at Kingston penitentiary; staff relied on an educated convict to teach the inmates. Just before Emma Woikin and Kathleen Willsher arrived, the inmate who had been performing this function was discharged. A man who taught in the men's prison was assigned to fill the gap temporarily, conducting classes at the women's prison three afternoons a week. In the summer of 1946, the teacher, H.B. Patterson, reported to the warden of the men's prison, R.M. Allan, who also was responsible for the women, that he had eight students at the women's prison, six of them at the elementary school level.

"The greatest attention had been given to the teaching of illiterates," he wrote, adding that two hours an afternoon three times a week were not sufficient. In a letter dated 22 July, 1946, he appealed to be hired full time.

Allan rejected the application on the grounds that his budget was insufficient. Besides, he thought the education of women was a low priority. "The education of female convicts, while desirable," he replied to Patterson, "does not present as important possibilities when consideration is given to the male convicts set-up."

Allan's problems with the education of women were solved with the arrival at Portsmouth of Kathleen Willsher, the prison's first inmate to hold a graduate degree from the London School of Economics. Patterson was moved back to the men's prison and Willsher began teaching the women. The number of pupils expanded rapidly to twenty, half the prison population. Emma Woikin was one of the twenty, working at high-school level. She augmented Willsher's instruction by taking a correspondence course at which she earned an A standing and honours.

The correspondence course ended abruptly a year later. In October, 1947, her picture was in the papers and she was denounced for wanting an education. A story in the *Montreal Star,* written by the paper's Ottawa correspondent, James A. Oastler, appeared under a three-column headline: "Red faces around the D.V.A." Oastler wrote:

There are a lot of red faces around the Department of Veterans Affairs. It all came about as a result of Emma Woikin, former civil servant now serving a penitentiary term for espionage in connection with the spy probe, writing an examination for veterans in Latin.

Miss Woikin is in Portsmouth prison.

Some time ago the Department of Veterans Affairs took over the Canadian Legion's educational service, including the text books. These educational services included a number of correspondence courses, including some on Latin.

Then the Department of Veterans Affairs got busy. They made all these courses available to veterans including those who were in penitentiaries or reformatories. There were quite a number who applied and were given the courses. Everything was fine until it was found that Emma Woikin had not only got one of the veterans' courses but had actually taken an examination in Latin and got very high marks. From all reports she was not the only civilian who had the advantage of one or more of these courses.

Today the Department of Veterans Affairs says, "It is all a mistake. It was a clerical error. But people should be in favor of rehabilitation of penitentiary inmates whether they are veterans or not. Really, these courses did not cost the country anything. We got them from the Legion."

Perhaps so, but a more careful check will be made in the future.

Ned Mazerall studied Spanish during the more than three years he spent in Kingston and Collins Bay prisons. Just before his discharge he wrote to C.D. Howe, who was showing an interest in Canadian investment in South America, and inquired if there was a chance of a job. Howe wrote what Mazerall described as "a nasty letter," stating he wasn't in a position to find jobs for people.

The Emergency Committee for Civil Rights renamed itself the Civil Rights Union and continued to attack the government's treatment of the detainees. In February, 1947, C. Brough Macpherson, the acting chairman, published an open letter to J.L. Ilsley, the new minister of justice, asking for a parliamentary committee on civil rights "to investigate violations of civil rights in Canada." Macpherson listed the areas to be examined:

RCMP methods; the conduct of the Royal Commission; the presumption of guilt in certain sections of the Official Secrets Act. The open letter also asked that circulation of the Royal Commission report cease, and that the government make reparations to those "found guilty in the reports but acquitted in court."

Six of the detainees who were found innocent were learning that their careers were as ruined as if they had been proved guilty.

Eric Adams, a brilliant economist who had represented Canada at Bretton Woods in July, 1944, when the International Monetary Fund was established, and who was being groomed, people said, to be the next governor of the Bank of Canada, discovered that he was unemployable.

Fred Poland had hoped for a diplomatic career in external affairs but found all government doors closed to him.

David Shugar, suspended from his position at Health and Welfare when he was put in the barracks, was fired on the day of his arrest. He asked for an explanation and received a letter from G.D. Cameron, the deputy minister, that "this was considered necessary in view of the report of the Royal Commission." When he was acquitted in December, he applied to be reinstated and was refused. A blizzard of letters to Health and Welfare and appeals to Mackenzie King produced a solid wall of rejection.

Israel Halperin, who had been assistant professor of mathematics at Queen's University, was found innocent of all charges in March, 1947. That summer he won a grant, offered by Princeton, for a year of study at the Institute for Advanced Study. He applied for a visa but was refused under legislation excluding "anarchists, advocates of force and violence for the overthrow of governments, and advocates of assassination."

The Civil Rights Union asked the government to compensate those acquitted for their legal costs. "They have been put to heavy legal expenses, suffered severe damage to reputation and in some cases lost their jobs." The government was silent.

The letter also examined some of the gaps and errors in Gouzenko's testimony. Frank Park, the civil-rights lawyer who spent much of his life studying the aftermath of the Gouzenko defection, believes these errors occurred not because Gouzenko was misinforming the court but because the RCMP fabricated some documents. Park is particularly suspicious of a notebook Gouzenko produced listing all the cover names, which Park thinks was the work of a Mountie who was anxious to reduce some of the confusion and ambiguity in the documents Gouzenko brought from the embassy safe. The index certainly was a convenient reference, but it had many errors.

Eric Adams, for instance, was said to be code-named "Ernst," but "Ernst" was described as Jewish, which Adams is not. Kathleen Willsher was said to be code-named "Elli," but Gouzenko spoke of an "Elli" who was not in Canada.

Even the conservative Canadian Bar Association complained, especially about the treatment of Mazerall by the Royal Commission. The protection of the Canada Evidence Act should be automatic, it noted icily, and not operative only when the person being questioned knows about it.

Concerning Emma Woikin, the Civil Rights Union observed:

It is doubtful if her contempt sentence is valid. It should be made clear that she is serving the original sentence only. It would be appropriate to review her sentence in the light of the fact that her conviction was only possible because of answers extracted from her by the police, which led to her subsequent guilty plea. The same consideration as in the Mazerall case is applicable here.

Despite the bleakness of prison, the ever-present threat of attack, the food she found almost impossible to eat, and her loneliness, Emma Woikin presented herself as an optimistic, friendly, helpful person. She became the darling of the staff, which softened her time in prison considerably. When she was ill she received such extra attention as lemon and honey to soothe her cough and was allowed the bliss of staying in the infirmary. She was even permitted to receive art supplies from her family and to keep them in her cell.

One matron, Mrs. Cherry, was so devoted to Emma that they corresponded for many years afterwards. Once when Mrs. Cherry was travelling to the west coast by train, she broke her trip to stay overnight in Saskatoon with Emma and Louie.

All inmates were required to work in the kitchen, the laundry room or the sewing room. The easiest work was in the sewing room, where Emma was assigned. Fourteen convicts laboured there making pillow-slips, kitchen whites for the cooks, shirts for the guards in the men's prison, and other articles as were needed. The women inmates did much of the housekeeping duties for the men's penitentiary. Women did the laundry of the male convicts, as well as the personal laundry of Warden Allan and the chaplains. Inmates who worked in the kitchen of the women's prison cooked for women prisoners and matrons and also served lunch to the chaplains and the prison psychiatrist.

There is no evidence that Emma Woikin played a role in the confrontations between the matrons of Portsmouth and their most difficult prisoners, Doukhobor women of the Sons of Freedom sect who were serving sentences for arson and nudity. The Doukhobor women succeeded in disrupting the routine by simply refusing, *en masse*, to have anything to do with it. Their protests are documented in the files of the National Archives. The first Doukhobor women had arrived at the prison on 12 June, 1944, from the Oakalla prison farm in British Columbia. Kingston had been advised that the women were vegetarians and would not eat the regular prison diet. To accommodate them, a make-shift kitchen — two hot plates — was provided in the basement. They were also given a supply of vegetable oil, since they would not cook with lard.

The Doukhobor women were placed in adjoining cells on the north side of the cell block. The small prison resounded to Doukhobor voices lifted in Russian psalms and prayers. In other respects, the matron reported to Warden Allan, they were "adjusting themselves in a satisfactory manner."

The "adjustment" lasted only until the prison required that the arrivals be photographed and finger-printed. The women objected; the guards insisted. The women promptly stripped. Matrons wrapped blankets around them and summoned male guards, who carried the protesting Doukhobors to the office of the part-time dentist, where a photographer waited. The head matron, A.M. Gibson, advised the warden that the pictures probably would have to be taken again because the Doukhobors had yelled and sung throughout the process and wouldn't hold their heads still.

On 27 August, 1945, thirteen Sons of Freedom prisoners were released under tickets of leave but refused to go. They would not sign receipts for the $1,182.35 paid for their train fares from Kingston to Slocum, British Columbia. They announced they would stay in Kingston until they could leave without signing documents.

To the dismay of the overworked staff, Doukhobor women continued to arrive from British Columbia. In September, 1945, the Doukhobor women refused to work. They were threatened with loss of remission time, ten days for every month of refusal, but they weren't impressed. Matron Gibson reported desperately that her problems were compounded by the fact that most of the Doukhobor prisoners spoke no English.

Another group was due to be released in January, 1946. Warden Allan issued a pained warning: "From past experience, we anticipate that these women will not cooperate to the fullest extent in the effecting of their release."

The Salvation Army was asked to assist in Toronto, where the women would wait for several hours in Union Station to change trains. To the astonishment of the prison staff, the Army reported that there was no problem at all.

On 10 January, 1947, Emma wrote her brother Alex:

Mine eyes, my brain, my heart are sad — sad is the very core of me. I'm lonesome and tired and how I wish I could somehow reach out to you across the many, many miles.

Because prison regulations allowed her to send only two letters a month, Emma inserted messages for others in the family in each letter. In one letter she requested Alex to thank John and Lena for chocolates sent to her and to Kathleen Willsher, whom the Konkins seem to have taken under their kindly wing. She also mentioned receiving gifts from the MacDonalds, the Ottawa family who had befriended her on her first day in the city and who remained staunchly loyal. In return she had sent the MacDonalds some socks she had knit. She continued to Alex:

When I start writing you Pearl is on my mind from beginning to end. I consider it an unearthly pleasure to see a creature like her. I love her dearly. . . .

P.S. *"Mens sona in corpore sano"* — therefore to keep my body from deteriorating I walk out in the fresh air, wave my arms and run. Good things don't last forever; I shall not be a visitor of the Canadian government forever, and somewhere there probably is either a potato field to dig up or thoughts to think.

One letter begins with a reference to "neighbours to the south," which seems, from the context, to concern neighbours of the Konkins who were critical of Emma. She writes:

My darlings, why do you worry about the neighbours to the south, etc.? Do you think I don't understand anything and do you think that I have ceased to think and remember?

I remember when sister Annie, who was like a mother, dressed Agatha and Emma in the same kind of dresses; and when Alex came in to see me before they went to bury my baby. He proved so kind and comforting. I remember father on March 18, 1942 [the day Emma's husband Bill Woikin killed himself] covered me up with a coat and put his arm around me and begged me to sleep and try to rest. . . .

I know I'll be very happy, not in the carefree happiness of childhood but the kind of happiness that wrings your heart. . . .

Please tell father to dry his tears and not worry about me. I am very fortunate being a prisoner . . . Tell him though I'm sorry for having caused him uneasiness I am at the same time grateful for such a loving family.

Emma had been in Kingston for a year and a half when the matrons learned that eleven more Doukhobor women were on their way, some to serve sentences of eight years. The newcomers seem to have been absorbed into prison routine with scarcely a ripple; there is no further mention of them in the matron's correspondence with Warden Allan. Perhaps Emma Woikin helped this quiet assimilation, which was a marked contrast to the arrival of the next batch of Doukhobor women, two years after Emma's release.

The 1950 Doukhobors are mentioned in letters between Kingston's Warden Allan and R.S. Douglass, warden of the New Westminister prison, where the women were housed temporarily before their removal to Kingston. Observed Douglass laconically, "It would now appear that we have mutual Doukhobor problems."

When the fourteen women arrived in Kingston, they were

placed, as usual, in separate quarters in the prison basement. All refused to cooperate; they would not even give their names. Allan was obliged to ask Douglass to send pictures so he could identify his prisoners. Allan also wrote a letter of complaint about them on 2 November, 1950, addressed to the commissioner of penitentiaries in Ottawa.

"When received," he commented in a tone of exasperation, "they were in the nude and have consistently refused to wear any clothing since their arrival." When the naked newcomers arrived at Kingston, the eight Doukhobor women already in the prison promptly undressed too.

Other inmates complained about the substantial sound of twenty-two Doukhobor voices raised in songs of worship. The prison psychiatrist was called and administered injections of apomorphine, a sedative, "to calm them down." When they were to be photographed and finger-printed, the women set a fire in their cell block. The desperate matron placed them in solitary confinement; the prisoners went on a hunger strike.

Allan wrote Douglass: "The only trouble we are having here is that they won't put their clothes on," he said. "However, there is a cold winter coming up. . . ."

The doctor was called to treat burns suffered by the nude women, who huddled close to steam pipes to avoid freezing. After seven days without food, they were examined again by the doctor, T.N. Tweddell, who took a humourous view of the situation; he commented that they "didn't seem to be suffering from a lack of nourishment."

The finger-printing finally was done. The National Archives has the results: fourteen forms that are totally blank except for a complete set of smudged fingerprints on each page; the identities of the women were still unknown.

On 5 June, 1947, Emma wrote to Alex and Annie. She had been in prison for a year and two months and faced more than a year more. She wrote with unaccustomed self-pity, first complaining that Alex hadn't written for a long time and then apologizing for seeming critical:

I am a convict and therefore have no right to force my attention upon anyone or demand anyone's attention. So that is the way a prisoner's mind reasons. In our shrunken world, our minds circle around like caged rats. . . .

She was more cheerful on 3 August, 1947, when she again wrote to Alex:

Weekend is always the most pleasant time of the week because we spend more time alone.

She described a visit from Mary and Al Conkin of Toronto and mused:

I could never express exactly how much it means for one in my position to be remembered. It reminds you that you are a human being, an individual, that once you were a child, and that you are not just a "poisonous toadstool in surroundings of darkness and gloom" with your brighter past or a more hopeful future.

She said that the MacDonalds had come to visit her but for the second time were refused permission to see her because they were not relatives. They left her fruit and cake, which kindled memories of their past kindnesses:

Grannie MacDonald would visit me with her guitar and we would sing. I always found it so restful to look at Granny's face. She has snow-white hair and a beautiful kind face. She is about 70 years old. . . .
   I have no hope (nor peace within, nor calm around) still I don't feel too bad ("Yet now despair itself is mild. I could lie down like a tired child and weep away the life of care.")

She had managed, with the help of sympathetic staff, to resume taking correspondence courses. The seclusion she found on weekends in her small, dark cell enabled her to study, and also protected her from Evelyn Dick and from the testiness of other inmates.
   Emma wrote her brother Alex on 16 February, 1948, thanking him and Annie for a dress they had purchased for her and for the offer of a vacation trip on her release; both gifts were intended, apparently, to help Emma's increasing despair. Annie was particularly alarmed, her daughter Agatha Kardash recalled, because Emma's once-pious nature was changing.

Emma seemed to find no comfort any more in prayer. She wrote:

Just now I feel I would like to do something more useful than have a holiday [on her release]. I want to do something worthwhile, even if it is raising a bushel of potatoes, or feeding a single calf, or just anything. . . .

She explained that the uproar over her Latin course with the Department of Veterans Affairs had been resolved:

Last year I did my studies completely on my own. I had no one to correct my lessons or anything. I just wrote my June exam and that was corrected by the Department of Education. Since last fall we have had the opportunity of taking correspondence courses offered by the Department of Veterans Affairs. . . . Besides Latin and science I am taking first year university English and history. In the two advanced courses I have to do an enormous amount of work. I doubt whether I'll be successful but it is character building to do something hard, almost beyond your strength, every day.

She was delighted to hear that Alex and Annie had moved back into the homestead, which had been deserted for the winter:

I didn't like to think of "our Home" being empty and I'm glad I didn't see it that way. You know that place always seemed alive with activity. . . . I am so dreadfully lonesome for you. I can't think of anything else but home, home, home. This more than likely will have to be the last letter I write to you from here. . . .

I am leaving prison on the 24th of August, so don't mail me any letters after the 17th of August. . . .

I doubt that Pearl will know who I am. It is three years since I have seen you. . . .

As Emma and Kathleen Willsher were spending their last few weeks behind bars, the matron of Kingston prison was deploring the quality of inmates who were replacing them. In a letter to Warden Allan asking for more staff, she pointed out that the prison population had swollen to seventy women, twenty more than the building was designed to hold, and that "the type we are getting is more difficult to handle than several years ago."

Emma Woikin and Kathleen Willsher were discharged on 24 August, 1948; both had received the maximum remission of their three-year sentences for exemplary behaviour. Remission, at that time, consisted of six days for each month of the first year in prison, and ten days for each month served after that — a total of about thirty-four weeks for each woman.

Judge Lazure's edict that Emma serve her six-month contempt sentence in a Quebec prison was not followed. The sentence was not rescinded, but she was allowed to remain in Kingston.

When they left prison, Emma was twenty-seven years old and Kathleen Willsher was forty-three. Despite the dissimilarity of their backgrounds, they had become close friends. They kept in touch for the rest of their lives, though Willsher returned to England as soon as she was freed.

"She was such a lady," Louie Sawula said of Willsher. "She was so high-class. She used to dance with lords."

There was real mourning when Emma and Kathleen left prison; Emma was missed because she was so sunny and Kathleen because she was a superb, and free, teacher. Matron Gibson wrote Warden Allan sadly on 4 October, 1948: "Since the release of female convict Willsher, certain studies instituted for the Prison for Women are now considered to be handicapped, due to the lack of a qualified person being available . . . to conduct the classes."

Emma Woikin and Kathleen Willsher were the first of the detainees to go to prison, but not the first to be released. Raymond Boyer, the millionaire chemistry professor from McGill, had been sentenced to only two years, the shortest sentence of the seven detainees who went to prison. When Boyer emerged from prison, his career in chemistry was shattered. He became a criminologist.

Chapter Twelve

For her departure from prison, Emma Woikin was dressed in prison-discharge clothes chosen by the government from the Simpson's catalogue: an overcoat that cost $8.97, a suit for $10.71 and a pair of shoes for $2.99. She signed a receipt for her train ticket to Saskatoon and left Kingston forever.

The train journey took most of two days and two nights, a long, reflective time for the Doukhobor woman; a space in which to prepare for the reunions and awkwardness that awaited her. She was not alone in the world. Her family would be loyal and she could count on their love. She would have to find a job, probably in Saskatoon. Maybe she would marry, someone safe and dependable this time.

Her father and all three brothers were waiting in Saskatoon. They were shocked to see the changes two and a half years in prison had made. Emma was dreadfully thin and her hair was mostly grey; she looked much older than twenty-seven.

John and Lena were living in a farm a quarter mile away from the homestead; Alex and Annie Konkin had taken over the original Konkin homestead. Bill and Hannah were still in their rambling house on the edge of the village of Marcelin. Emma's father, Alex E., was living in Blaine Lake. Her sister, Mary, and

Mary's husband, Pete Perverseff, were a short drive from Marcelin.

Alex E. wasn't pleased with the way the land had been shuffled. John had two sons who would need farms; John should have stayed on the homestead he complained. Alex, with three daughters, had less need for a big place. But Alex was the scientific farmer in the family and loved land, while John was never a man for hanging on to things. It wasn't his style.

Emma stayed with John and Lena. She remained indoors, away from prying eyes. "She looked like a dog does when he's had a licking," her nephew Fred Konkin recalled. He was sixteen when Emma got out of prison, almost finished school, living at home and working with his father in the fields. "A dog'll come back to you shy and ready to run if you lift your hand again. That was Emma."

Fred thought the family felt shamed by Emma's time in prison but Mary stoutly denied it. "I still don't think she had anything to do with all that," she said spiritedly. "I figure it was just because she was Russian. In Ottawa they figured Russians would stick together, that they were one for each other, sort of thing."

Some say Emma Woikin was a bit of a hero among the Doukhobors, who were long accustomed to being outcasts and could admire defiance. Mary spoke with pride of the eligible men who flocked around the Konkin household to see if Emma was interested in marriage. But Emma was listless and didn't appear to notice them. Mary's theory about her sister's deepest feelings is that Emma never stopped loving Bill Woikin.

Fred Konkin observed, "It wasn't that she was a traitor, we never thought that. But there was a feeling of resentment that she had done something to put herself in prison and cause pain for the family."

He felt that the Konkin name was somewhat tarnished in the Blaine Lake community. His father, John, was a respected man, a school trustee, an elder in the Doukhobor prayer home. His mother taught Sunday school. The two were always called when there was a death in a Doukhobor family. It was John or Lena who washed the bodies, plaited the hair of the women, and dressed the corpses in finery. When someone died, almost the first person notified was John Konkin.

"Put it this way," Fred explained, "it was Emma's life, she

could do whatever she liked with her own life, but not when it hurt other people. She let the family down. People don't have a right to do those things. There is a set of guidelines to live by and you just don't pull off capers like that."

The attitude of people outside the Konkin family seemed the same, but not the same. When they saw Emma in town they avoided her and appeared uneasy. "Emma was snubbed, really," Fred said. "People didn't want to run into her if they could easily avoid it."

She went to Sunday services in the prayer home. Her sister-in-law Annie was disturbed that Emma clearly had lost her faith. Her letters from prison often mentioned her longing to believe and to find comfort in religion, but she seemed to have given up trying.

In September when the harvest was finished, Fred returned to high school in Blaine Lake. He was grateful that his friends sensed he didn't want to talk about his notorious aunt. Emma, who had been so close to Fred, felt his hurt and was careful not to press him to relent. "We talked, but it wasn't like it had been, not as open and easy," Fred reflected. "And I never mentioned jail."

People who did bring up the subject of her prison life in Emma's presence got a quick brush-off. "That's over, let's forget it," Emma would reply with an impatient gesture of her hand. She distributed the paintings she had made in her cell. One of them made a lasting impression on everyone who saw it. It was a pretty scene of ships on Lake Ontario, the water dancing in the sunlight, but there were grim prison bars in the foreground.

After staying with John and Lena, Emma moved back into the homestead and lived with Alex and Annie. Her niece Pearl Konkin Sherstobetoff, who was eight, saw her for the first time since Emma had visited Blaine Lake four years earlier. Annie said to Pearl, nudging the child's memory, "This is your auntie." Pearl stared. The woman in front of her didn't look anything like the laughing woman she remembered.

The homestead was full of excitement because Agatha, the oldest of the three daughters of Alex and Annie, was getting married in November to William Kardash. Emma pitched in to help with the cooking and began to feel herself again.

Alex and Annie decided not to tell people that Emma was

staying with them. Pearl remembered thinking how strange that was, because her parents usually loved to have the neighbours drop in whenever they had a guest. "This was a quieter time," Pearl observed. "The people who did come would sit and stare at her, not knowing what to say."

On an impulse one day Emma wrote a letter to Marguerite Choquette. It was the first time she had tried to communicate, except for the phone call to ask for her schoolbooks, since the raw February morning when the RCMP took her to the barracks. She thanked Marguerite for her kindness, sent her love to the children, said she missed them greatly, and added that she wanted to explain some day what had happened.

The letter upset Bert Choquette. He told his wife not to answer. She agreed, but still regrets the decision. "I had my job to think of," she explained, her face troubled. "It might have got me in trouble to answer, so I didn't." She shrugged. She's a practical woman: what's done is done.

"And I never heard from her again," she concluded flatly.

Emma spent the autumn days in her brothers' home painting in oils. In December, 1948, a reporter from the Saskatoon *Star Phoenix* came to interview her and reported that Emma had sold some paintings and intended to become a professional artist. She hadn't yet decided where she would establish her studio, she told the reporter, who wrote: "Still youthful and good-looking, she does not like talking about her experiences and adventures and will deftly turn the conversation to some safe topic such as weather or the crop prospects."

Despite the brave talk about making a career in art, Emma was trying to find a job as a typist, and was having no luck at all.

"People said she would never get a job, but she did!" Mary Perverseff said, her eyes blazing with triumph.

It happened in January, 1949. Emma once more seemed to be her old optimistic, determined, friendly self, hugging children and filling plates to overflowing. On a job-hunting trip to Saskatoon she saw a help-wanted sign in a drugstore window, went in and applied, her manner confident, and got a job as a clerk.

Her employer was Isaac Elik, a man slightly outside parochial Saskatoon society because he was Jewish. He was undeterred by Emma Woikin's reputation as a traitor. He paid her about ten dollars a week and she found a cheap room in a large, impersonal rooming house and joined the anonymous working poor.

Soon after she began her job, a Royal Canadian Mounted Police officer visited Elik.

"Do you know that you've got a spy working for you?" he asked the druggist. "Emma Woikin is just out of prison."

Elik defied the policeman. "I know all about her," he snapped, "and she's a good worker. Leave her alone."

Other detainees did not find such defenders. When Ned Mazerall emerged from the penitentiary at the end of November, 1949, he realized he would never be hired again in radar research, a field in which he had shown astonishing ability. He decided to start over in a new profession in a new place.

Sipping tea from a china cup in his Winnipeg laboratory almost thirty-four years later, he commented quietly, "The consequences of the arrest for me were that my career was destroyed. I think my colleagues consider me a good engineer, very good indeed. When I came to Winnipeg with a former colleague at the National Research Council we set up the world's first electronic instrument to measure the moisture of grain. And also the first scintillation counter, which is used to detect radio-activity. Both are very useful devices so we had the impetus to get together and form a company."

For a while everything went well. Mazerall began to relax, believing he would be allowed to pursue creative engineering projects so long as they were not military. He took out a patent on the moisture reader in his name and was pleased that there was great interest in it in the United States. The partners agreed it was time to open a branch in Indianapolis and Mazerall was delegated to go there and study the situation.

A careful man, he went first to the Winnipeg office of the RCMP and told them his travel plans. He asked if he would have any problem crossing into the States. He was assured that he was free to do as he pleased.

"So I went," Mazerall related. "It was about 1950, or maybe 1951. The train had hardly got underway when a United States customs and immigration man came along, took one look at me, sat down and said, 'Have you ever been in prison?'

"Here am I, dressed in a good overcoat, and a homburg hat, a proper tie, all that. The last person on the face of the earth you would ask if he had ever been in prison. If I had been a scruffy-looking character in jeans and T-shirt, yes."

He sighed. "So I knew right away what had happened. The customs man said, 'You're not going to be allowed into the country. I would appreciate it if you would get off at the next station.' So I did."

Mazerall went back to the RCMP in a fury. He said he told them, "I'm not in the news. There is no way someone in the middle of the prairies is going to know that someone named Mazerall even exists." The RCMP denied that they had anything to do with the incident.

"I didn't believe that for a moment," Mazerall commented with quiet resignation. "I never again told them when I wanted to travel. I went to the States many times over the years for holidays, but I never told the RCMP I was going. And I never again had any problem."

Unfortunately Mazerall and his partner were under-financed and the company went broke. It was acquired by Canadian Aviation Electronics, which offered to keep Mazerall on. Mazerall worried because CAE had some government contracts.

"The president knew all about me, of course," Mazerall continued. "Because I had no security clearance it was understood that I would work in some areas but not in others. Nevertheless, within less than a year an RCMP officer came to CAE and said, 'You're going to have to get rid of Mazerall.' I later learned he had no authority to do that, that he did it entirely on his own. But he did it. It was done. And I lost the job."

Emma Woikin's feisty employer, on the other hand, protected her. She went on with her job, selling nail polish and headache pills, unaware for years that her job had been threatened.

One night a craggy-faced man about ten years her senior came into the drugstore and spent a long time watching her. He was Lucas Sawula, a labourer on the Canadian National Railway, looking for a wife. He liked what he saw: a bright, cheerful woman, not too pretty, a hard worker, nothing loose about her.

Louie Sawula has no vocabulary for complexity in either of his two languages, Ukrainian and English. He lived his long life by simple, immutable principles such as loyalty, thrift, and honesty. He understands honour: you give your word, you keep it; you have a job, you work your head off. He adopted early in his life a capacity to observe the slippery behaviour of employers with a measure of amusement. It is fundamental to his canny view of the world that working people get shafted every time. He has no existential doubts, no pool of unresolved longings; he is comfortable in his skin. He is, recognizably, a thoroughly decent, untroubled man.

When he first saw Emma Woikin he was forty-one years old, with a long, mournful nose, a broad square forehead, and the body of a man who could swing a pick-axe all day, which he did on CNR road gangs. He had an accent thick with his Ukrainian heritage, showed a bold sexual confidence in his expression, and was courteous as a count.

Louie Sawula was one of seven children of impoverished Ukrainian Catholic farmers who barely sustained themselves on a bit of land near L'vov, close to the Polish border in a part of middle Europe that has changed its rulers a few times in every century. Louie, born on 2 October, 1908, was sixteen when he left home to join his brother Peter in Saskatchewan.

The teenager arrived in the fall of 1924 at threshing time and went to work in his brother's fields the morning after he got off the train. His brother had some schoolbooks and taught him some elementary words in English, but Louie Sawula never had an ear for the grammar. He speaks English straight from the Ukrainian in his head, his sentences devoid of articles and sparse in adverbs and adjectives.

Three weeks after his arrival in Canada, the boy landed a job on the spare board of part-time workers of a CNR road repair gang, which is one of the most brutal of all labouring jobs. Though he believes the arthritis in his hips comes from working on the open prairie in temperatures of forty below, the work seems to have agreed with him. In 1983 he was seventy-five years old but looked ten years younger. His thick hair was mostly grey, his teeth were worn stubby, with some gaps, and he was a little hard of hearing, but he was full of good humour and could walk a brisk mile.

When he was twenty-one he married a Ukrainian woman of nineteen who was five months pregnant. The marriage was a mistake. He knew it almost from the beginning, but to Louie a bargain is a bargain. He built a small wooden house for his family with his own hands and the couple had a son, Ernest, born in 1930, and then, four years later, a daughter, Lorraine, whom the family called Lorris.

Louie described his first wife with due regard for the feelings of his children. "I hear something about her, you know," he explained carefully. "She wasn't very honest with me." Other men? "Yaw," he replied. Finally, with an effort, he said it all: "To tell the truth, I hated her. I started to hate her so much I would do anything to get rid of her. I joined the army to get rid of her."

He served in World War Two in a tank-repair unit that followed the armoured corps all through Sicily, Italy and Belgium. He came home with the same rank he had when he left, private. On his discharge he hired a private detective and got evidence of adultery, the only permissable grounds for divorce at that time. Though his wages on the CNR were meagre, he saved enough to pay a lawyer and get a divorce.

"She not a good mother," he explained, as if that was the final straw. "When I was overseas my girl was in Saskatoon living with some Ukrainian people, my son was on the farm with my brother. My daughter got sick, sick, very sick. The lady who was looking after her went to my wife, she was in about the third house away, and she says Lorris is very sick. You think she come to see her? No! She was with bootleggers and that kind of a bunch people, you know. Drinking and that, but she didn't come to see Lorraine."

With no change of inflection, he added, "She's dead now."

His son was sixteen and working on the railway, having lied about his age, but Louie's daughter was only twelve when his divorce was finalized. The judge gave Louie custody and he placed Lorris with some Ukrainian nuns in Saskatoon to finish her schooling, since his rooming house was unsuitable for the child.

The arrangement worked for a time but then the nuns began hinting strongly whenever he came to visit that he should get married and make a proper home for his daughter.

Louie could see the wisdom of that but he wasn't keen to marry the woman he was dating. He let it be known, in his practical way, that he was looking for a solid, dependable woman to marry. A friend called him and told him to come over. She had just the woman for him, someone living in her rooming house: Emma Woikin. Louie learned where Emma was working and went to the drug store to look her over. He decided at once that she was the one.

The next night he dressed in his best and went to Emma's room. He found her playing cards with two men. One was a Russian who seemed to be Emma's boyfriend. The other, Louie discovered, was a car salesman who was just hanging around, looking the situation over. Louie introduced himself and politely asked Emma to deal him in.

"I liked her personality," he explained, struggling as everyone does to analyze what it is that attracts people to one another. "And what she went through . . . ." His face showed sympathy. "I felt sorry for her, to tell the truth. She was so poor when she came from that jail, wearing her jail coat, so cheap that coat. I used to take her groceries when I went to see her." He grinned. "Lots of groceries."

He didn't know, that night of the card game, that Emma was the woman who had figured in the spy trials. Later, when he learned of her past, it seemed irrelevant. He had decided to marry her.

It was a matter of indifference to him that Emma's Russian boyfriend seemed to have the inside track. He continued his courting, bringing bags of food, letting her get used to him. He knew that his friends in the rooming house were assuring Emma that Louie was a steady and true man.

"They talk to Emma," he explained. "They say we both need, they tell I came from old socialists, you know. So she hear that I'm a good man, and things like that." He gave a "hoo-hoo" laugh, which he uses to cover embarrassment; he didn't want to seem immodest. Talking about his pity for her, the jail coat, the groceries, he did a lot of hoo-hooing.

A few weeks after their first meeting, Louie went along with Emma, her brother John and their niece Mabel Konkin, second daughter of Alex and Annie, to a Ukrainian concert. The men found themselves alone together for a few minutes on the sidewalk outside the concert hall. "If things go right," Louie told John seriously, "I'm going to be in the family, you know."

John considered this a moment and nodded. When he got back to Blaine Lake, he told his wife Lena, "Louie's a good man, steady, hard-working. Emma would be all right marrying him."

Doukhobors prefer that their kin marry Doukhobors, a sentiment common in all clans of the human tribe, but for them a Ukrainian isn't so bad. John's own daughter Lily married a German, which took real adjustment. Fred recalled that the German suitor came calling with a bottle of whisky, which he and John shared for some time before Gunther said, "I'm going to pop the question."

John replied doubtfully, "Hitler and Stalin never got along."

Gunther, unperturbed, observed, "That's right."

John sighed. "But I guess we'll have to get along with you," he said, extending his hand.

Louie took Emma to meet his daughter Lorris, then fourteen. Lorris Sawula was an independent teen-ager, accustomed to fending for herself after a lifetime of neglect; Emma was a young woman of twenty-eight who had her fill of upheaval and wanted peace and order. There was no warmth between them.

"Emma liked children," Lorris commented with chilling insight, "but she wasn't maternal."

"Lorris didn't say nothing bad to me," Louie mused, "but I don't know whether she like Emma or not. The boy met Emma too. They wouldn't told me they don't like her." He added loyally, "But Emma like them."

He proposed to Emma less than a month after they met. She said yes without hesitation.

They were married on a Saturday night, 5 March, 1949, in the living room of the house of Louie's brother, Peter Sawula, in Saskatoon. As a divorced man, Louie couldn't have a Catholic ceremony, which didn't have much meaning for him anyway. The service was performed by a controversial Saskatoon clergyman, the Reverend C.P. Bradley, an Australian who had arrived in Saskatoon in the midst of the Depression. Bradley occupied the pulpit in one of the city's grander churches, St. Andrew's Presbyterian, which enjoys a splendid river view and an establishment congregation.

Bradley's politics were far too radical for his parish, and his parishioners ejected him, saying he hadn't been properly ordained. He subsequently launched what he called the People's Church and became president of the local Canadian-Soviet Friendship Council.

"He was for working people," Louie Sawula explained.

"Hard times in the thirties. Strikes, relief. Bradley was a good man."

Louie's nephew Orest was best man and Mabel Konkin was her aunt's attendant. Alex E., Emma's father, attended, and so did her brothers Bill and John and their wives.

Bill wasn't much impressed with his new brother-in-law, then or ever. "I still don't know why she married him," he grumbled, sitting in his farmhouse in Marcelin one October afternoon in 1983. "He wasn't her type really. He had nothing to say."

The tiny Sawula house was packed with some twenty-five guests. The room was so steamy that the wedding photographer had to wait fifteen minutes before his camera lens was free of fog.

The wedding picture shows Emma wide-eyed, an enigmatic smile on her face. She is wearing a small hat tilted over her right eye and a dress reminiscent of her first wedding dress in its abundance of fussy detail. Louie looks serious and resolute.

The photograph appeared in newspapers across the country. Louie was astonished and delighted when a friend told him he had seen it in a Winnipeg paper. In several cities the picture was labelled "Convicted spy marries," and the accompanying story mentioned the dead child, the husband who committed suicide, Gouzenko's defection and the two and a half years in prison.

Louie and Emma moved into a larger room in Emma's rooming house while he looked for a house. There was no question of Emma quitting her job; they needed the money. She had found something that paid better than the drugstore, an office job with a man from eastern Canada who sold his own brand of cold cream.

Louie had the impression that there was something unsavoury about that operation, because Emma left after a short time. Her next job was in the office of a collection agency.

They rented a house until Louie could manage the modest down-payment required to buy a government-subsidized "war-time house" — a small pre-fabricated building. Thousands of houses were erected in Canada to accommodate veterans. Lorris Sawula moved in with Louie and Emma; it was an arrangement neither woman liked very much.

"She didn't need a fourteen-year-old daughter," Lorraine, now married and living in Toronto, said forgivingly. "I'd never had a parental figure and when you don't have it, you don't miss it."

The family struggled along uncomfortably for two years until Louie and Emma had saved enough money to buy a better house. Louie's son, Ernest, was newly married and wanted to take over the war house at 1709 Victoria Avenue. Until Louie and Emma moved, nineteen-year-old Ernie and his bride lived upstairs.

Louie and Emma hoped to relocate in what he called "a nice neighbourhood" but they couldn't afford any of the houses they liked. In the end they bought a modest bungalow at 425 Avenue G South, a pleasant street of small houses well kept by loving owners.

Louie broke the news to Lorris that Emma didn't want her to live with them. Though it meant Lorris had to leave school at sixteen, she accepted the decision with some relief. "I wanted to be on my own," she commented without bitterness. "And I was lucky enough to get a job right away as a bookkeeper with a magazine distributor."

Louie signed the Victoria Avenue house over to his son. Strictly speaking, these houses were supposed to be only occupied by veterans. There was a small flurry of bureaucratic indignation as inquiries were made as to whether Louie had attempted to resell the house to another veteran. After a while the matter was dropped. "It was the same name, it was still in the family, so they let it go," Louie explained.

Emma continued to look for a job that would pay better. She was drawn to the field of law; her court appearances had impressed her with the dignity and intelligence of lawyers. One day just before the move to the house on G Street, she spotted an advertisement in the help-wanted column of the *Star Phoenix* for a secretarial job in the firm of Kyle, Ferguson and Hnatyshyn. It might have been the Ukrainian name, Hnatyshyn, that gave her confidence.

The partner who needed a secretary, however, was George Ferguson, a formidable and proper man who was a brigadier general in the Canadian army, newly discharged after commanding the army's demobilization. Emma knew the name and the man's reputation for stiff propriety; some of her Blaine Lake neighbours retained George Ferguson when they needed a city lawyer.

Ferguson interviewed Emma and seemed impressed with her skills.

"Where did you get your experience, Mrs. Sawula?" he asked.

"I worked for the civil service in Ottawa," she replied.

Ferguson smiled as he joked, "Did you know the famous Emma Woikin?"

Emma said bleakly, "Don't you recognize me?"

Ferguson belatedly put it together. His face reddened and he was too stunned to speak. Emma rose.

"Perhaps it wouldn't be good for your firm to have me here," she offered graciously. "Think it over. You can call me in the morning."

That afternoon Ferguson conferred with John Hnatyshyn. Hnatyshyn was a passionate prairie Tory who later was appointed to the Senate when his friend John Diefenbaker was prime minister; Ferguson was a staunch Liberal. It was 1951 and McCarthyism was at its peak in the United States, where careers and lives were being destroyed by the mere hint of Communist sympathy.

There could not have been a less auspicious time for a convicted Canadian spy to be seeking a position in a prestigious, politically astute legal firm in a righteous prairie city. John Hnatyshyn and George Ferguson are dead; Hnatyshyn's son, Ramon, a member of Parliament, never was told what transpired in the partners' discussion about Emma. However, their decision to hire the ex-convict, a confessed traitor, speaks highly of their fairness and decency.

The next morning Webster told Emma to report for work as soon as possible.

Years later Emma told Doreen Konkin, the wife of her nephew Fred, how to get a job. "You just walk right in and sell yourself," she advised her. "You don't fool around. If they ask you a whole lot of questions, just disregard them and tell them what they want to hear. That's the way to get a job."

It was Doreen's impression that Emma was describing her manner during the interview with George Ferguson. If so, it sheds another light on the near-miracle of her employment. All accounts of Emma Konkin Woikin Sawula stress the extraordinary energy that radiated from her. If she was in top form for her interview with Ferguson, her vivid blue eyes snapping, the man could not help but be dazzled.

Ramon Hnatyshyn, who was a member of Cabinet when Joe Clark was prime minister, was in high school when Emma was hired by his father's firm. Interviewed in the summer of 1983 in his handsome office on Parliament Hill in Ottawa, he thought that his father must have reasoned that the firm didn't work in areas where a security clearance was needed. Also, he said, grinning, Emma Sawula was just about the best secretary anyone had ever seen.

"What she did, she did with vigour," he recalled affectionately. "She was a first-rate typist and smart as a whip. She could look after everything. Talk about para-legal, she was the predecessor of para-legals. You could give her the name of the client in any regular routine transaction, give her the essential details, and she would prepare the documentation while the lawyers went out for coffee. Or whatever."

John Diefenbaker often dropped in to see his friend and loyal supporter John Hnatyshyn. Emma considered Diefenbaker a windbag and wore a look of disapproval until he took his leave.

Other regular visitors were the Royal Canadian Mounted Police, who came in plain-clothes to lean on the lawyers about Emma. Ray Hnatyshyn estimated that these calls went on for fifteen years. They were still happening when he graduated from law school and joined the firm. They asked him about Emma's friends, whether she was active in any political organizations, what he thought her political views were, whether she had made any notable comments about the government.

He was certain that Emma was perfectly aware of the identity of his callers. There was something stiff about the way she moved while the Mounties were on the premises. Neither of them ever discussed it.

Chapter Thirteen

Emma Sawula was perfectly suited to the 1950's style of woman. Like her housewife counterparts she was a product of the Depression who had known hunger and shabbiness and was now transfixed with gratitude to have a home of her own with sparkling windows and a neat front lawn, a car in which to take Sunday drives in the country, a refrigerator full of food, and a closet that contained clothes no one else had worn.

In appreciation, women of that era devoted themselves with a passion to waxing floors to a high shine, learning from *Chatelaine* magazine how to prepare casserole dinners for guests, and enfolding their husbands in adoration.

Every woman was a paragon; it was the style. Marion Woodman, a Jungian analyst in Toronto, wrote a book in 1982 that touched on the compulsion to be blameless. The book, *Addiction to Perfection*, described such women as Emma. "She is starving. She has to perform perfectly in order to be loved. Her emotional stability is determined by another's reaction. . . . She cannot depend on a love which accepts her for who she is . . . the only way she can alleviate her dependence on that judgmental voice [within] is to be perfect enough to shut it up. But there is no shutting it up."

Marion Hilliard, an obstetrician at Women's College Hospital in Toronto, wrote a runaway best-selling book in the fifties, *A Woman Doctor Looks at Love and Life,* based on a series that ran in *Chatelaine* and sold out every issue. She advised a woman who was too tired by the end of the day to want sex to "put her Thespian skill to work at convincing her husband he is desired. . . . By nourishing her husband's ego, she ensures his contentment which, in turn, will ensure her own."

As feminists were later to complain, that kind of advice made all women actresses. Whatever it cost to be the perfect bedmate, the resourceful nurse of three children down with measles, the neighbour with the unfailing sponge cake and the organizer of the annual Fun Fair to raise money for the Home and School Association, women kept their doubts and despair hidden.

Chatelaine also contained articles about a puzzling phenomenon in the midst of such domestic bliss: the prevalence of nervous breakdowns among housewives.

From childhood Emma had found herself in a situation where there was a need for her to be perfect in order to feel sure of acceptance. Because of her clouded parentage, reflected in her physical differences from other Konkins, she exerted herself from an early age to be helpful, charming, loving, appreciative and thoughtful beyond reproach.

That conditioning carried her into a marriage where her husband's family was not entirely welcoming, so she laboured harder in the fields than any of them, despite her frailness, to protect herself from criticism. In Ottawa, where she was a country cousin, a Doukhobor on top of that, she was crisp, efficient and willing, a star in the office.

She even coped with the adversity of prison by being a cheerful, friendly, co-operative presence who identified with the staff, not with other prisoners. Though close family members saw her pain in the months following her discharge, until she was dying, she never showed her despair to anyone.

She sailed into her new life in Saskatoon with all flags flying. All she had to do to keep afloat was to be the best legal secretary in the office and make Louie Sawula the most contented man on earth. For a woman of Emma's ability and determination, both were a snap.

"It was 'my Louie' this and 'my Louie' that," her brother Bill complained.

"Louie was a little fussy about some things," Doreen Konkin observed, "but Emma would do anything to please him. If he didn't like what she served, she'd jump up and make him something else."

Emma quickly became aware of John Hnatyshyn's large brood of bright children and took them under her wing.

"She practically baby-sat all those kids," Saskatoon lawyer David Beaubier commented.

Ray Hnatyshyn agreed. "It was evident she had a frustrated maternal streak," he said. "She had wanted children and she was very fond of children. Greta and I were married quite a while before we had a child and when we finally did, Emma was right there. She had a maternalistic streak, to put it mildly."

The Hnatyshyn children learned about Emma's background from their father, bit by bit, at dinner conversations. The children were excited by the drama but they grasped that they were never to speak of it outside the house, and certainly never to Emma herself. Despite the closeness that developed between Ray Hnatyshyn and Emma, neither ever referred to her trial or the years in prison.

The propriety of the office was established by George Ferguson. The younger Hnatyshyn always called Emma "Mrs. Sawula," never "Emma," and he was Mr. Hnatyshyn to her even when she was his mentor during his articling period.

"I was told, but I don't believe it, that she was apprehensive about people who knew about her past," Ramon Hnatyshyn reflected, sitting in his shirt-sleeves in his Ottawa office in May, 1983. "I don't recall having any sense of that myself. But I was talking to a guy who is on the court of appeal now, a judge who is a friend from law-school days. When he was articling in Saskatoon he recognized Emma because he used to teach in the Blaine Lake area. He felt her tense when she realized he knew that she was Emma Woikin. I never saw anything like that but maybe I was too naive to notice."

Emma appeared carefree. She picked out the furniture for the small house on Avenue G and supervised renovations to make two decent-sized bedrooms out of three tiny ones. The Sawulas also added panelling in the living room and glassed in the front porch. Emma made quilts for the beds and pillows for the brocade sofa. She painted on black velvet and gave the pictures to anyone who admired them. She made hundreds of Doukhobor head scarves, *"platoks,"* hand-painting each with flowers and birds, and gave them to family and friends.

When she needed a new dress, she and Louie would shop together on Saturday afternoons. Both were critical about clothes. The fit and quality had to be just right. Emma would model one after another for him, finding the neck wrong with this one, the price too high on that one, the colour wrong in the others. Finally she would select some fabric, pick out a pattern, bounce home and run up a new dress in time to wear it that evening.

To Louie's delight, she loved his Ukrainian friends. The house was full of guests who were made thoroughly welcome by the hostess.

"What a wonderful woman, oooh boy," Louie remembered appreciatively. "So smart. Everybody like her. How many parties we had in our house, big parties. Ooh boy."

Louie's daughter Lorraine Bertram agreed without hesitation. "Emma was excellent for my father, just excellent," she said.

Bill Konkin was not as enthusiastic. "After she married Louie Sawula I didn't see her much," he said disgustedly. "She was so involved with the Ukrainians. They just play dumb cards, that's what they do. Nothing! I went house, they playing cards. That's what I didn't like. That's what they did all the time, that's stupid!"

Emma's sister, Mary, got along fine with Louie Sawula but she never saw him as a real husband, not the way Bill Woikin had been. "I don't think there was too much there," she observed, not unkindly. "They were just, well, good partners."

Louie Sawula was ecstatic to be married to Emma. A wise man, he asked no question to which he didn't want the answer. It was more than enough to accept his good fortune; he felt no need to inquire if she loved him.

People speak of how she "spoiled" him. She never uttered a word of criticism, but admired everything he did, went everywhere he wanted to go, kept his clothes pressed the way he liked them, cooked the Ukrainian dishes he loved, asked anxiously while he ate if everything was all right.

Louie was in Toronto in the summer of 1983 to attend the wedding of his grandchild, Connie Bertram. Sitting by the lake one afternoon, watching sea gulls glaring with yellow eyes at bits of litter, he was asked if he and Emma ever quarrelled, did he ever think of a divorce. He was astonished by the question. "Divorce!" he repeated, incredulous. "With Emma!" The questioner must be crazy. He shook his head and finally, still stunned, said, "Never. Never."

Most of the Konkins found Louie easy to like. He sat with a friendly face at family gatherings, content to listen and enjoy the *varenikis,* pastry stuffed with cottage cheese or potato or sauerkraut, and topped with melted butter or yogourt or sour cream.

Emma fed guests as if they had just been rescued from a famine. She could produce a dozen dishes, all freshly made, and never forgot anyone's preference.

Fred Konkin's favourite was Boston cream pie. If he and Doreen dropped in unexpectedly, Emma would slip into the kitchen and in only minutes produce a feast that included Boston cream pie.

Strangely, Emma lost her interest in painting. The first time Doreen saw the painting Emma had done of Kingston harbour seen through the bars of her cell, she exclaimed over it. Emma seemed distant. "That's in the past," she told Doreen curtly. Doreen, still marvelling at the painting, missed the signal and went on, "Do you still paint, Aunt Emma?" Emma replied, this time in a distinctly cold voice, "No, that's all in the past."

It was a long time before Doreen realized that her extraordinary aunt suffered from a poor self-image. "She considered herself very homely," Doreen said with sympathy in her voice. " 'A plain Jane' is what she always called herself. 'Nobody could be as homely as I am,' she would always say. I would cry out, 'But Aunt Emma, you're not homely!' but she didn't really believe that."

The Sawulas built an idyllic life in the pink-and-white bungalow on Avenue G. Louie planted a shade tree in the front and tomatoes against the sunny garage wall in the back, where they grew to a height of six feet and were a source of wonderment to strollers along the rear lane. An ornamental fence kept dogs off the perfect lawn and Emma maintained a vegetable garden in which a weed never lasted a day.

Inside the house the floors shone with wax, the artificial fruit on the coffee table never lacked dusting and cut-glass bowls shattered sunlight into rainbows.

In summer the Sawulas vacationed with friends. Once they drove to Winnipeg in a caravan of cars, stopping at picnic grounds where Emma and the other women unpacked the food while the men sipped whisky in the shade. Once they went east on the train and Emma found the MacDonalds, the people who took her into their home the first day she arrived in Ottawa.

A few times a year they drove to Blaine Lake and made the rounds of the Konkin farms. Their favourite vacation was to take the train to British Columbia and soak in the Harrison Hot Springs.

A few times they drove to North Battleford on Highway 16, which passes Langham. One time Emma indicated, with her head, a weedy looking place on a hill-top near the road. "That's where Bill Woikin and my baby are buried," she said. Louie asked if she would like to stop. She said no.

Louie's seniority on the railway eventually earned him a better job, repairing engines in the yards. He was devoted to Ukrainian friends who worked with him on the railway. Evenings and weekends they played kaiser together, a card game like hearts.

Louie was puzzled that they hadn't any children. "We didn't do anything to stop it," he explained delicately, "but Emma didn't get pregnant." Did they every talk about it? He can't remember that they did.

Emma was as accomplished and indefatigable at the office as in her domestic life. She was the fastest typist; she had an excellent memory for precedents; she greeted the shy clients. She became, by all accounts, almost a member of the Hnatyshyn family, doted on by the children and greatly respected by the parents. John Hnatyshyn paid her the compliment of being tactful in her presence about his political views.

"Those damned Communists!" he would roar, reading in the *Star Phoenix* about the latest activity of Tommy Douglas's CCF government. Then, looking guiltily at Emma, he would clap his hand over his mouth. "Excuse me, Mrs. Sawula," he would apologize.

Emma's performance never slipped but symptoms of strain were beginning to show. In the early fifties she had an operation on her gall bladder. In 1954 she went to Doctor Donald Boyd, a general surgeon in Saskatoon, whose father had been the Konkins' lawyer in Blaine Lake. Boyd was also Louie Sawula's doctor. Emma complained of chest pains; she said her ankles were swollen at night.

Her heart was tested and found to be sound. Boyd told her that he could find nothing to explain her symptoms. He noticed a curious thing: Emma was a different person in his office. She was edgy and anxious, not at all her usual buoyant self.

In the summer of 1956 Emma's father, Alex E. Konkin, died of a heart attack at the age of seventy-nine. At the time he was living with his third wife. He left little land, having given most of it away to his sons long before.

Three years later Emma was back in hospital again, this time with a peptic-ulcer condition. Emma was convinced that she had stomach cancer. Louie had never before seen her frightened and was alarmed. Her fears mounted when the general practitioner they consulted sent her to the cancer clinic at University Hospital, Saskatoon's largest, for tests. She seized Louie's big hands and cried, "Save me, Louie. Save me!"

Louie, eating lunch on a summer day in 1983 in the sedately spinning CN Tower restaurant, said sadly, "How could I save her? Dr. Peterson made operation. After, I said 'Doctor, what is it? Is it cancer?' 'No,' he says, 'Ulcer. Very bad ulcer.' 'Are you sure?' I say. 'Maybe you don't want tell me.' The doctor say, 'I tell you sure, it's very bad ulcer. I took eighty percent of her stomach out.' "

Emma didn't believe that Louie and the doctor were telling her the truth. She was thirty-eight but she seemed obsessed by the belief that she was dying. Louie had to tell her again that it was an ulcer, not cancer; slowly she began to accept that he wasn't deceiving her.

Louie was the only one to know of those few days of terror. As far as the rest of the family could see, Emma was blithe as ever.

"She came through the ulcer operation smiling," Doreen Konkin related. She added thoughtfully, "That's pretty much the Konkin style, really, to act like everything is okay on the outside. Konkins share their troubles with very few. They are pretty secretive about their real feelings.''

Kyle, Ferguson and Hnatyshyn welcomed her back gratefully. No one knew like Emma Sawula where papers were filed and which clients needed mothering more than they needed a lawyer.

Emma's brother Alex A. Konkin also had a horror of cancer. After a visit to a relative dying of the disease, he instructed his family not to tell him if he happened to develop cancer. "I want to have hope," he instructed Annie. "If you tell me it's cancer, that'll be it for me." In 1962 he was diagnosed as having cancer of the pancreas. As he had requested, the nature of his illness was never discussed with him.

He and Annie lived at the Konkin homestead only in the summers. Like the other brothers, he had moved into town. John and Lena were in Blaine Lake, in a big five-bedroom house that had belonged to her father, and Bill and Hannah were in Marcelin.

As Alex declined visibly, the family pretended nothing was wrong. His daughter Pearl doesn't believe he was fooled. One day he said gruffly to Annie, "You have to be a real fool not to know when you're not getting any better."

Like all the Konkins, Alex had obsessive work habits. When he was in his fields he would eat his lunch without leaving the machine. The summer of 1962 was the first time anyone had seen him stop working to eat. When Annie brought his lunch, he climbed off the combine, sat down heavily, and ate what he could.

He was taken to St. Paul's Hospital in Saskatoon, where Emma visited him every day. All the Konkins were at his bedside when he died on 16 December, 1962, at the age of fifty-seven.

The homestead where Bill, Alex, John, Mary and Emma had been raised, where Alex and Annie had raised their three daughters, was abandoned. It was still standing in May, 1983, when Fred Konkin paid a visit. It looked as though the last tenants, Alex and Annie, had departed one load shy of emptying the place.

There was a big bed in the room where Emma had slept. A faded purple dress hung on a hanger behind the door, stirred by the wind that howled through the broken windows and caused the green roller blinds, cobwebbed with cracks, to clatter. An orange crate, upended and covered with a cotton curtain on a string, held an Eaton's catalogue (Spring-Summer 1955), a Band-aid box, a bottle half full of cough syrup and some patched and mended denim work pants.

The bedroom across the way was littered with Pearl's toys. A doll with a cracked bisque face stared palely at the rafters and a hollow rubber ball, one side crushed, rolled once in the wind. Downstairs a sofa spilled its stuffings beneath a 1955 calendar that promised "You can be *sure* if it's Westinghouse." In the summer kitchen there was a wood-burning stove and some chipped enamelled basins. Alex's old peaked cap was hanging on a nail.

Fred Konkin said, "One day we'll just run a bulldozer through here and burn it all."

When Emma's niece Agatha Kardash, returned to the homestead in October to assist in a picture-taking mission, she was torn between nostalgia and distress. Her concern, typical of a Konkin, was that the place didn't look fit to be seen by a visitor; she had to restrain herself from tidying up.

She closed the torn screen door with regret and relief. "There was a lilac bush over there," she said, nodding in the direction of a stubbled field, "and the flowers were here. Oh, you're not going to take *more* pictures!"

There had been great changes in the law firm of Kyle, Ferguson and Hnatyshyn just before Emma's brother died. Kyle and Ferguson had died within six months of one another. Ramon Hnatyshyn, who was in Ottawa serving as executive assistant to Walter Azeltine, government leader in the senate, returned home to help his father keep the firm together.

When John Hnatyshyn died in 1967, the sons took over the firm. There are ten lawyers in the firm now, three of them sons of John Hnatyshyn. "Three brothers and seven referees," is how Ray Hnatyshyn describes the situation.

Emma Sawula gave no sign that the changes affected her but apparently she didn't feel the same after John Hnatyshyn died. Louie Sawula said she was discontented about money. The Hnatyshyns, he said, were tight about wages. Periodically Emma would announce that she was giving notice because she needed a job that paid better, at which she would receive a raise. "That's no way to get what is fair," Louie commented. "She shouldn't have to ask."

Ray Hnatyshyn prefers to think it was because Emma simply wanted a change. Or maybe that she wasn't feeling well. In any case, one day she encountered Marcel Cuelenaere, senior partner in a nearby law firm. Cuelenaere's brother John was John Diefenbaker's partner in Prince Albert. Marcel and Emma knew one another slightly and stopped to talk about John Hnatyshyn's death.

One of them commented that Emma might be thinking of leaving the firm. Cuelenaere needed a secretary and was aware that Emma Sawula was considered one of the best legal secretaries in the city. He mentioned a salary and noted that she was startled and impressed. "I'll let you know," she told him.

A few days later she telephoned him. "Okay, I'm coming," she said.

There are conflicting stories about Cuelenaere's awareness of Emma's criminal background. He said he didn't know, and that he accepted her without asking any questions because he assumed that a man of George Ferguson's character would have investigated her thoroughly. His partner, David Beaubier, had a different recollection. He recalled that he and Cuelenaere had a discussion about Emma's lurid past, wondering if it would pose a problem for them.

"What the hell," Beaubier said breezily. "We just run a simple little law practice, so who cares? She can't do any harm here."

Cuelenaere agreed and observed that Emma's maturity and tact were a great asset, and, besides, he needed a secretary desperately.

They hired her for more money than she had ever made. To Emma's intense gratification, her raises came automatically.

Ramon Hnatyshyn admitted he was deeply shocked at her departure. "It was traumatic when she left," he remarked, his voice choking. "We were all depressed. It was a tearful goodbye. I was depressed particularly." He stopped, clearly moved.

Despite her resignation, Emma continued to visit the Hnatyshyns, bringing preserves and vegetables from her garden. By mutual consent, they never discussed her reasons for leaving.

The offices of the firm Cuelenaere, Beaubier, Walters, Kendall and Fisher, a middle-sized law firm, are on the third floor of the Permanent Building, 210 21st Street East, the city's main street. They are reached by means of a slow old elevator. The offices are devoid of the alarming opulence that marks some big-city legal suites. Even the corner office occupied by Cuelenaere, the senior partner, is as spartan as that of a high-school principal.

Cuelenaere and Beaubier were delighted with their new secretary. "Emma worked more for Marcel than she did for me," explained Beaubier, a big, affable man leaning back in his chair with his foot resting on a open drawer. "I think she may have got along with me better than with him; at least she sent her relatives to me. I have a very direct way of doing things and Emma liked that."

Her work with Beaubier mainly concerned estates. "She was good at estates," Beaubier observed. "Hell, she was good at everything. She was very good with people. Often I'd be tied up and someone would come in and they would want to know something about an estate. What you want for that is a secretary who can walk over and tell them the right thing and not the wrong thing, and send them on their way. They're happy, they've been served. It works."

He shifted in his tipped-back chair. "Emma had enough sense in her head to make a judgement call as to what these people need and should have," he continued. "Like sometimes you don't want to tell people how serious something is because it distresses them. They know they have a problem but they don't know how serious it is. Well, that's why we would have someone like Emma. Someone experienced and tactful."

Soon after she changed employers, in 1967, Trofem Kurchenko, the man who may have been her natural father, died. After years of working for the Konkins, Kurchenko had saved enough to invest in a farm of his own, a quarter section, which he left to Emma, complete with a house and a respectable sum in his bank account. Emma and Louie picked out a handsome gravestone, the best the cemetery had to offer, and made the funeral arrangements.

For the first time in her life, Emma had funds that belonged to her alone, something beyond the income she had been pooling with Louie's wages. She put her inheritance in the bank. At some point, maybe even on the day she learned of her inheritance, she made up her mind: she would visit Russia.

Chapter Fourteen

Emma emerged from Kingston penitentiary no more or less political than she had been before. Emotionally and spiritually, she was drawn to the USSR because it was the homeland of her people and because, to no little degree, the Sokolovs had presented the country as a place where Emma's baby would have been born alive and Bill Woikin would not have committed suicide.

As persistent RCMP inquiries discovered, Emma did not join any of the Communist splinter groups in Canada. Her views were moderate-left. (Ramon Hnatyshyn, a Tory, suspected that she voted for him out of friendship.)

Her decision to visit Russia was not an unusual one. In Saskatchewan, where many Doukhobors and Ukrainians have become relatively prosperous, tours to the Black Sea are advertised by many travel agencies.

"There are members of the Saskatoon Club who have been to Moscow," Donald Boyd, Emma's surgeon, commented. "It's not considered to be something suspicious."

Emma mentioned such an excursion a few weeks after she became Marcel Cuelenaere's secretary. She was chatting with the other women in the office and noted that a friend of hers was leaving for Russia in a few days. Marie Klassen, who was a bookkeeper and legal secretary with the firm for sixteen years, asked innocently, "Isn't he afraid to go?"

Emma's habitual mask of agreeableness slipped. "She flared," Klassen recalled. "She really tore a strip off me. I thought to myself that we would never get along but we did. She acted as if nothing had happened and I never made a remark like that again."

Klassen had a feeling that Emma was at heart a Communist. "I don't know what gave people that idea," she added thoughtfully. "I don't remember that she ever talked politics or commented on events, but still it was there."

Telling only Louie of her plans, Emma contacted a travel agency and booked herself into a twenty-one-day tour to the Soviet Union. She would sail on the Soviet ocean liner *Pushkin*, which was crossing the Atlantic in the summer of 1969.

Emma wanted to make the pilgrimage alone. Louie never questioned her decision to go by herself. It was all right with Louie Sawula; anything Emma did was all right with Louie Sawula.

The editor of a Russian-language paper, *Iskra*, learned of Emma's plans, probably through the travel agent, who provided names for the writer's column of social notes. He knew Emma Sawula was no ordinary Canadian tourist. He contacted the Soviet Embassy in Ottawa and told them that someone identified as a spy by Igor Gouzenko, someone who had become a martyr in a Canadian prison, was about to visit the Soviet Union.

Emma sailed on the *Pushkin* as an anonymous member of her group but after the boat docked she received special treatment. She was assigned a personal guide who took her wherever she wanted to go. Doctor Boyd thought he heard that she was presented with a medal, but Louie Sawula knew nothing of this. She sent postcards to friends and relatives. Marie Klassen kept the one that came to the women who worked in the law firm. Dated 29 June, 1969, and illustrated with some glorious scenery in the Black Sea region, it read:

Hello, all of you. This is the sort of countryside
we are spending time in. Today is the last day at
Socki, a city that spreads 145 miles along the Black
Sea, and tomorrow we go to Tbilise and then Moscow

and then *HOME*. The trip is most enjoyable but I am looking forward to being home again. Emma.

Something awful happened to Emma in Russia, something that struck at the foundations of her being. Perhaps she learned that the country she had imaged as free and great was really repressive; perhaps she met the Sokolovs again and was crushed by their betrayal. She confided in no one, but after her return from Russia Emma Konkin Woikin Sawula began to drink herself to death.

When she returned she told everyone in her usual warm and enthusiastic way that the trip had been wonderful. Those who knew her best detected a false note in her glowing reports. She admitted to Doreen and Fred Konkin, for instance, that the voyage on the *Pushkin* had been the best part of the journey; the Soviet Union had been a bit of a disappointment.

Doreen said, "There was a change in Emma when she returned. Something was bothering her. Something was not quite right."

Emma's sister, Mary, had a theory that Emma went to Russia because she knew she had cancer and she was hoping that a certain fabled women doctor there could save her.

"She didn't talk about it, even to me," Mary remarked sorrowfully. "She wouldn't tell anybody. She didn't want people to know she was sick. When she came back from Russia she wouldn't say anything too much, but I knew she had given up hope. She didn't want to go to the doctor any more."

With Louie Sawula's permission, Emma's doctor, Donald Boyd, revealed that Emma did not have cancer when she went to Russia — or ever. In 1969 her health was normal. There was no sign of any malignancy.

In the Soviet Union, Emma sat for a studio photograph with an unidentified woman. Mary believed that women to be the famous doctor Emma went to see; others say that woman was Emma's personal guide. Perhaps the woman was Lida Sokolov.

Emma's usually small appetite grew even smaller, then seemed almost to disappear. She continued to cook huge amounts of delicious food, but took only a taste for herself. Some days she made a meal of two oranges sliced on a plate.

"She couldn't eat anything," mourned Mary. "She would

cook all this food and invite people to a party, her friends more or less, and then eating nothing, nothing. They liked her so much. And she'd made the best of meals and she couldn't eat a thing.''

She told Louie that the Soviet Union was a wonderful place; he should go too and visit his sister. The next summer he went. She did not accompany him.

Doctor Boyd's office nurse, Irene Irwin, lived not far from the house on Avenue G. On fine days Emma and Irene Irwin both enjoyed walking the near-mile to work, taking a route along the wide and beautiful South Saskatchewan River.

During the ten years of their casual companionship, Emma mentioned bits of her past: the baby who died, the husband who killed himself. But she never mentioned anything that happened after she went to Ottawa. Irwin judged Emma to be a happy and contented woman, devoted to Louie, about whom she talked incessantly, but after Emma's visit to Russia something changed.

"She told me that life in Russia was not all that bad," Irwin recalled. "She talked about going to the theatre and concerts and mentioned that transportation was good there, but she seemed very let down somehow. Her disposition changed. She became quieter, and depressed. She had been very excited before the trip but afterwards she seemed disappointed by something."

Emma invited Irwin to her home to see her souvenirs from Russia. The nurse accepted the invitation and the two women shared a pot of tea. At that time, Irene Irwin said, there was no sign that Emma already was a heavy drinker.

Emma had always been a social drinker; she would have a drink with Louie or when friends gathered. She had a notable capacity to drink along with others and show no sign of being drunk. Still, it was apparent to a few in her family that Emma was beginning to drink more, much more, than they did. Mary and others put it down to the cancer theory they were developing — that Emma had cancer and was drinking to relieve the pain. They could think of no other reason for Emma to make herself drunk.

Emma helped the myth along by referring to her "indigestion." "There's something wrong with my stomach," she would complain, pushing her plate away.

In the beginning of the decline, her employers had no evidence that Emma had become an alcoholic. David Beaubier found her invaluable in settling estates that involved relatives in the Soviet Union. When a Ukrainian-born or Russian-born Canadian leaves something in his or her will to someone in the Soviet Union, the Russians create a horrendous amount of red tape. The estate can be depleted by as much as fifty percent before it reaches the heir.

One lawyer in Winnipeg had become proficient at settling such estates and most estate work was routed through him — until Emma Sawula entered on the scene. The Cuelenaere firm became a short-cut and money-saver many were grateful to find.

"She would whack off a letter in Russian," David Beaubier explained. "And she was really great." He described one occasion when Emma advised the relatives in the Soviet Union to allow her to purchase goods for them in Russia rather than send them the money directly; her idea saved them a considerable amount.

"She got catalogues from a little store," Beaubier recalled. "I think there were only two kinds of cars that were available. She phoned long-distance to straighten out which one they wanted. It was very thoughtful of her, because she knew that ordinarily Soviet citizens have to wait for years to buy a car, unless they are a party functionary. The heirs were thrilled. With the money left over Emma bought them other things, gas coupons I think."

Beaubier and Emma conferred closely on this and other cases involving Russia. Her attitude towards Soviet bureaucracy, he said, was no more respectful than her attitude towards Canadian bureaucracy. Her feeling seemed to be that authorities are the same everywhere: difficult.

Emma was highly regarded outside the office as well. Once Louie Sawula attended an office party with Emma. As was his custom at such functions, he kept in the background, content to admire his wife's fancy friends. A judge sat beside him and, on learning Louie's identity, told him seriously, "You know, your wife knows more about law than some lawyers."

Louie gave his hoo-hoo laugh, enormously gratified that his wife was so highly regarded. "A judge!" he emphasized. "A judge said that!"

Emma had a new concern, the health of her brother, John Konkin, the one closest to her. John was suffering from a serious heart condition he had decided to ignore.

Of the three Konkin brothers, John was the questing one. His life was marked by bad luck and poor timing, a combination not improved by his impulsiveness. Burned out of the first farm his father gave him, he later transferred the homestead to his brother Alex.

Then John moved into Blaine Lake and lived in a big house, where his natural grand hospitality had full scope. Fred remembered that sometimes all five bedrooms were full of guests. Fred would come home some evenings and find his own bed occupied by a stranger. People who came to Blaine Lake to visit Doukhobors or to study Doukhobors always seemed to stay with John and Lena Konkin.

One of the Konkins' most celebrated guests was Stefan Sorokin, who stayed with them in 1949. Sorokin was a Russian who thought the Sons of Freedom were the truest Doukhobors and won the loyalty of many of them. Blaine Lake's Independent Doukhobors gave him a courteous reception but rejected his exhortations that they stop educating their children and give up private ownership.

Sorokin suggested that he was the legendary Doukhobor leader known as "The Hawk." Fred Konkin was assigned the task of accompanying Sorokin to the sauna to look for the distinguishing hawk-shaped mark the leader was supposed to have on his body. Fred reported to the elders that Sorokin had no mark. Though the Russian remained in Blaine Lake a while longer, his power to influence those Doukhobors was gone.

John Konkin traded the big house in Blaine Lake for a garage and some land in Marcelin. He lived there for three disastrous years. Business was poor, and one day he locked the garage door and walked away from the business. For a while he took over a big flour mill in Blaine Lake which had been abandoned, but he couldn't get the business on its feet and had to give up.

"He liked being in business rather than farming because he wanted to be with people," his daughter-in-law Doreen Konkin explained. "He wanted something more interesting to do than sit on a tractor by himself."

His next venture was a Shell bulk dealership. He took delight in driving the huge delivery truck to farms and service stations, and hanging around afterwards to chew the fat. If people couldn't pay, John Konkin was willing to barter. He'd take some cattle or a bit of used machinery instead of money.

He and his brother Bill jointly owned a herd of Aberdeen Angus. Bill commented disgustedly,"They are fence-busters from the word go. You just can't keep track of them." Early in 1969 Bill and John were chasing cows when John sat down abruptly, his face white. Bill ran for help and an ambulance took John to St. Paul's Hospital in Saskatoon. When Mary went to visit her brother there, she found him already talking about getting back to Blaine Lake in a hurry. He had big plans, he told her; he wanted to buy a combine.

"You'd better slow down," she advised. "Sell the cattle and slow down."

He laughed. "I'll be all right," he assured her.

In September 1969 he had another attack. Doreen telephoned Mary and told her that this was a very bad one. Soon after John reached hospital, his heart stopped. St. Paul's cardiac-arrest team succeeded in getting it started again, but in the process they broke some ribs. John was amused. When Mary arrived at his bedside he told her he was thinking of suing them.

Bill Konkin issued orders to keep closed the curtains in John's hospital room. John's crops were still in the fields and Bill didn't want his brother worried about adverse weather. "People say, 'Don't worry about it,' but you do worry about it," Bill remarked. "That's easier said than done, not worrying."

Bill sighed heavily and went on: "It was the beginning of October and someone opened the drapes. It was snowing. In twenty minutes John was dead. It was a bastard." He shook his head. "It's stupid to worry about material things like a crop but, there you go, how can you stop a guy?"

Fred and Doreen, who had been living in Saskatoon with their two daughters, returned to Blaine Lake to take over the Shell dealership. Fred found that the books were a mess, the result of John's casual bartering habits; they could not be straightened out. Eventually John's farm holdings proved a failure too. Fred and Doreen stayed in Blaine Lake anyway, in their snug and gleaming bungalow across from the rink. Doreen took a job working in the office of the Blaine Lake

RCMP detachment and Fred became an insurance agent for Pennsylvania Life, a job that kept him on the road collecting premiums on hail insurance all over northern Saskatchewan.

Emma was devastated by John's death. Most people saw little change in her usual energy and gregarious good spirits but those close to her were concerned that something was wrong. "She was a lonely woman," her nephew John Konkin observed shrewdly.

Marie Klassen, who saw her in the office, was coming to the same conclusion. Emma knew hundreds of people, Klassen noted, but there was no one close to her. She had no confidante, no intimate — friend or relative — with whom she revealed her real feelings.

One day in the spring of 1971 Marcel Cuelenaere spotted a small bottle of some clear liquid he took to be vodka in the drawer of Emma's desk. She gave no appearance of drinking on the job, and he decided it was none of his business.

Cuelenaere remembered an afternoon when he and his wife accepted Emma's invitation to visit her home on Avenue G. He could still recall vividly the perfection of her garden, everything lined up in docile rows and not a weed to be seen. When Emma went into the kitchen to prepare the tea, he thought she was gone overly long. Later, remembering the vodka bottle, he decided she must have been having a drink.

David Beaubier disapproves of office socializing after work. He was wary of the cosiness Emma sought. "I have no doubt that she wanted to baby-sit my son, move right in there," he said, not without affection. "I wouldn't allow it because I think there should be some distance between people who work together."

For a woman with a prison record, Emma Sawula had developed an astonishing sideline: she was sought by Saskatoon judges to be a court interpreter for Russian or Ukrainian people whose English was poor. Beaubier richly enjoyed the irony. "All the good and true Conservative judges were happy to have her," he grinned. "I'd run into a judge on the street and he'd say, 'By the way, I'll be needing Emma next week.' We'd give her time off."

Marie Klassen described Emma as a person who always displayed high spirits and a sense of playfulness. "There was lots of zip and fun to her," she reflected. "She seemed to have a zest for life. She could laugh with people. Did she have empathy? Oh, no. I would say that she needed empathy."

Emma was having problems with her menopause. A hysterectomy was performed in City Hospital and the surgeon found both her Fallopian tubes blocked, possibly the reason for her sterility. The blockages were caused by an old pelvic inflammation.

Emma returned to work, seemingly her old self. Louie talked happily about the good times they were having, playing cards almost all night sometimes.

"We would drink and drink," he remembered fondly. "I could drink forty ounces of whisky and feel good, not drunk. I was strong. I could drink and still drive home. Emma never learned to drive. Emma would keep up, drinking with me, and the next day she never said she had a headache. She never didn't feel good. Oh no. She was just the same."

Doctor Boyd commented somberly, "You see it sometimes when a hundred-pound wife is drinking with her husband, who is two hundred pounds, matching him drink for drink. The woman can go down very fast."

Some may have wondered about the drinking, but no one felt comfortable to comment. People who cared about Emma complain that she was a hard person to help. "She was always doing things for other people but she was embarrassed to have you do anything for her," Doreen Konkin observed. She told of a time when she and Fred were invited to dinner with Emma and Louie, and brought a bottle of wine. Emma seemed shocked by such largesse. "You shouldn't have done that!" she kept protesting.

Doreen and Fred feel there is a balance to be struck in the matter of hospitality. Doreen is the kind of woman who brings a jar of borscht when she visits, and Fred reaches for the cheque in a restaurant. They found Emma's resistance to receiving a gift a real problem.

Another time the Konkins brought Emma corn on the cob, which she loved. Doreen had frozen some from her garden and gave Emma a bag of ears. "She couldn't get over it." Doreen laughed. "You'd think I had given her something wonderful. Oh my."

Fred recalled a day when Emma was visiting in Blaine Lake

and asked if Fred could get her some fresh pork. She didn't eat pork herself; she wanted it for Louie. Fred had a friend who had just butchered a pig, and Fred had bought half of it. He went to his freezer and handed Emma a roast. Emma hunted for her handbag and asked how much she owed him.

Fred was offended. "If I can't give something to my aunt as a present I'm going to take it back," he told Emma. Seeing he meant it, Emma accepted the roast. Doreen could see that she was uncomfortable.

Louie encountered the same difficulty. One Christmas he bought Emma some jewellery at Birks. Emma was horrified to see the familiar blue box in which the store has packaged gifts for generations. Even before she opened it, she was scolding Louie for spending too much money on her.

Her one luxury was a coat of dark-brown mink paws and a hat to match. She loved that coat. Even so, she bought it under protest. Louie was with her when she went shopping for a fur coat and disapproved of the cheap one she selected. "It looks like hell," he told her, thinking of the jail coat, and picked out the one made of mink paws.

Louie never saw Emma cry, he said. If that is true, Emma was a consummate actress. All her other relatives speak of how easily she cried, how sentimental she was and, at the end, of her sadness. Her niece Pearl recalled one evening when Emma began to cry at the dinner table. "All of a sudden, she got depressed and started to cry," Pearl related. "My mother asked, 'Why are you crying?' Aunt Emma answered, 'Well, my two brothers have passed away. I miss them. It's so sad.' "

Pearl added matter-of-factly, "She'd had a few drinks, and all that."

In the fall of 1972, Emma began to telephone Marie Klassen in the evenings. Though the two women worked together amiably enough, Marie never thought of herself as Emma's friend, so the calls seemed odd: they were also pointless. She could hear music in the background as Emma explained that she was calling because she was having a wonderful party.

"We're having such a good time," she would tell the puzzled Marie. "Do you hear the music?"

Once when she called there was no party sound; Emma appeared to be alone in the house. She told Marie that she was depressed and wanted to talk to someone. They chatted about inconsequentials for a while and then Emma hung up. Marie thought Emma had sounded drunk, but she wasn't sure.

Louie Sawula retired from the CNR after forty-seven years. His friends gave him a farewell dinner and he made a brief, embarrassed speech. Emma then spoke and by all accounts what she said was unexpectedly passionate and moving. David Beaubier, who heard this from several people who were there, heard she said the CNR was nothing without its workers, that the people who fixed the track and loaded baggage were the railway.

One morning in the spring of 1973 she called the office to say that she wasn't well enough to work. She had indigestion, she said. After that there were many days when she didn't appear in the office.

People who went to the house on Avenue G found Emma frightfully weak. She couldn't stand for long and would lower herself into a chair with a deep sigh of exhaustion. Still, she insisted on cooking and serving huge meals. The family watched in consternation as she would refuse to eat and sometimes left the table to go to the bathroom and vomit.

"Maybe it's my ulcer again," she offered weakly.

Louie pleaded with her to see a doctor; everyone did. She said there was nothing a doctor could do for her. They thought she was talking about cancer.

In November, 1973, almost a year after the hysterectomy, her sister Mary came to visit. She was alarmed to find that Emma had collapsed and was too weak to move. She called Doctor Boyd over Emma's protests and he advised taking her to the hospital. Mary, Pete and Louie carried Emma to the car. Mary told the nurses in the emergency department that Emma hadn't eaten in a month. She was gratified when Donald Boyd ordered intravenous feeding.

Boyd's notes of the diagnosis make no mention of an ulcer. Her condition, as he described it, was "anorexia and chronic depression." He added, "alcohol suspected but not admitted." His examination of her liver, which was distended, convinced him that Emma was drinking heavily. She denied it vehemently.

Irene Irwin, who worked for Boyd and knew the diagnosis but shared her employer's respect for confidentiality, went to

visit Emma in the hospital. She was amazed at Emma's mood.
The woman seemed indifferent about living. "I had thought
she was so happy," Irene commented in a conversation about
Emma in October, 1983. "When I saw her in hospital she didn't
seem to care if she got better or not."

Dave Beaubier also paid a visit to the hospital. He and Emma
talked idly for about a hour, mostly about the office and people
they knew. He thought Emma seemed wistful and defeated.

"I don't mean she was saying 'Poor me' or anything like
that," he hastened to add, "but she was really sorry for herself.
I think she knew the jig was up. There were some tears."

Beaubier comforted her, saying she would be back at work in
no time, her old self. Neither believed it.

Reflecting later on that visit, Beaubier observed flatly, "I
don't think Emma really enjoyed her life from the time she got
out of prison until the day she died."

A few days after Emma's hospitalization, Boyd took Louie
aside. "Is Emma drinking?" he asked.

Louie replied evasively, "Yeah, I guess so."

"How much?"

Louie shrugged. "I donno, I don't see. Maybe she drinks in
the night. She gets up in the night."

Boyd told him to hide the household's liquor. Louie thought
the measure was extreme. He couldn't believe that Emma was
an alcoholic. He was convinced then, and remained convinced,
that the drinking was Emma's way of coping with terrible pain.

"She was drinking because her stomach bother her," he said,
and then added thoughtfully, "Maybe she feel bad, so bad she
wants the alcohol. I don't know. I think she kept to herself lots."

Nevertheless, he obeyed the doctor. He hid the whisky in the
kitchen but Emma found it immediately. Next he put the
bottles in the fruit cellar behind the jars of preserves.

One night he wakened to the sound of someone falling down
the basement stairs. He ran, sick with dread, and switched on
the basement light. Emma was sprawled at the foot of the stairs,
still holding a cup in her hand.

"She missed the step in the dark and was going down, still
holding the cup," he said, not knowing whether to laugh or
cry. "I come up and say, 'Oh Emma' and pull the cup from her
hand. 'You're not supposed to drink,' I say to her."

Emma got up, walked briskly up the stairs without a word and got back in bed.

Louie added, mourning, "If I had known she was going to die, I would never stop her. I wouldn't take the cup away, I would let her drink."

She returned to work, but only occasionally. There were no bloodshot eyes, no hang-overs; Emma never had a discoloured nose or slurred her speech or staggered. Beaubier, who had a relative who was an alcoholic, was amazed that there were none of the classic symptoms he associated with drinkers. "Looking back on it," he commented, "over those last two years she occasionally had a flushed face. But I didn't put that down to alcohol."

Between the hospitalization and Emma's death, Beaubier had the impression that Emma was anxious to tell him about what happened in Ottawa. She brought up some aspect of it a few times but he always discouraged her. He's an open, friendly man but he didn't want to hear about Emma's experience as a spy.

"It wasn't that I didn't want to sit around and spend some time with Emma," he explained. "I'm fairly casual and if one of the girls wants to come in and spend fifteen minutes pouring her heart out, well, that's fine. I'll see what I can do. But I thought there was an episode in Emma's life that we were specificially not going to get into; you know, the less said about it the better."

The admission made him uncomfortable. "At the time, I'll be perfectly clear, I thought she was going to sit down and tell me her life story," he went on. "And I didn't want that." He added, "If you'd come to Saskatoon to interview her then, you could have had Emma Sawula on a platter."

The absences from the office became more frequent and lasted longer. Marcel Cuelenaere would telephone Emma at home, distracted because he couldn't find a file or needed an address or wanted a name. Mary, who was there for some of the calls, was satisfied that her sister was indispensible.

Emma was refusing to see her doctor. Donald Boyd encountered Mary on the street and asked after Emma's health. When Mary told him how weak Emma was, he was concerned. Mary passed his comment along to Emma. Emma's reply was, "Tell him to go to hell."

Mary was amazed. It wasn't like Emma to talk that way. Besides, she knew Emma had a high regard for Boyd.

Emma's diet consisted almost entirely of oranges and alcohol, and her physical condition was worsening rapidly. Louie went one day to visit his son Ernie in The Pas; Ernie wanted his father to help him find a house. When Louie returned the next evening he found Emma passed out in the kitchen. She had taken a taxi to the liquor store.

He picked her up in his arms, frightened at how thin she was. He estimated she had lost perhaps thirty pounds from her customary one hundred forty. Still she was a dead weight, so limp that he had difficulty putting her to bed.

After that she stayed in bed most days, remote and uncaring. Mary said that she cried a lot; Louie never saw tears.

Their twenty-fifth wedding anniversary was 5 March, 1974. Emma rallied enough to dress. She wore her bedroom slippers, safer than shoes with heels. About twenty friends filled the small living room; they brought flowers, gifts and food. Louie placed Emma tenderly on a footstool in the centre of the room and afterwards cursed himself for his thoughtlessness. Before anyone could reach her, Emma leaned back and fell on the floor.

"I should have put her in a chair with a back," Louie grieved.

He lifted her gently, led her to the bedroom and helped her into bed.

She was admitted to St. Paul's Hospital on 9 April. Doctor Boyd noted that she had jaundice and was emaciated, with the distended abdomen common to women alcoholics. Her liver was greatly enlarged but he wasn't pessimistic about her recovery. He prescribed steroids and was pleased to see improvement in her condition.

Emma prepared to die. She was brusque with visitors, urging them to leave almost as soon as they sat down. When someone from the office telephoned she asked that no one come to see her. One woman who disregarded the instruction reported that Emma told her coldly that she didn't want visitors, and turned her face to the wall.

When her sister Mary went to visit, planning to spend a sociable afternoon with Emma, she received the same treatment.

"Why don't you go now," Emma said abruptly, soon after Mary had taken off her coat.

Mary thought Emma was just being polite. "No," she replied, "I want to stay with you."

Emma looked impatient. "You must be sick of sitting there," she suggested.

Mary shook her head. "No, I'm not. I'll stay with you a while longer."

Emma glared at her. "Really," she said, "I mean it. Please go."

Mary went downstairs to the hospital lounge, where she encountered other Konkins on their way to visit Emma. She wasn't surprised that they were back in the lounge a minute later. One of them said she had asked Emma what she wanted, what they could bring her, and Emma replied bitterly, "What does a dying woman need?"

"I went to see her often," Mary sighed, "but she never wanted me to stay."

Doreen and Fred Konkin were given the same reception. They went regularly, not staying long, until one day Emma told them with finality, "You have better things to do. I don't want you to come any more."

Donald Boyd was amazed at the rapidity of her decline. He talked about it one Sunday morning in the spring of 1983 in the nurses' lounge, on the second floor of St. Paul's Hospital. He had been called into surgery to mend the head of a heavy young man who had fallen off a trampoline in the small hours of the morning. Boyd had just changed from his surgical gown and looked weary. He spoke in quick bursts in a raspy, low voice, looking blankly at a low table in front of him, which bore a jar of apple juice, a mottled banana, two ashtrays, a pack of Medi-Wipes, an electronic pager and a tube of silicone cream.

"She went down so fast," he said quietly. "She died a lot more quickly than we thought she would." He said he couldn't understand it, that when he told her she should stop drinking she seemed to drink even more.

Louie was by her bed, holding her swollen hand, the night before she died. She was unconscious. After a while he went back to Avenue G to get some sleep. Early the next morning, 22 May, 1974, Boyd called him. Emma had died without regaining consciousness.

The autopsy report was brutally blunt. It noted that Emma Sawula was fifty-three years old and died of "florid fatty cirrhosis with pulmonary edema. The body was that of a thin, limp, jaundiced woman."

Emma had requested a Doukhobor service and Louie complied. He went shopping for her funeral outfit. "I was looking for some kind of nice dress," he explained earnestly. "I wouldn't mind to pay, I could afford, I had money. You know, for a funeral dress got to be high-necked. I look but I couldn't find anything like that, so I bought some kind of suit."

The service was held in the Saskatoon Funeral Home, one of the city's largest. The crowd overflowed the chapel; some people stood outside in the cold. Almost everyone from the Cuelenaere, Beaubier law firm was there. They found the ceremony decidedly strange, over-long and aimless. The Konkins feel it suffered somewhat from Louie's unfamiliarity with Doukhobor style.

Some of the singing and prayers were in Russian and some in English. Bill Konkin, the family spokesman at ceremonial occasions, gave a brief eulogy. Fred Konkin spoke about the cookies Emma used to make for him. Some of the contributions, however, were disjointed. "If Aunt Emma had seen what happened at her funeral," Doreen Konkin said delicately, "I don't think she would have been too pleased."

Louie Sawula was delighted with it. He declared he also wanted to be buried in the Doukhobor way. "It's not like ministers and priests, who do dah-dah-dah," he explained. "Doukhobors, they have a choir there, the singing's so nice."

Emma Sawula is buried in Plot 628 in Saskatoon's Wood-lawn Cemetery, a vast, peaceful place that stretches beside the railway tracks near the Robin Hood Mills and some grain silos. Ukrainian and Doukhobor names are scattered thickly among the McNultys, Kerrs and Fishers of Saskatoon's English-Scottish founding stock. Part of the cemetery is reserved for the Chinese community, and many markers bear the name Mah, Lee or Eng; another section is for children; still another has row on row of crosses dedicated to men who died in wars.

Ernie Sawula went with his desolated father to select a tombstone. Louie wanted the best for his Emma. They picked red granite on which Louie had engraved:

SAWULA
IN LOVING MEMORY

EMMA
1920–1974
EVER REMEMBERED, EVER LOVED

Louie stayed in the house on Avenue G after Emma's death, but he was a lost man. He put an advertisement in the paper to sell Emma's coat of mink paws. The woman who bought it exclaimed, "I know who wore this. It was that little woman who worked for the senator."

After that, he moped. "I was kinda lonesome, I'll tell you," he related. "I had a home, I had a car, I got money, I had everything. That's all right in the day. But at night comes, sit, you know. Just sit in your house."

A year after Emma's death, his friends told him about a wealthy widow who was looking for a husband. He drove over to see her at her cottage near Flin Flon. She was in the garden picking peas. She was a Ukrainian from Manitoba, he learned. Her husband had owned a fleet of taxis and left her wealthy enough to maintain big houses and travel to the Orient.

They decided that marriage was a practical solution to their common problem, loneliness. Louie, anxious to protect his inheritance from Emma and his own substantial savings, went to Cuelenaere to draw up a prudent marriage contract, so that in the event the union failed he would keep his money and his new wife would keep hers.

He sold the little house on Avenue G and moved into her huge home, where there was an acre of grass to cut. They drove to Florida together in a Cadillac that first winter. She criticized his driving; he wasn't used to being criticized. He missed the little bungalow.

"You should never live in somebody else's property," he commented ruefully. "The bed is always cold to you."

One day, thirteen months after the wedding, he said to her, "Let's not be married any more."

She replied, "Okay."

Louie moved into a condominium apartment in a twenty-two-storey building in a residential area of Saskatoon. The building is full of well-to-do retired people who appreciate the accessible barber shop, hairdressing salon, pool-room and recreation program. The women, most of them tired of cooking after lifetimes in farm kitchens, are grateful that there is a diningroom on the top floor, which affords a magnificent view of the lazy South Saskatchewan River and the flat prairie beyond the city. In winter, when supper is eaten after sundown, Louie is enchanted by the lights of Saskatoon. "Like a fairyland," he says.

He didn't care much for the food served in the building's dining room; no cooking anywhere is as good as Emma's was. After the evening meal he would return to his apartment and watch television, often falling asleep with it on. He grieved that Emma had died so young. Sometimes when he saw an old woman struggling across the lobby in a walker, full of pain and not enjoying life, he wondered why she was alive and his Emma, who was so happy and loved to laugh, was dead.

In 1980 the award-winning CBC radio show "Ideas" broadcast a fictionalized account of the thirteen people in the barracks. George Sherstobetoff, a bright eleven-year-old living in Blaine Lake, came home and asked a question. He said to his mother, Pearl, the daughter of Alex Konkin and niece of Emma Konkin Woikin Sawula, "There's a kid at school who heard on the radio last night that there was once a spy who came from Blaine Lake. Who was that crazy woman who was a spy?".

Pearl looked at her mother, Annie. Neither knew how to answer him.

The boy persisted. He remembered the name of the spy. "It was Emma Woikin," he told his mother. "Did you ever know her? Did you meet her?"

Annie Konkin diverted the boy while Pearl sat stunned. While George ate, the women had a whispered conference. Annie advised her daughter to tell the truth. Pearl said she didn't know what to say. Annie said she would handle it.

She sat down beside George and said simply, "Emma Woikin was your mom's auntie."

A few days later Pearl pulled out the family snapshots and showed her son pictures of Emma. She told him how kind Emma was, how loving, how she used to hug children.

"That's supposed to be something bad, eh?" she explained to Doreen Konkin later. "Going to prison is pretty bad? So I made out it was nothing bad, and I showed him all the presents she gave me."

George was teased about his spy aunt by his friends, who learned who Emma Woikin was from their parents. He endured it in stoic silence. A few days later, the taunts stopped.

Thirteen people went to the RCMP barracks in February 1946. Thirty-seven years later, ten were still living. They were a disparate group, scattered across the globe, with little in common but the accident of history that ground them down. They share something else: an abiding bitterness.

When the National Film Board and the Canadian Broadcasting Corporation film crews were preparing a documentary of the events surrounding Gouzenko's defection, only one of the detainees agreed to appear in it.

Fred Poland, who died in 1982, a respected journalist who specialized in scientific matters, managed to erase his involvement in the spy trials from his biography. His obituary, which appeared in newspapers across the country, made no mention of his time in the barracks.

Gordon Lunan had withdrawn into anonymity in a small Ontario town. David Shugar lived part of the time in his native country, Poland. Raymond Boyer, the oldest of the group, could talk about what happened to him with some dispassion, but bore an underlying soreness. Eric Adams, the economist with the brightest future of them all, was living in Montreal, a quiet, fierce man. There is an account of his trial in Jack Batten's book *In Court*. Joseph Sedgwick, Adams's lawyer, is quoted in Batten's book. He says he met Eric Adams on the street one day and found him "very shabby."

Fred Rose died in March, 1983, in Warsaw, Poland, at the age of 76, still asserting that he was "proud to be a Canadian" though Canada had refused to allow him to visit even when his daughter was married in Montreal. The country also refused to allow his ashes to be buried in Canada, as his widow requested.

Israel Halperin is living a life of distinction and good works at the University of Toronto. He is a Fellow of the Royal Society of Canada, secretary of the Canadian Committee of Scientists and Scholars, former vice-president of the Canadian Mathematical Society and a persistent fighter for the release of political prisoners and Jews in the Soviet Union and elsewhere.

Halperin was tried and found innocent. But he was still so

sensitive about the pain and indignity he suffered that one afternoon, when a young law student approached him in his office to ask about Gouzenko to assist her research in a legal action, Halperin didn't pause to be civil. He jumped to his feet, opened the door and asked her to leave.

Ned Mazerall is still so wracked by quiet fury at what happened to him that he sometimes finds himself shaken by fantasies of violent revenge.

"It destroyed my career," he said quietly in his University of Manitoba lab in the summer of 1983. "My life was restricted by it. After the RCMP stepped in and I lost my job, I never felt confidence enough to leave Winnipeg. I always felt that wherever I went, they would interfere. I've had a lost thirty-five years since I came out of prison. They might have been useful, but I can't do anything to change that now."

The experience also destroyed his marriage. He hadn't seen his daughter since she was sixteen. His wife had the daughter's name changed legally so she wouldn't be reminded of the man who had been disgraced, and that blow finished him.

Mazerall was dismayed to learn that talking about the barracks, the trials, his years in prison, still had power to make him weep. When the NFB-CBC crews were putting together the documentary film, he thought he was in control and was the only detainee who agreed to be part of it. Out of curiosity, he asked the producer to send him a copy of the newly released transcript of his interrogation by the Royal Commission. When he read it he was devastated. He knew he couldn't keep his composure on camera, so he cancelled.

Kathleen Willsher married in England and died there, her demise unnoticed by the press. Emma Woikin's death, also unmarked, followed soon after.

For twenty-five years Emma Woikin maintained the valiant illusion that she was a happy, light-hearted woman. Towards the end, the effort of keeping all the balls in the air was no longer worth the trouble. She had buried a child and a beloved husband; she had been betrayed by a man who dazzled her; she served more than two years in federal prison. To pretend that none of that mattered must have been exhausting.

Louie Sawula often wished he could have found a finer tombstone for Emma, something more monumental. She deserved that, he felt, but nothing that grand was available. Instead, like Emma, he simply did the best he could.

Index